Living, Dreaming, Dying

Living, Dreaming, Dying

Practical Wisdom from the
Tibetan Book of the Dead

ROB NAIRN

Foreword by His Holiness
the Seventeenth Karmapa

Shambhala
Boston 2004

Shambhala Publications, Inc.
Horticultural Hall
300 Massachusetts Avenue
Boston, Massachusetts 02115
www.shambhala.com

9 8 7 6 5 4 3 2 1

First Shambhala Edition
Printed in the United States of America

∞ This edition is printed on acid-free paper that meets the American National
Standards Institute z39.48 Standard.

Distributed in the United States by Random House, Inc., and in Canada by
Random House of Canada Ltd

Interior design and composition: Greta D. Sibley & Associates

Library of Congress Cataloging-in-Publication Data
Nairn, Rob.
Living, dreaming, dying: practical wisdom from the Tibetan book of the dead/
Rob Nairn.—1st Shambhala ed.
p. cm.
Includes bibliographical references and index.
ISBN 1-59030-132-3 (pbk. : alk. paper)
1. Karma-gliṅ-pa, 14th cent. Bar do thos grol. 2. Intermediate state—
Buddhism. 3. Death—Religious aspects—Buddhism. 4. Funeral rites
and ceremonies, Buddhist—China—Tibet. I. Title.
BQ4490.K373N35 2004
294.3'423—dc22
2004000602

Contents

This book is humbly dedicated to

Ogyen Trinle Dorje

His Holiness the Seventeenth Karmapa

FOREWORD

The *Tibetan Book of the Dead* is part of the profound teaching that Guru Rinpoche gave to the world. It is a guide to liberating the mind from illusion in the bardo of death. In order to accomplish this, it is necessary to train the mind in this life by developing kindness, compassion, and wisdom. Without these qualities the mind cannot be free.

The great teachings on enlightenment are always the same in essence, but the way they are expressed can be adapted in an infinite number of ways, which depend on people's needs, understanding, and mentality in different times and cultures. In *Living, Dreaming, Dying*, Rob Nairn is offering a modern psychological perspective with the hope that it will be easier for people to understand and apply these ancient teachings to their lives in a practical way. Rob's work to benefit beings has my blessing.

The Seventeenth Karmapa Ogyen Trinle Dorje
May, 2002
Sidhbari, India

*The Seventeenth Karmapa and His Holiness
the Fourteenth Dalai Lama.*

Preface
What's the Use?

What *is* the use of all the information provided by the *Tibetan Book of the Dead* and all the other profound publications pouring down on us from the pens of Tibetan translators? How does it all help us?

"It gives us information," we cry. And this, after all, is the age of information. We feel secure with it: We have the answers; we know. So we must be okay.

And since we have the answers, when we die we will be okay.

No, we will not.

Mere information, knowledge, intellectual cognition, is deficient. What is needed is a deeper thing—at the very least, the beginning of some personal experience that carries us across the boundary between head and heart.

That's the problem with our information-knowledge civilization: We have all the flashy, glamorous wrappings, but we don't know how to eat the contents. So we starve while surrounded by mountains of food. As T. S. Eliot put it in "Choruses from 'The Rock'":

Where is the Life we have lost in living?
Where is the wisdom we have lost in knowledge?
Where is the knowledge we have lost in information?

The published material in English and other languages on life, dream, and death is fascinating, instructive. It tells us what goes on in the different dimensions of our existence and what we can do about it. What it doesn't mention is that most of us carry within ourselves the causes that block the inner journey—the journey of doing what has to be done. Because of these causes, most people go through a cycle. First—hope, excitement: Here are the answers at last! They study, gather the knowledge, and try to apply it to their lives—let's say in dream training or meditation. Then comes a slowly dawning bewilderment: It doesn't seem to be working. At first these searchers won't admit this "not working" either to themselves or to others. More strenuous efforts might be made, but still there is disappointment. Then begins the final stage, according to personality type. Introverts usually conclude there is something wrong with them, so it doesn't work for *them*. Extroverts angrily attack the teachings or teachers and debunk them as inauthentic. Both give up and go away.

What a shame. The door was there; they couldn't walk through.

Why? Because the full picture of how we are as humans was not seen and understood: our complex makeup with its unseen psychological forces working at many levels—some neutralizing others, some preventing us from being able to do what we long to do, some driving us to despair.

This is confusing. All the necessary ingredients *seem* to be there, but somehow it doesn't work.

I remember once reading about the Toronto zoo. Apparently they had a pair of rhinoceroses who were kept together in a large cage. The hope was that they would breed. The years rolled by and nothing happened—no baby rhino. The zookeepers were puzzled because the two seemed to get along well enough; they were both young and healthy, and no reasons could be found for this failure. Baffling. Until one spring day an attendant was sweeping the path outside the cage. A commotion within drew his attention. The male was trying to do his stuff, but every time he reared up to mount the female, his horn struck the roof and made it impossible for him to get farther. Who would have thought it! An unseen obstacle. All the ingredients were there, but it wasn't working!

Books on life, dream, death, can outline principles, but the step from there to applying them is a big one because all the unseen obstacles in our minds can't be anticipated. This step is crucial, so we need some form of bridging.

That's what is being offered here.

In the years since I began giving courses on this subject, it has become steadily clearer to me that it is essential for us to take account of and uncover, experientially, our personal psychology and how it plays out in our lives, dreams, and death. Unseen psychological forces such as projection and habitual mind patterns govern how we are and what we can or cannot do at every level of our being, but we are unaware of them. Most of us more or less stumble through life without learning about these projections and habits, but none of us can progress in life, dream, or death without doing so, because the forces that prevent change and progress within the personality are located within them. So a certain amount of psychology is needed.

Everything fell into place for me one day when Lama Yeshe Losal, our retreat master at Samye Ling Buddhist center in Eskdalemuir, Scotland, was talking to us about the Six Yogas of Naropa. Quite casually he said, "If you want to know what state your consciousness will experience in the death *bardos*, just look at your dreams."

When I heard this, all the elusive nuances of "dream work" fell into place, and I felt I had a workable angle on the subject of life, dream, and death. This gave me confidence to offer my experience of more than forty years in this field and in modern psychology in the hope that it will help people to approach death more peacefully and beneficially.

Here it is in a book that has been brewing since 1980. It attempts to make accessible the ancient Tibetan teachings on living, dreaming, and dying. Without presuming to change the teachings, I am presenting an approach and a perspective that I hope will make it possible for you to understand and apply them in your life—your ordinary everyday life, without taking off into the frozen Himalayas to sit in a cave.

Much of the focus is on the psychological issues you undoubtedly have operating in your mind at this very moment of reading and how these prevent you from being happy, from being able to do what you want to do . . . from becoming enlightened.

Because I am of a practical disposition, I have devised tricks and ways of working creatively with these mind states. Over the years many students have found these helpful—some have walked through the door.

May this effort bring peace, happiness, and liberation to countless beings, including you—because it has all been done for you, for your happiness, dear reader.

Kalk Bay, South Africa
April 2002

Introduction

Living, dreaming, dying, account for the totality of our experience. We are doing them all the time. The unusual question is: How well are we doing them?

Mostly, we drift through these states without realizing that we are constantly creating the conditions — physical, psychological, spiritual — for our future. If suffering, pain, happiness, or joy is experienced, we ourselves are accountable, not some external force. If happiness is to be found, we have the power to create the conditions for it. That is a world perspective, but Buddhism offers an even vaster perspective: As humans we have the potential to become something extraordinary — enlightened. Enlightenment takes us beyond the sorrows and joys of the human state to something indescribably grand.

Having become enlightened, we have limitless power and ability to help others in ways known and unimaginable — to help them to freedom and happiness. Bodhisattvas live only to do this.

This is living, dreaming, dying well. Anything less is pointless.

Many Westerners are fascinated by dream and its potential for new experience and spiritual growth. Few are drawn to the idea that death can be a creative and liberating experience, but the fact is that death offers more spectacular opportunities for enlightenment than life. So does dream. We must train while living if we want to recognize and take advantage of these opportunities.

The purpose of this book is to introduce you to the main principles of training and acquaint you with some of the age-old Buddhist teachings on liberation through living, dreaming, dying. We will also examine how the "ordinary person in the street" can best prepare for death and thus die skillfully, and also how to help others who are dying or have already died.

Most Westerners have difficulty gaining perspective on the Tibetan teachings in this area. As a result they struggle to integrate them effectively into their experience. To help overcome this problem, we will examine material from neuroscience and psychology that parallels and illuminates the Tibetan teachings, particularly on dream.

The most important single message to emerge from the Buddhist teachings on this topic is simple and powerful:

If you want to be happy and become enlightened, give up all forms of selfishness and harmful behavior. Live to help others. Above all—try to be kind.

Chenrezi, the Bodhisattva of Compassion.

The Greater Scheme of Things

In part 1 I have attempted to present the themes of the Tibetan Book of the Dead *so that anybody can understand them and, more important, learn to identify the psychological patterns that dominate our lives and determine how we experience the moment of death and the bardos of death.*

Once we understand that life and death are as interconnected as waking and sleeping, we will largely overcome our fear of death.

Although death leads us into new experiences, they arise out of our own mind; they do not come from an external source. If we train and make friends with our mind in life, we have a chance of recognizing what is happening in death. This recognition can result in enlightenment.

1

Being Fully Human

I am awake.

—*The Buddha*

The words above were the Buddha's response when asked about himself.* Was he a god? No. Was he an angel? No. A magician? No. So who or what was he? The Buddha said simply, "I am awake."

So, if we are not awake while we are awake, what are we? And what could we wake up to?

OUR LIMITLESS HUMAN POTENTIAL

The human condition brings with it a potential. It's the potential to become something more, to finally free ourselves from the limitations we impose on ourselves through the illusion of our conditioning.

In psychological terminology we are capable of realizing much more than we normally do. We could live a more fulfilled life, be happier, more caring and loving, wiser and more compassionate. We could be more at peace with ourselves and with the world. In the spiritual terminology of Buddhism, we could become awakened or enlightened. This

---

* "Buddha" is a title derived from the root *budh*—to wake. Thus *buddha* literally means awakened, developed, and enlightened. Each one of us has the potential to become a buddha. The historical Buddha was Prince Siddhartha Gautama, who became enlightened and taught in north-central India some twenty-five hundred years ago.

means the ending of all suffering and unhappiness and the lasting man-ifestation of our highest human potential.

It begins with finding out how to be happy, because that is what we want most in life.

I WANT TO BE HAPPY

We all want to be happy. Sometimes we are; often we are not. Why haven't we already attained permanent happiness? Because we don't know how. We are trapped in misunderstandings about ourselves, a form of ignorance that causes us to look for happiness in the wrong places.

Ignorance leads us to focus outward. We come to believe that happi-ness and peace of mind are to be found only "out there," that something has to be added to "me" before I can be happy. This eternal wild goose chase accounts for what most humans are doing—seeking happiness in externals such as a relationship, wealth, power, fame, possessions, beauty, or some ultimate experience. Some people may find temporary satisfaction in these endeavors but never true, deep, lasting happiness and peace of mind. Never the real thing.

What we achieve instead is disempowerment of ourselves. If I believe I can be happy or have peace of mind only if something external is added to my life or my self, the clear implication is that I am lacking. I lack that something; I can't be happy unless I find it. And so the desper-ate search commences.

This so tragically misses the point. Happiness is not out there; it is in here, in our own heart and mind. The Tibetans have an old saying:

> If your mind is at peace, you will be happy regardless of outer circumstances.
>
> If your mind is disturbed, you will be unhappy regardless of outer circumstances.

Most of us can understand this, at least intellectually. But for some reason it is difficult for this understanding to penetrate deeply enough to become realization, so we do not act on it. We continue, life after life, pursuing our elusive, phantom goals.

This book offers a different life perspective, a chance to change the scenario. It talks about enlightenment, or waking up to what we really are and what we experience when we do wake up. We experience the profound peace of mind that is our true nature. It's here right now, but we aren't experiencing it because we are ignoring it by fixating outwardly, looking outside for happiness.

Let's turn the situation around and begin to look within—not in a morbidly introspective way but in a joyful, creative way, exploring options we may not have seen before. We can look at life with a different perspective.

THE TWO DIMENSIONS OF REALITY

> Relative truth refers to the way something appears. Ultimate truth is what actually is.
> —*Tai Situ Rinpoche*, Relative World, Ultimate Mind

The basis of Buddhist philosophy and psychology rests on the understanding that we exist simultaneously in two dimensions: absolute, or ultimate, and relative, or conventional.

The *absolute* refers to us as enlightened beings, so we might say it is our "true" state. It is present at this moment, just as the sun is present even when it's obscured by clouds. *Relative* is the state that knows only clouds and doesn't realize there is a sun. It comes into being when separate, egocentric thinking, also known as dualistic thinking, dominates consciousness. Its existence is rooted in obsessive-compulsive thinking, and there is only one word involved—*me*.

The path to enlightenment is the path of dispelling the clouds that obscure the absolute, so that slowly we begin to experience what was always there. It's not mysterious. We don't have to import anything new into our lives. We simply retune to what we really are, which is the absolute. It is our true inner nature. It is what is prompting you to read this book. It has said to you, "I need to find out something about my real inner self." If it weren't for that you might be watching television or diverting yourself in some other way. So the absolute is affecting us all the time but in ways that we don't normally perceive.

It is the negative aspects of the relative that most significantly obscure our experience of the absolute. In the earliest Buddhist teachings, these negative aspects are identified as "unwholesome courses of action" and the consciousness associated with them. They are rooted mainly in greed, hatred, and delusion and have unfavorable karmic results: They contain the seeds of unhappy destiny or rebirth. That is why in Buddhism a lot of attention is given to identifying and freeing ourselves from unwholesome mind states and assiduously cultivating their opposites — generosity, love and compassion, and wisdom. When we are able to do this, the mind is closer to the experience of its true nature: the awakened state, awakened to the reality that we *are* the absolute.

Negativity is entrenched in our stream of consciousness at unconscious levels and therefore affects us in unseen ways or as unconscious tendencies: habitual patterns and conditioned reflexes. Levels of conditioning are deep and endure not only for this lifetime but for many lifetimes. They dominate our lives if we do not expose and integrate them so that we free ourselves from all conflicting emotionality. Interestingly, we don't get rid of the negative, because everything is relative and absolute simultaneously. Within every negative is an enlightened opposite. We train ourselves to transform the negative so that the enlightened opposite, which is positive, can manifest.*

WHAT IS ENLIGHTENMENT?

"Enlightenment refers to an individual's awakening to the mind's true nature."[1] What does this mean?

In his teachings Ringu Tulku explains:

The path of understanding our own mind consists of going through layer upon layer, deeper and deeper, unfolding and unfolding.

---

* *Transforming negativity* is a term used to describe the process, taught in Buddhism, that empowers practitioners to meditate in the presence of negative states in such a way that the positive, which is always within the negative, can be brought out — like turning a coin over to see and examine its opposite side. This topic is discussed further in the sections on purification and tonglen.

Enlightenment is not something we try to achieve—some striving to become better and better, like climbing a mountain. Although we say that in order to become a buddha we need to become enlightened, develop our wisdom, compassion, and positive qualities, this does not mean "going higher" or accumulating more and more. It means letting go of more and more, because each letting go frees us from a layer of projection and brings us closer to the underlying reality—the true nature of our mind.[2]

Sogyal Rinpoche has described buddha nature:

It is in the sky-like nature of our mind. Utterly open, free, and limitless, it is fundamentally so simple and so natural that it can never be complicated, corrupted, or stained, so pure that it is beyond even the concept of purity and impurity. To talk of this nature of mind as sky-like, of course, is only a metaphor that helps us to begin to imagine its all-embracing boundlessness, for the buddha nature has a quality the sky cannot have, that of the radiant clarity of awareness.

As it is said: It is simply your flawless, present awareness, cognizant and empty, naked and awake.[3]

The Dalai Lama defined enlightenment from a different perspective: "Enlightenment is the ending of rebirth, which means a complete non-attachment or non-identification with all thoughts, all feelings, all perceptions, all physical sensations and all ideas."[4]

The Dalai Lama's definition isn't nihilism. It's a statement of how our grasping manifests and prompts us to identify with thoughts, feelings, and perceptions. That is where the glue comes into being. If we let go of grasping, our attachment to thoughts, feelings, perceptions, sensations, and ideas falls away and the clouds part. We experience the enlightened state. We experience and manifest total compassion, total wisdom, clarity, love. All those positive qualities are obscured now because we are enmeshed in an illusion of self that accompanies grasping. But we *can* attain the enlightened condition.

This is a simplified presentation of the Buddhist worldview. The overriding concern is how to help beings realize their enlightened potential, because until we do, we are constantly haunted by the certainty that good times will not last forever and suffering will ensue, that we do not always get what we want and may at any time be afflicted by what we fear most. Even as we seek new distractions and cling to our comfort zones, we are aware at some level that any self-centered happiness we may find is as ephemeral as the morning mist. A vague but all-pervading sense of dissatisfaction casts its shadow over even our sunniest moments. That is what the Buddha called *duhkha*, living in a state that is inherently unsatisfactory and stressful.

The Buddhist focus is to help beings become enlightened, to cease activity that causes suffering. We can make a commitment to ourselves to become someone who lives to benefit others and the world we live in: that is, a bodhisattva, or spiritual warrior.* The archetypal concept of spiritual warrior is not one of confrontation. Rather, it is someone who unflinchingly faces each situation without deflection or escape, using everything as fuel on the path to enlightenment.

It doesn't mean we become obsessed with suffering; it means we understand that we don't have to have a hard time. We don't have to have ill health, wars, killing. We can, as human beings, be marvelously happy and compassionate and joyful and have a lot of fun. This is what happens when we become enlightened, when we free ourselves from all the attachments the Dalai Lama mentioned above.

The Buddha said that there are many paths to enlightenment—in fact, the figure eighty-four thousand is quoted. This is thought to refer to the size of the crowd he was addressing and may be regarded as another way of saying that every one of us can find the path that suits us best. The Buddha said many times, "You yourself must make the effort—Buddhas only point the way."[5]

The path this book examines is the path of training in mindfulness

---

Bodhisattva is derived from the words *bodhi*, which means "awake" or "awakening," and *sattva*, meaning "hero" or "warrior." According to Jamgon Kongtrul in *The Great Path of Awakening*, "This term can be translated as 'awakening warrior': *awakening* because the process of purification and growth that will culminate in buddhahood has been set in motion, *warrior* because of the courageous attitude that overcomes all obstacles and difficulties encountered in this way of life."

and recognition in living, dreaming, and dying. We will look especially at dream and death. Since we all dream and we're all going to die, why not develop the liberating potential of these states? But remember — dreaming and dying are not isolated from living, so we will explore the potential of them all.

THE ENDLESS CYCLE OF OPPORTUNITY

Living

Most of us accept the idea that it is possible to change the state of our minds while we are alive. That is what most spiritual traditions explore. We call it spiritual growth or inner unfoldment. In essence, it investigates ways to realize our full potential while embarking on some form of training or discipline. This allows the manifestation of the potential that leads to enlightenment. There is no greater experience in life. So we train for enlightenment while we are alive.

Dreaming

The role of dream in revealing our inner world is central to analytical psychology. Carl Jung taught that while dreaming, we might encounter ancient symbols arising spontaneously in the unconscious mind. These symbols, called archetypes, seem to occur in all the world's myths and religions, albeit in culturally different guises.

Neuroscience has also begun to explore the potential of dream, and it is generally acknowledged that dream offers great opportunities for learning and for understanding the deeper levels of the mind.

In Tibetan Buddhism knowledge of the fact that dream has great potential has been known for more than a thousand years and has been put to good use. In Buddhist thought, sleep consciousness is seen as a parallel to the consciousness experienced in death, and dream yoga was developed as a way of becoming enlightened. Yogis enter the dream state consciously; they have learned that through meditation it is possible to become enlightened while asleep.

Dying

Most spiritual traditions teach that death is not the end, that there is something more—a continuation of life in a different form. Despite this, many of us view death as some frightening termination of all hope and life, "that grand and gaping enigma."[6] It is not to be talked about but, rather, is to be denied and ignored for as long as possible.

Others, such as Carl Jung, look at it differently: "The spiritual climax is reached when life ends. Human life, therefore, is the vehicle of the highest perfection it is possible to attain; it alone generates the karma that makes it possible for the dead . . . to abide in the perpetual light of voidness without clinging to any object, and thus to rest on the hub of the wheel of rebirth, freed from an illusion of genesis and decay."[7]

THE TIBETAN BOOK OF THE DEAD

What a difference—death is our greatest opportunity. This is really what *The Tibetan Book of the Dead* is about. "The book is not a ceremonial of burial, but a set of instructions for the dead, a guide through the changing phenomena of the bardo realm."[8] But the book does not stand alone as some kind of manual or road map that we pick up on our way to the grave. It is part of a comprehensive system of training that commences in life. Death is a continuation and potential flowering of our life's training. This point is always to be borne in mind: Life and death are integral elements of one great cycle. Energy is constantly passing from one to the other and back again. Life and death are not separate episodes existing independently of one another.

THE SIX MINDS OF LIFE AND DEATH

We are more complex than we realize. We have six minds, which manifest in six different states: three of life and three of death.* In Tibetan there is a specific term for each of these states.

---

* The term *six minds* is used for convenience. We have only one "mind." What I want to emphasize, however, is that the mind has six aspects or modes. For simplicity I call these aspects minds.

The consciousnesses, or minds, that manifest in the bardos of life are:

Kyene: conscious, rational, logical, intellectual

Milam: dream

Samten: meditation

The consciousnesses that manifest in the bardos of death are:

Chikai: the process of dying (sometimes called the moment of death)

Chonyi: the first days of the bardo of death

Sipa: the second stage of the bardo of death: seeking rebirth, drawn by the need for embodiment

In life we go through three distinct states of consciousness: apart from the waking state, which most of us are experiencing now, there are sleeping and dreaming, and a third state, meditation.

Then there are three states of death: the mind of the moment of death, the death mind of projections (the first days of the bardo of death), and then the mind of becoming: the mind driven by karma toward a new life. There is a distinct and definite transit every time we pass from one mind into another.

We repeat continuously these cycles of living and dying. According to the Buddha, we've done this billions and billions of times. So we've died billions of times. The curious thing is—and this is the teaching—if we get it right when we die, we can become enlightened and thus end the cycle forever. It would be like waking up in the morning and realizing that we have been dreaming, that the dream is over, and that endless possibilities lie before us as enlightened beings who can help others in every imaginable way.

THE SIX BARDOS OF SAMSARA

Bardo Thodol is the Tibetan title for the *Tibetan Book of the Dead.* The word *bardo* may be translated in various ways, but it needs to be defined. *Bardo* literally means "gap," "interval," or "between," denoting time between two events. Traditionally the term is used to designate the *state* we are in while dying and while dead: "The intermediate state that follows death and is prior to one's next rebirth."[9] But it also has a more extensive meaning: "More broadly speaking, the term bardo can refer to any of the six transitional processes of living, dreaming, meditative stabilization, dying, reality-itself and becoming."[10]

Our total existence in samsara* encompasses six bardos referred to in the previous paragraph: three of life, three of death. Each bardo thus corresponds to one of our six aspects of mind.

Thus far the concept of bardo is fairly easy to grasp. But there are two further components we need to understand: (1) Moving from one bardo to another requires a specific transit; (2) each bardo is not just a state of consciousness but includes being in a different realm, where different conditions, potentials, and limitations apply.

Transits

To leave a bardo—life, for example—we need to "dissolve" out of it. In this way consciousness divests itself of the elements that enabled it to function in that bardo and held it there.

While we are alive and awake, consciousness remains in place because a certain configuration of subtle elements is present, holding it and binding it into the central nervous system. Certain experiences, such as a blow on the head or a sudden shock, can cause these elements to fall apart, and we may become dizzy, disorientated, or even unconscious.

The same thing happens more gently when we fall asleep. As sleep approaches, we become drowsy and feel we are slipping away. The world we know recedes and another state approaches. This experience arises because the elements are dissolving and releasing their hold on consciousness. It's a bit like taking off our clothes and being naked. While we are "naked" we are neither here nor there: no longer awake and not yet fully asleep.

Sleep comes when we enter dream bardo. Consciousness becomes

---

*Samsara is the endless cycle of life and death in which we are trapped. "When the nature of the mind is obscured by delusion, it is called samsara. When it is recognized, it is called nirvana" (Dilgo Khyentse Rinpoche, quoted in *The Tibetan Book of Living and Dying* by Sogyal Rinpoche, San Francisco: HarperSanFrancisco, 1994).

anchored once more by the elements, but this time they have come together in a different configuration, less dense. The result is that the mind we experience in dream differs from life: It's more flexible.

Each transit entails these distinct elements:

- Dissolution (removing our clothes)
- Neither here nor there (naked)
- A new configuration of elements (putting on different clothes)

The "neither here nor there" is a very special place to be, because while consciousness is there, it is not subject to the limitations imposed by the bardos that precede or follow it. It's a place of great potential for finding out about pure consciousness and even becoming enlightened. Neuroscientists realize this, and research is exploring this state, which, in the sleeping and waking context, is called drowsiness.[11] This suggests that every transit from one bardo to another is significant because it is a crack between worlds. If we would pause long enough to peep through the crack, we might find ourselves staring directly into our enlightened minds.

Bardo as a Realm

While we are alive and awake we are in the bardo of life, this world we all know. The state of life contains potentials and limitations. We can do a lot of things with our minds and bodies here. Most important, this is the prime realm of being able to initiate things, because we have freedom of will and intelligence, and this realm operates in a fairly orderly, linear manner.

This means we can begin training—in meditation, for example— follow through consistently, and experience the results. There is the potential for focus, which enables us to achieve things. The downside is that we tend to make everything very solid, in the sense of attributing significance and identity to thoughts, ideas, and feelings. Also, this is where the elements come together in their densest form, so our mind tends not to be very sensitive to spiritual or finer realms. It means that our spiritual or enlightened nature is quite cut off and we have difficulty penetrating and experiencing the spiritual realms. This difficulty is also due to negativity in our karmic streams.

When we enter dream, things change. Different laws apply. Time and space operate differently and dream lacks the solidity we fall into in life. As a result, as we will see in chapter 3, the dream realm offers great potential for meditation if we learn to dream lucidly.

We are different in each bardo, and the world of each bardo is different. We could take a science fiction view and say it's easy to travel to different worlds. All we have to do is step out of the body-mind that holds us in this world and step into a different body-mind that will enable us to function in the other world. When we are in one of these bardos *we believe it is reality*. This belief traps us and makes us subject to the conditions of that bardo.

From the point of view of enlightenment, this waking life and its realm are the most significant, because it is here that we are able to set in motion the forces that lead to liberation from all the realms. The training we undertake here will bear fruit also in the other bardos, particularly those of death, and that is the whole point of the *Tibetan Book of the Dead*, where we are told about the death bardos so that we can understand the need to prepare ourselves for the opportunities that arise in death. If we are diligent, we could become enlightened in this life. If not, the effects of our training will not go to waste but will make enlightenment easier in those other bardos where the veils of ignorance are not so densely wound about us.

Now we know.

The final and perhaps most important feature of the bardos is that they are all like transit camps. None of them is the final resting place. There is no such place for the unenlightened mind. It has no option but to roam from one state to another and back again, endlessly. This is why the Tibetan lamas so often use the phrase "wandering in samsara." That's what we do—and will continue to do until we finally attain liberation.

THE PARADOX OF BEING HUMAN

> Although we all have a fundamentally pure nature, it is
> not easy to get in touch with it. The gross way our mind
> ordinarily functions drowns out this deeper, more subtle
> vibration to such an extent that we generally remain

unaware of its existence. If we truly want to connect with this subtle essence, we need to quiet all distractions and loosen the hold our ordinary appearances and conceptions have on us.

—*Lama Thubten Yeshe,* Introduction to Tantra

While we're living in this world, we are conditioned to think that our predominant mode and our predominant power are rational, logical, and perhaps intellectual. We require the world around us to operate according to laws of rationality.

Science and technology are great expressions of human intelligence, but "scientism" can make us into mechanistic beings, leading us to equate ourselves with machines, particularly computers. So we put a huge value on the rational and intellectual, on external and material progress, and discount or devalue other human dimensions.

But in reality, the most powerful part of the human being is not rational. It may not be irrational, although it very often is, but it is nonrational, and the nonrational is what is in charge most of the time.* The nonrational is a manifestation of the unconscious mind, that part of the human being which is powerful and instinctive and works according to its own rules. It's more honest than the rational and more directly in touch with human reality, and it doesn't mask the existence of conflicting forces within the mind. Conflicting forces produce negativity. Negativity not faced within a human psyche is projected out to destroy and harm others.

That is the paradox. We think we are rational beings. We conduct our lives and plan them as though rationality rules, but all the time, the nonrational is more in control and, therefore, is upsetting us.

The rational perspective dictates that we focus only on what we can perceive. We limit our understanding to effects and results rather than their causes, which are often in the unconscious. As a consequence, we get out of touch with ourselves, for example, in the manifestation of

---

* "Nonrational" is an authentic state, like dream, that is governed by rules other than rationality. "Irrational," by contrast, would be behavior within the realm of the rational mind that does not conform to rules of rationality. Such behavior would be aberrant or deviant.

depression, anxiety, stress, or any unwanted negative state or unexpected mood. Because we are out of touch, we don't know why they arise or where they come from.

While we are out of touch in this way, we are unable to grow psychologically or spiritually because our subtle inner energy systems are dislocated and we are unable to understand ourselves. So we need to acknowledge and come to terms with this paradox and live it rather than ignore or deny it. Then we begin opening up to and accepting these strange—sometimes disturbing, sometimes blissful—forces that also constitute "us." This is the beginning of true spiritual creativity and is what is commonly termed the spiritual path.

It's a spiritual path because it results inevitably in a weakening of egocentric grasping and a corresponding flowering of enlightened qualities. The main seat of this grasping in the beginning of our journey is the rational mind, which seeks to hold everything in place. Acknowledging and allowing integration of deeper forces changes that inclination because the control freak becomes unseated.

Carl Jung described this when talking of individuation and the stripping away of the layers of personality:

> In this way there rises a consciousness which is no longer imprisoned in the petty, oversensitive, personal world of the ego, but participates freely in the wider world of objective interests. The widened consciousness is no longer that touchy, egotistical bundle of personal wishes, fears, hopes and ambitions which always has to be compensated and corrected by unconscious countertendencies; instead it is a function of relationship to the world of objects bringing the individual into absolute binding and indissoluble communication with the world at large.[12]

This discussion of the human condition is offered as a prelude or background to the living, dreaming, dying scenario, because it's our humanness in its many dimensions that is involved in the journey through the realms. If we view ourselves as something limited and static, that point of view will restrict us psychologically and spiritually. We won't be able to move beyond it. By standing back and seeing ourselves as more complex and even multidimensional, we make space for a broader and more spacious perspective. This is the basis for change in life and dream, and it is also the basis of our training for liberation in the bardo of death.

Of course, the rational mind has an important role in life; it is the mind that identifies us with a high degree of continuity in this world, and this enables us to perform across the spectrum of human activity. It also enables us to remember to do all the daily commonsense things. But it's only part of our whole psychic makeup.*

If we don't understand this complexity of our psyche, we will not be able to integrate the totality of our energy and harmonize our deeper energy systems.† Our ability to train in dream is hampered if we do not begin the process of integration. And this lack of integration has an even greater impact when we die: Any conditions in the unconscious that have not been integrated will manifest in death and create difficulties for us, as will be discussed later.

As a consequence of understanding the complexity of the psyche and integrating energy, we can accept that the human condition is a paradox. We move away from the stance that the rational world is the only authentic one, and we acknowledge and learn to work with our unconscious forces so that an integrated mind can emerge.

MEDITATION: THE WAY OF AWAKENING

One way to begin the journey of integration and beyond is to meditate.** Meditation is the high road into every avenue of the human psyche, right to the deepest stages we experience in death. Why is that? Because when we meditate we bring the mind into focus in the instant. In meditation we develop a latent faculty: mindfulness. When mindfulness is

---

*Our entire psychic makeup—all psychic processes, conscious as well as unconscious— is encompassed by the psyche.

†Integration is a psychological process that enables unconscious material to be recognized and accepted by the conscious mind, thus resulting in the energy of the unconscious becoming part of conscious experience.

** "And beyond": Once the psychological process of integration is under way, depths of conscious experience begin to open up. These depths are limitless and result finally in the experience of enlightenment.

present, the mind naturally comes into focus, enabling the fragmented energies to integrate, which they will do spontaneously when appropriate conditions are created. They are naturally drawn together by the power of meditation. It's like a magnet. We magnetize our enlightened potential through the effort to meditate, naturally drawing every aspect of the mind into a harmonious integrated state that penetrates all the levels of our humanity. It penetrates the waking mind, the dreaming mind, and the mind we experience during and after death. That is why, of all the methods offered in Buddhism, meditation is emphasized as the most important. It is the one training that changes the mind at all levels.

This, then, is a look at the human condition. If we want to fulfill our human potential and be happy, which is what most of us do want, we can do so. It is possible. We begin by becoming realistic about ourselves and making some attempt to understand and come to terms with the way we are.

We free ourselves from the crippling arrogance of rationality and accept our contradictory, paradoxical nature. We accept that the rational, cognitive mind—*this* mind, the mind that is reading these words—is not in charge. It thinks it is, but it is not. It is the weaker member of a partnership, the stronger member of which is the vast, powerful, little-known unconscious. Within the unconscious abide deep, powerful habitual tendencies and other forces that constantly play upon and mold the rational mind.

The path to happiness is a journey of inner unfoldment, inner discovery, opening up to the unconscious and learning to go beyond it. The journey cannot commence if we refuse to release our hold on limiting assumptions about ourselves and explore this inner reality.

Now we start to learn, cognitively and experientially, about other aspects of our complexity: our many minds and the cyclic nature of our existence—moving, always moving, in circles through different states of consciousness and back again. On and on and on.

The teachings on living, dreaming, and dying identify opportunities for liberation that we can all understand and apply to our lives—our human condition. We just have to do it, and the doing begins with training in mindfulness. Some call it meditation.

2

Freedom through Recognizing

> Spirituality means waking up. Most people, even
> though they don't know it, are asleep. They're born
> asleep, they live asleep, they die in their sleep with-
> out ever waking up. They never understand the
> loveliness and beauty of this thing that we call
> human existence. They are having a nightmare.
> —*Anthony De Mello*, Awareness

We know that we are living in a potentially endless cycle of living and
dying. It will continue until we do something to bring it to an end. We do
this by waking up to our true nature, by becoming enlightened, liberated
from the cycle or wheel of constant becoming.

It is the fundamental grasping action of the mind that keeps us en-
slaved. The remedy is to free ourselves from that which prevents enlightenment, namely, grasping. This involves freeing ourselves from our
precious egocentricity. We have made our separate identity paramount,
so we cannot imagine giving it up. It's like a dagger we have plunged into
our own heart: It's the source of continual pain and suffering, but because
we are familiar with it, we don't want to take it out. We cling to our pain
and shut out our true nature. That is the effect of egocentric grasping.

FUNDAMENTAL IGNORANCE

From the Buddhist perspective, we are dealing with fundamental ignorance, which is one of the three mind poisons: greed, hatred, delusion.

Delusion is fundamental ignorance, a nonrecognition of the way things really are. This is not intellectual or factual not-knowing but a fundamental unwillingness to see, because the act of seeing, the act of waking up, may require effort and discomfort. It requires going out of the cocoon of comfort we are always trying to secure. It challenges the ways we've been conditioned to see and experience life. While we're conscious, this manifests as a tendency not to see what's happening in ourselves and around us, not to face our own psychological processes, not to face our projections or the real implications of external events around us. We are trapped in this fundamental unwillingness to see. It is the basis of our unenlightened state and manifests in our daily experience as an emotional resistance to accepting the obvious in life.

Tai Situ Rinpoche says strongly, "Ignorance is the result of not seeing things deeply, as they actually are, but merely seeing the surface. Most of the time we don't even see the surface accurately."[1]

Swimming Upstream

Waking up from our ignorance is like learning to swim upstream. We are reversing our direction, turning around and going against the instinctive and familiar ways. This does not mean that we have to give up everything. It means that we start to change our way of seeing. We start to look at the surface more clearly, more accurately, and then deeper layers start opening up to our view. Do we choose to live for our own limited selves in our smug but rather stuffy cocoon, or do we see ourselves as part of a dynamic, limitless interaction of all life? We have the capacity to live our lives in such a way that we are a beneficial presence in the world. This is a difficult choice for most people, but sooner or later we all face it. We are all going to become enlightened—and sooner, we hope, rather than later. But there are no quick methods. The key, as Ringu Tulku says, lies in "awakening the heart by opening the mind."*

---

* This is the slogan of Ringu Tulku's organization, Bodhicharya.

The main principles for opening the mind, for learning to look and see more skillfully in life, dream, and death, are intention, awareness, and recognition. Awareness makes recognition possible.

INTENTION

The first step in opening the mind is to establish strong intention. We need to generate a powerful motivating energy that will sustain the effort to be aware, to recognize what is happening. The act of seeing may not be easy. But if we instill in our stream of consciousness a very powerful intention to recognize in life, dream, and death, this gives us power over a situation and liberates us from illusion. It will carry through from one life to the next, and it will bear fruit—if not in this life, then in another.

AWARENESS

The capacity to see life clearly is dependent on awareness. Awareness is that quality of mind that naturally and effortlessly knows what is going on within and around it. It develops out of being present in the moment: what we call mindfulness. Mindfulness is being completely present with whatever is happening while it is happening, and at the outset we need to keep constantly before us the clear intention and resolve to persevere with the meditative practices that will establish these qualities.

Awareness is an uncomplicated and natural perception of events, situations, or mind states that does not require thought. It is not the result of thinking but arises out of mindfulness. Because we understand life in terms of thought and concepts, it's difficult for us to understand the subtle quality of awareness.

Mindfulness training entails resting the mind in the moment and allowing it to remain there without distraction. Although this is a very simple thing to do, we find it difficult because we always want to grasp at things mentally. This draws the mind away into thinking, and because we think and react so much, we miss the fact that a brilliant clarity of awareness is arising in our minds all the time. Every time we perceive or sense something directly, clarity or pure experiencing arises an instant ahead of the mind's action of naming or recognizing.

We may glance out the window and see a beautiful sunset. The power of the beauty transports the mind and we experience a moment of pure joy. Without our realizing it, the mind then grasps that experience and tries to make it "mine." It tries to possess the experience. In that moment the purity is lost and the experience becomes something less.

William Blake understood this when he wrote "Eternity":

> He who binds to himself a joy
> Does the winged life destroy;
> But he who kisses the joy as it flies
> Lives in eternity's sunrise.

The innocence of joy is simply the absence of the grasping, controlling mind that tries to take possession of every experience and appropriate it to self—to make it "mine." The innocent, unconditioned mind is able simply to rest in the magic of a moment without ending it by performing an act of ownership.

Mindfulness training can lead us toward a pristine state of clarity, to this free openness that we may have glimpsed in childhood, before "Shades of the prison-house begin to close / Upon the growing boy."[2] The bars of the prison house have, in the Buddhist view, been fashioned over many lifetimes, but they often seem less solid in childhood.

It is helpful to look at two diagrams showing different life scenarios to understand what effect awareness has on our experience of the world and our mind states. First, in figure 1, we consider a life situation where awareness is weak. In figure 2 we consider a life situation where awareness is present.

The two dotted lines, which I call mind streams, represent most people. Mind streams passing through time and space: That's us.

The top mind stream is the conscious, rational, cognitive mind, the one that is functioning at this moment. It is the most superficial stratum, which I have depicted as floating on clouds of ignorance—about itself and, in particular, about the underlying unconscious mind factors.

LIFE SITUATION 1: Awareness weak

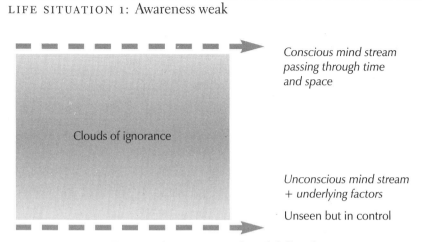

Figure 1. Awareness weak and diffused.
When awareness is weak, the mind cannot penetrate ignorance.

The bottom dotted line represents the unconscious mind—unseen habitual tendencies that are largely unconscious—which is present with the conscious mind. This unconscious dimension, though unseen, is largely in control. The unconscious is more powerful than the conscious mind. If we look at the big picture of our lives, we can see the extent to which unconscious forces are constantly surfacing and dominating situations. That is why people who want to be good, loving, kind, and constructive very often do the opposite in their lives. They can be harmful or destructive without necessarily intending it.

It's as though there were a double track, and we're in touch only with the top one. These underlying mind factors are the source of the negative and conflicting emotional states that arise unbidden in our mind. So there people are, floating along, their deeper energies masked by ignorance. When awareness is weak and diffused, the inherent intelligence of the mind is not able to penetrate the ignorance and discover and integrate those unconscious forces.

When we train in mindfulness, awareness begins to develop. Where there is awareness, what we call penetrating insight begins to arise in the

LIFE SITUATION 2: Awareness developed

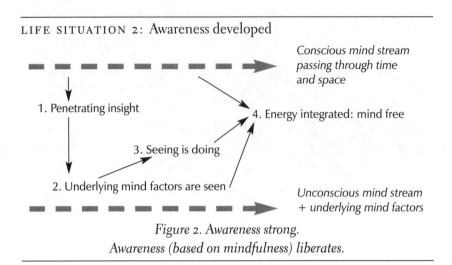

Figure 2. *Awareness strong.*
Awareness (based on mindfulness) liberates.

mind. It first arises at the level indicated by the top dotted line and becomes a characteristic of the mind, enabling it to penetrate the clouds of ignorance: to see into its own depths and connect with the underlying mind factors.

Stage 1: Penetrating insight. By its very nature, awareness begins to dispel ignorance. We could use the analogy of turning on a light in a room.

Stage 2: Underlying mind factors are seen. The light reveals the room's contents. As awareness develops, we begin to get a sense of our own mind, hints of what's going on there. We begin to come face-to-face with ourselves as we really are. That happens as we dispel that intermediate band of ignorance.

Stage 3: Seeing is doing. The third stage is what Krishnamurti calls "the seeing is the doing." This is an area where our psychological landscape differs radically from our physical one. Physically we see something, then we have to do something if we want it to change. I could be driving down the road and see a dog in front of me. I must brake. Just seeing the dog is not enough. If I don't do something, I might kill it. Psychologically it is not like that, because the act of seeing is itself an act of power in relation to our own mind states. When we see what's happening in our minds, the mystery is removed and the psychological hold of the state we have seen is lost. Unresolved psychological factors can dominate the mind only while they are unseen.

This is a theme often found in fairy stories and myths. For example, when warlocks or witches fight, a sure way to defeat opponents is to discover their true name and then say that name. This will subdue them. It's as simple as that. The act of naming is an act of power. It seems also to be a psychological truth: The act of seeing unmasks the condition and removes its power. That begins the process of integration. No more need be done: We recognize the reality or truth of a situation.

Stage 4: Energy integrated. Stage four illustrates that the seeing robs these mind factors of their autonomy. They have no option but to surrender and give up their energy, which is then integrated into conscious awareness.

The two mind streams, conscious and unconscious, then come into harmony, and wisdom begins to develop—"wisdom" because we are connecting with the deeper levels of the mind.

This is a brief sketch of how mindfulness training gives rise to awareness, insight, and wisdom naturally and spontaneously. Some call it a natural unfolding.

Awareness in Dream

The same principle of awareness applies in dream. In the beginning of our training, the dream controls us because we have not seen it for what it is and have not named it. We have not yet penetrated to that deeper level of understanding. So consciousness is dominated by the autonomy of the dream state. When we recognize dream, we are free and can do what we like—fly through the air, go through mountains, change landscapes, turn monsters into angels—because the dream is ours. We have removed its autonomy and integrated its power.

This parallels our waking experience, where if neuroses and the underlying mind factors go unrecognized, they naturally remain autonomous, which means they have the power to overwhelm consciousness. As soon as there is recognition, there is the beginning of freedom.

Awareness in Death

We should not be surprised to learn that the same awareness principle applies even in death. The death process, and the after-life experience, trigger automatic changes. As the elements begin to disintegrate and consciousness starts separating from its physical components, very powerful manifestations naturally arise within the mind of the dying person. The untrained person will not recognize these for what they are and will almost certainly experience confusion and fear. But if we can recognize what is happening, the recognition overcomes the autonomous nature of the experience. The moment we are able to perform a total act of recognition in relation to what is happening, the rest of the death process is short-circuited, and enlightenment is possible.

Forming the *intention* is the training; *recognition* is the key. This is what we will consider next.

RECOGNITION

If we are aware of what is going on, important consequences follow, as is illustrated by my favorite story of the cobra and the rope.

Imagine you are in Africa, in Zimbabwe. The Buddhist center in Harare has a beautiful location on the slopes of a rocky hill clustered with indigenous trees. The hill is famed for its teeming population of cobras that live in crevices among the rocks. I built myself a retreat cabin there, a wooden structure with a cool, thatched roof. The cabin is raised on stilts to discourage casual visits from these particular neighbors, who aren't too choosy about where they shelter when tropical rains flood their homes. Farther down the hill is a large, oval meditation hall, also thatched and therefore somewhat dark.

One evening you walk into this hall through the front door. By chance you glance down and see in the dimness a large, squiggly shape, at least six feet long. One end, thicker than the rest, lies no more than six inches from your foot. You feel great fear. Suddenly this becomes a significant moment in your life, because you are now facing death: If a cobra bites you, you have only about twenty minutes to live. Maybe you are trying to remember how to approach death, when someone comes in and switches on the light.

This "snake" that has held you frozen with fear isn't a snake after all; it's a piece of rope. Your fear vanishes, death is forgotten, you breathe a sigh of relief and laugh.

What changed? Simply recognition. You saw the situation as it really was. That recognition liberated you.

This is liberation in life, where we experience two dimensions: outer, or practical, and inner. At the outer level, the person who recognizes a situation is in a better position to deal with it. At the inner, or psychological, level, recognition is a prerequisite for resolving psychological conditions. In both instances the mind is freed from bondage.

In dream, recognition dispels the illusion of the dream state and results in lucid dream, where unusual possibilities open up.

The effect of recognition is most dramatic in death, where it can result in enlightenment. Recognition is the key, above all others, to liberation in life, dream, and death.

Recognition in Life

Why is it so difficult to recognize in life? To see relative things for what they are? To be aware of our ultimate nature?

Most of us see only what we want to see. The mind has unconscious suppressive mechanisms that keep a great deal of knowledge, understanding, and experience out of our conscious awareness. This knowledge is there and the potential for knowing it is always present, but for various reasons—usually fear and attachment to our egocentric sense of separateness, both of which manifest as emotional resistance to seeing what is really in the mind—we prefer not to know it and therefore ignore it. This produces inner fragmentation, causing us to lose touch with parts of our inner self. When these parts reveal themselves in our consciousness, we turn away; we "turn a blind eye." This obscures our ability to know what is happening in our mind while it is happening. The effects will still be felt, but the cause will not be seen or known. This is the state of most people's minds. Because we do not see or recognize what is going on in our minds, we cannot recognize ourselves. We are strangers to ourselves.

The stone shrine outside the cave of the Delphic oracle in ancient Greece held the inscription KNOW THYSELF, which pinpoints both the human dilemma and the solution. If we don't know ourselves, we cannot be happy and fulfill our spiritual potential. The way out of this dilemma is to turn within and commence the inner journey of discovery. This is part of the swimming upstream that we find so unappealing because it's difficult and runs counter to our desire-based inclinations. It's like taking medicine: We don't like the taste, but it leads to healing. So we take it.

This inner ignorance can manifest psychologically as neurosis, the causes of which are embedded in the unconscious. Most people are not in touch with this level of self and are therefore unable to do anything about their neurotic forces, which may cause depression, anxiety, phobias, or other dysfunctional states.

Therapy helps us get in touch with the original event or circumstance that gave rise to the neurosis and has been repressed and denied. Therapy may lead to catharsis when the mind "lives" what happened at that particular time or age. In that moment the memory reenters consciousness with all the emotional force of the original experience, enabling the now adult mind to understand. It sees, knows, and understands a great deal about the neurosis that was never known before. This contact with the repressed memory results in a rush of energy from the unconscious into the conscious mind, allowing all aspects of the early experience to be acknowledged and accepted. The actual energy of the experience is thus integrated into consciousness, freeing the mind from both the pressure and the neurosis that resulted from the repressed memory.

Ignorance about the cause keeps us in a state of bondage. Discovering and integrating the cause frees us. In any situation, those who recognize and know what's going on are in a stronger position than those who do not, because they are able to avoid difficulties and optimize opportunities. It is a great advantage in life, at every level of activity, to know what is going on while it is going on.

Recognition in Dream

If we are not aware that we are dreaming, we will be overwhelmed by the dream condition. Unless we develop the power of lucid dreaming, we think the dream is reality and suffer within the dream as though it were real. The mind is totally absorbed in the illusion of the dream, because we have not recognized the nature of the situation; we have not recognized that this is a dream. Within dream, the training begins with recognition, and this topic is dealt with more fully in chapter 3.

Recognition in Death

The same principle applies to death. When we start to die, we go through a series of very definite psychological experiences that, if we don't recognize them for what they are, overwhelm the mind. If we can recognize and face them, we find ourselves looking directly into what is taking place psychologically and discover there is more than we would have seen otherwise.

If we are not seeing, we are overwhelmed and trapped in a belief that the illusion is real. If we see, we have a chance to recognize and thus free ourselves from the illusion. Recognition is the key, and we would be well advised to train for it.

Training in Recognition

Mindfulness is the crucial connection between living, dreaming, and dying. It is a deeply powerful faculty that not only changes the waking state but also carries through into dream and death. While living, we have the power to train the mind. In dream, unless we've accomplished lucid dreaming, we don't have that power.

In death, if we haven't trained in advance, the power of the situation is so great that we will have almost no chance of recognizing what is happening.

What can we do? It's very simple: We prepare now. We can have a trial run at death every single night when we go to sleep. We can begin training to fall asleep consciously and to dream lucidly. The process of falling asleep parallels the process of dying, while dreams parallel the bardo of death.

This training is not only crucial for successful dying, it is also crucial in life. To be mindful liberates us from a great deal of unnecessary suffering and can lead to enlightenment in life. We are not postponing everything until death comes along. We are looking at training that is crucial in life and carries over into death.

To give a practical dimension to what has been discussed, I have devised this simple awareness exercise, which will help you to recognize how perception, and thus awareness, can arise without the need for thinking. It's the ground for freedom.

EXERCISE: Relaxed awareness

Sit comfortably with your eyes open or closed, whichever you find easier. Relax, be quiet, and just be there without doing anything at all. Let go of any sense of having to do something. Be at ease.

After a while certain realizations will come to you, most of them probably in the form of sounds or sensations: The wind rustles the leaves, a dog barks, a car goes by and you hear the rush of tires on the road, a bird calls. Maybe a cool breeze touches your arm, or you feel an itch on your cheek. You may smell gasoline fumes or coffee being brewed.

When some time has passed, lie back in your chair and reflect on what has happened.

First: Did the act of sensing (hearing, feeling, smelling) require any effort? No. The sensations all came to you; they entered your awareness simply because you have ears, nose, and so on.

Second: Did the sensing depend at all on thought? Once again, no. Sensing happens without thought.

Third: Did you think about what you were experiencing? Almost certainly yes. This is the interesting part. The mind naturally thinks about whatever comes to its notice even though there is no need for it. This is grasping, taking hold of the experience.

Now repeat the exercise. Spend quite a long time at it if you like, and see if you can relax and be so lazy that you don't even bother to think about what comes to you.

Do this exercise a few times so that you begin to realize and understand two things:

- Sensing happens naturally and equally naturally gives rise to perception.
- Perception means that you know about it. But the act of sensing is not dependent upon thought.
- Despite this, we nearly always think about what we have sensed.
- That constitutes grasping.

See if you can perceive the thinking, grasping process in your own experience as you go about your daily activities. This will set you on the path to understanding grasping. It may seem simple—which, of course, it is—but it is surprisingly profound. Important: When you recognize grasping, don't blame or criticize yourself. It's natural and we all do it. So you're okay!

This is a beginning of understanding ourselves and how our minds work. We are automatically, naturally, performing acts of perception all the time. They come to us spontaneously via the senses. If we simply remained with the perception, the mind would be relaxed and at peace. But the mind will not permit that. It wants to interfere and possess the perception. So we have "me perceiving." This moves our experience from the realm of pure experience into the realm of grasping and thinking, which causes the mind to become disturbed: Grasping and thinking disturb the mind.

If you do this exercise a few times, you will discover interesting over-tones. For example, we often think that simply because we think, we have to think. There is a part of the mind that says, "Now, you've got to think, you must analyze, work it out, or know more about it." When we discover this impulse, we also learn that we don't have to believe this part of the mind. We then start to quiet down and relax.

If the mind is more quiet and relaxed, it is increasingly able to be aware and to recognize in life. We can train the living mind, and that training will carry over into the dreaming mind and the dying mind, be-cause we are developing a faculty that is deeper than those three minds. This training cuts through our conditioning, our habitual tendencies, to awaken inherent intelligence, courage, and wisdom. So we train our-selves to stay in the moment of purity, in the moment of brilliance. It be-comes part of our ordinary experience.

We live, we dream, we die, but life goes on, because our reality is that we are a stream of consciousness flowing through time and space. We endlessly experience similar conditions with ever recurring opportuni-ties for happiness, suffering, and liberation — and will continue to do so until we wake up and discover our inherent ultimate nature. But our normal way of living in the world does not generate the conditions for awakening. We have to work at it, and this involves a complete turn-about in our approach to life and ourselves.

To wake up to life, we start freeing the mind from fundamental ig-norance and grasping. This begins with developing mindfulness, which leads to awareness. Awareness is not a mysterious state, but it may not be easy to recognize because it is not dependent upon thinking.

Awareness is the basis for recognizing exactly what is happening within and around us. At a psychological level, recognition frees the mind. In dream, recognition results in lucid dreaming, and in death it can result in enlightenment. All our training is drawn into focus by the formulation of determined intention — intention to be aware and to recognize.

3

Dreams and the Path

Ultimately, you must forget about technique. The
further you progress, the fewer teachings there are.
The Great Path is really No Path.
    —*Morihei Ueshiba*, The Art of Peace

Now we will look at dream in relation to what I call the path. *Path* is a
term we often come across in spiritual literature where there's the idea
that we are stuck here and that we need to go to a better place somewhere else: The idea arises that we have to undertake a journey in order
to reach our goal.

THE PARADOX OF PATH

The Buddhist perspective is that there is no need for a path because
we're already there, we are already enlightened—the only problem is
that we haven't realized it. But we use the term anyway because it con-
veys the idea of moving toward something different. We are freeing ourselves from the illusion of not being enlightened so that we can
experience the enlightened state that is our true reality.

Although there is nowhere to go, we nevertheless need to free our
minds from what are called the two obscurations: negative and conflicting emotionality, and dualistic thinking.

Negative and conflicting emotionality is the product of negative activity that has produced negative karmic consequences. These are like

veils that obscure our awareness of the enlightened state. The effect is to trap us in an illusory understanding of ourselves, which results in dualistic thinking and egocentricity. We think of ourselves as the center of the universe; we think we're separate, something solid. It is this way of thinking that cuts us off from our fundamental reality, which is spacious and enlightened. As a result, we perform unskillful acts of body, speech, and mind, generating further negative karma, and so the process moves on, perpetuating itself until we do something to end it.

VAJRAYANA

There are various paths within the different schools of Buddhism, each one designed to suit the needs of different personality types. One is Vajrayana, which is the essence of Tibetan Buddhism.* Within the lineages of Vajrayana, a number of skillful methods of working with the mind have been taught over the past thousand years. These methods directly and radically cut through the fundamental grasping attitudes of the mind, not at superficial levels, but at the source. They purify karmic causes that are deeply embedded within the mind's karmic stream. These karmic factors manifest in our lives to determine our positive and negative tendencies and experiences; they also manifest within our conscious-

---

*Vajrayana, or tantra, is the form of Buddhism that flourished mainly in Tibet and is thus often referred to as Tibetan Buddhism. These are the distinguishing characteristics of Vajrayana:

- A body of highly specialized meditation methods that can be practiced only by students who have received initiation from a qualified master: These meditations sever the roots of grasping and desire at the deepest levels and can lead to enlightenment in a single lifetime.
- The crucial role of a qualified Vajrayana master: It is not possible for students to enter upon the path without the help and guidance of a master.
- Lineage: Vajrayana teachings and methods are preserved within the four great lineages of Tibetan Buddhism. The chief function of the lineages is to preserve the purity of the teachings and ensure the authenticity and accuracy of transmission of practice methods from masters to students. See also "About Buddhism" on page 262.

ness to determine and limit our way of perceiving and relating to life. They keep us trapped in illusion, preventing us from experiencing our enlightened state.

WE STRENGTHEN WHATEVER WE FOCUS ON

Within us is the potential to be whatever we choose.
—*Akong Rinpoche*

Within us is the potential to experience virtually any state of mind, ranging from the most negative and confused to full enlightenment. Those states on which we focus are those that we strengthen and thus experience more frequently and powerfully. Energy follows focus. When we understand this, we realize why negative habitual patterns are so problematic: They act as magnets attracting negative energy, reinforcing the habitual pattern. Habitual patterns support negative and conflicting emotions, so these also become reinforced. The training in life, dream, and death is to break the habitual focus and thereby free the mind from the habitual patterns. When we are able to do this, we are able to let go of what we think we are and discover that reality, in the form of our enlightened mind, is always staring us in the face.

While we're experiencing life in these bodies, we are enmeshed in progressive layers, or sheaths, that obscure the enlightened state. When we are embedded in our six senses, we see the world and experience reality through them.*

When we fall asleep and dream, one of these sheaths dissolves, so the dream state is less dense. Our enlightened condition remains veiled by ignorance but not so heavily as in the waking state. Therefore if we can access dream and introduce recognition into it, we open up a potential for becoming enlightened.

---

*Buddhism classifies the mind as a sense organ along with the five physical senses. So the six senses and their corresponding objects are: eye, visible form; ear, sound; nose, smell; mouth, taste; skin, sensation; mind, thoughts.

We can begin by understanding something about sleeping and the dream state. We will clarify how we enter dream—which happens by clearly discernible stages—and finally see how falling asleep and dreaming parallel dying and being dead. Then we will have the basis for understanding dream yoga, or training for enlightenment while we are asleep. What a pleasure!

THE STAGES OF SLEEP: TWO PERSPECTIVES

The Neuroscience View of Sleep

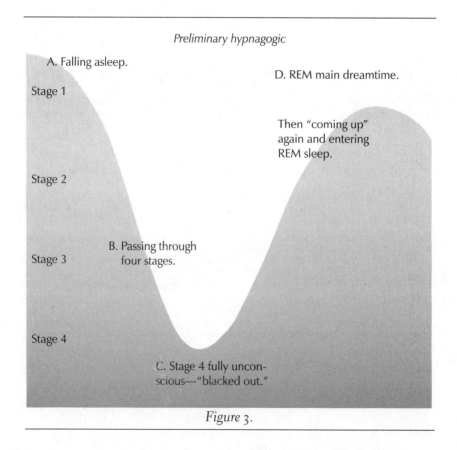

Preliminary hypnagogic

A. Falling asleep.

Stage 1

D. REM main dreamtime.

Then "coming up" again and entering REM sleep.

Stage 2

Stage 3

B. Passing through four stages.

Stage 4

C. Stage 4 fully unconscious—"blacked out."

Figure 3.

"Advances in research made it clear that sleep is an active phenomenon. It is a state of consciousness with its own laws."[1] Neuroscientists have developed methods of measuring the changes in brain waves as we enter sleep and dream. These changes correspond to changes in states of consciousness. A pivotal advance in mainstream sleep research was the discovery of REM (rapid eye movement) sleep in the 1950s, made possible by recording the electrical activity in the brain by means of the EEG (electroencephalograph).

In neuroscience, it is observed that we fall asleep in four stages, passing into an increasingly deep unconscious state. These stages are accompanied by changes in brain waves (see figure 3).

Stage 1. Fragmentary hypnagogic images arise.*

Stage 2. These images tend to be mental rather than visual, like a background or commentary.

Stage 3. We are becoming increasingly unconscious.

Stage 4. We are fully unconscious. A term often used is *blackout*.

Stage 4 represents deep, heavily "drugged" sleep. If somebody wakes us up shortly after we have fallen asleep, we feel as though we have come from a very deeply unconscious state. When we awake, we may be disoriented and have no sense of how much time has passed since we fell asleep. This is the deepest sleep of the night and usually lasts for about an hour. We experience it only once in the course of a night's sleep.

After stage 4 we drift up into REM sleep, which is the main dream time. We remain in REM sleep for some time, then drift down to stage 3, then back up to REM sleep. This cycle in and out of REM sleep repeats itself four or five times through the night, becoming shallower as dawn approaches.

By means of sophisticated equipment, various characteristics of the sleeper can be measured, including cerebral activity, heart rate, blood pressure, and breathing. It has been found that during non-REM sleep all activity quiets down, but during REM sleep the brain is more active than in wakefulness. "Thus sleep is not a single state, nor are its variations random. It is a pattern that is highly regulated over time and that includes distinct states of human consciousness."[2]

Hypnagogic means "associated with the drowsiness preceding sleep."

The Vajrayana View of Sleep

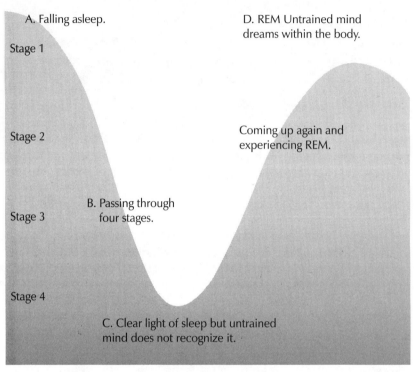

A. Falling asleep.

Stage 1

D. REM Untrained mind dreams within the body.

Stage 2

Coming up again and experiencing REM.

B. Passing through four stages.

Stage 3

Stage 4

C. Clear light of sleep but untrained mind does not recognize it.

Figure 4.

Vajrayana agrees entirely with neuroscience on the four stages of falling asleep, where the hypnagogic images and mental contents occur at stages 1 and 2, followed by progressively deeper unconsciousness to the deep sleep of stage 4. Vajrayana also agrees that REM sleep is the classic dream time.

The major difference is the status of stage 4, which from the point of view of neuroscience is largely an unknown quantity, whereas Vajrayana sees it as the most important stage in the sleep cycle. When consciousness is at stage 4, it is resting in what is called the clear light of sleep. This state is the closest we get to the enlightened mind, and in it the veils obscuring our enlightened nature are thinnest. However, without training we are almost invariably unconscious at this point and do not recognize it. Vajrayana training focuses on developing the power to enter this state consciously.

Neuroscience confirms the ancient Vajrayana view that there is a change in consciousness between waking and dreaming. And when it comes to the stages of falling asleep, scientific observers have confirmed with the aid of machines what Buddhism discovered more than two thousand years ago by direct observation made possible by meditation training.

DREAM: THREE PERSPECTIVES

To obtain a clear understanding of the nature and function of dream, we will review three perspectives.

- Neuroscience
- Analytical psychology: the approach of C. G. Jung
- Vajrayana: particularly as articulated by the Dalai Lama in one of his recent exchanges with a group of neuroscientists*

The Neuroscience View of Dream

According to neuroscience, dream is the arising of spontaneous, subjective mental or visual images. The images arise inwardly, inside the subject, inside us.

In terms of the structure of consciousness, however, we are going exactly 180 degrees away from our waking experience, where we focus on events that arise and come to us from outside in ordered, logical, predictable ways. An object doesn't suddenly appear in our line of vision.

---

*At the fourth "Mind and Life" conference, Dharamsala, 1992, as documented in Francisco J. Varela, ed. and narr., *Sleeping, Dreaming, and Dying* (Boston: Wisdom Publications, 1997). These dialogues between the Dalai Lama and Western scientists aim to promote cross-cultural scientific research and understanding.

We see, for example, a person walk into the room. External consciousness is fixed into frameworks that are fundamentally logical, rational, and sequential.

Dream, by contrast, is much freer. Things can happen out of time, in the past or the future. Places don't hold still for us. We could be in London one moment and in Bangkok the next. In dream it would not seem strange or out of place to us.

Mental or visual images arise in three states: in the state of wakefulness, in non-REM sleep, and in REM sleep.

In the state of wakefulness we can hallucinate. When that occurs, we see things that are not physically present. When we start falling asleep, we pass through non-REM stages. While still conscious of the room around us, we begin to experience fragmentary, hypnagogic images. These appear at the onset of sleep, and most of us are familiar with this state. Then we go through stages of experiencing fragmentary dreams, often of a more mental nature than visual, such as thinking or hearing a commentary running, before we become unconscious. After passing through stage 4, we move up to REM sleep.

REM sleep is the main dream time, when our dreams are vivid and sometimes meaningful and usually have a story line. The REM stage is closest to waking, so dreaming is very close to waking consciousness. "It is clearly true that vivid, visual, story-like dreams occur classically in REM sleep."[3]

Scientific research focuses chiefly on REM sleep, but the other levels are by no means ignored.

The Analytical Psychology View of Dream

Jung tells us that "dream is a fragment of involuntary psychic activity, just conscious enough to be reproducible in the waking state."[4] So dream is strong enough, or conscious enough, to penetrate consciousness when we wake up, but it is a "fragment of involuntary psychic activity." As Jung expands his work on dream, he makes it clear that dream arises out of the unconscious. It is involuntary because it is not normally subject to the control of rational thought processes. This is very different from waking consciousness, where we work on the premise that to be meaningful, things must be logical, rational, and under control. Dream cares nothing for the view of consciousness. In fact, dreams can be embarrassingly blunt and honest, often presenting in vivid detail images of thoughts and feelings the dreamer tries to suppress in life, frequently of a sexual or violent nature.

Jung also says that dreams are largely compensatory. We don't always get what we want in life, particularly emotionally. This may cause pain, sadness, or longing. The dream mind picks up on this and gives it to us in sleep.

I think what is most significant is that dream, from Jung's point of view, is mostly irrational and therefore difficult for the waking mind to understand. Many people regard dreams as adjuncts of the waking mind and seek to interpret them rationally. This misses the point, which is that dreams are complete statements on their own terms. Those terms are nonrational, and if we want to learn the language of dream, it's necessary to let go of the insistence on rational meaning. "Usually a dream is distinguished by 'bad qualities' such as lack of logic, questionable morality, uncouth form, and apparent absurdity or nonsense."[5] Dreams do not exercise censorship; they just throw up whatever is in the unconscious mind, and if we don't like it or can't understand it, we say, "That's bad." The fact is that the unconscious has not been socialized and may not subscribe to our ideas of good and bad.

Learning to work with our dreams entails learning the language of dream mind. One key is not to try to rationalize what the dream is saying but just to immerse ourselves in the underlying energy, the feeling, whatever is there, so that it can slowly communicate itself and soak into the rational mind. Doing this can be a lot of fun because we learn to let go of our rational, prescriptive thinking process and allow ourselves to drift into this wonderfully crazy realm of dream and connect with whatever energy is there. Intuition begins to play a part.

When looking at dream we should not forget that *we are our dreams*. We are the unconscious. It is not another individual; it is not some external being presenting us with this material. It's part of us, and dreams present us with imagery for specific purposes. They seek to establish balance within the psyche and to promote psychological integration, which conscious attitudes prevent. There is meaning associated with dream, but the problem is to understand it, because the language of dream is not the language of the waking mind.

The psychic structure of dream is unlike that of other contents of consciousness. It does not follow the same rules of time and space: It allows us to move backward and forward through time, to float in the air, and to be very quickly in one place and then another, which causes no surprise in the dream. People appear and disappear, events arise and change or vanish, landscapes change, and in dream we are quite comfortable with all this, because it accords with the psychic structure of the dream mind.

Ideas in dreams are linked in a way that is foreign to our logical thinking. The ideas don't move logically; they move fantastically. This is completely at variance with our waking experience, where most of our ideas move in a rational, logical sequence.

This is a brief Jungian perspective on dream. The important features are that in Jung's view, the dream consciousness is quite definitely autonomous, independent of waking consciousness. It is not subject to rules of rationality and logic. Dream arises from another place within us.

The Vajrayana View of Dream

Dream has been the subject of detailed study in Vajrayana for centuries. One of the important traditions, known as dream yoga, originated with the eleventh-century yogi Naropa.

The Dalai Lama says that in Buddhism the origin of dream is understood as an interface between different degrees of subtlety of bodies: the gross level, the subtle level, and the very subtle level.[6] Ringu Tulku mentions that it is accepted that there are several different kinds of dream, such as dreams reflecting daytime experiences, dreams resulting from physiological conditions such as changes in health, dreams due to the way the mind travels through the body's channels, and also prophetic dreams with premonitions.*

---

* In conversation with the author, London, 2001.

Buddhism sees the "mental factor of sleep" as the essential basis of dream. This means that waking consciousness is necessarily excluded from the dream state, and it is only if something quite peculiar happens to the mind that waking and dreaming can happen simultaneously. So Vajrayana does not include hallucination in the category of dream.

Vajrayana views sleep as a form of nourishment for the body, as is *samadhi*, or meditative concentration. "But if you ask why we dream, what's the benefit? There's no answer in Buddhism . . . other than its use in meditative practice," says the Dalai Lama.[7]

If we can dream lucidly, it becomes possible to engage in spiritual practice while dreaming. The dream mind has both advantages and disadvantages. On the plus side we learn that the act of *recognition* changes everything; as soon as we recognize that we are dreaming, we are able to take charge of the dream and change it in any way we choose. We can meditate in sleep and more easily reach deeper levels of meditative experience than we can while awake.

On the other hand, training to do this is not easy, because although the dream mind is more malleable than the waking mind, it is also less stable. The other factor is that "we" are controlled by dream. It happens to us. Even when we begin to dream lucidly, our ability to recognize the dream will be sporadic and patchy. Sometimes we recognize, sometimes we don't. And when we do recognize, in the beginning of our training the recognition may not be strong enough to dispel the autonomy of the dream state completely. Thus we dream, recognize that we are dreaming, but find that the dream carries on happening to us even though we try to change it. It's a bit like trying to control a wild horse: It keeps running off with us. The struggle is to maintain the recognition, like trying to keep our eyes open when we are very tired—they get heavy and droop, compelling us to fall asleep against our will.

Even though we succeed in recognizing dream, this turns out to be no more than a start. We have to keep hold of that recognition by strongly maintaining our focus. We find that we are struggling against the autonomy of the dream state.

Once we are established in lucid dream, we have the dream equivalent of the stable mind of meditation. Then great possibilities open up to us.

In essence, neuroscience detects changes in brain waves that correlate with different states of consciousness as we go into dream, but it does not extrapolate any human or spiritual potential from that, while Jung talks about a different psychic structure, with the potential for integrating unconscious elements. The Tibetan Buddhist picture is more radical. It says that when we go into dream we move out of the waking mind into another mind, the dream mind, and our waking mind falls dormant. However, an untrained person's mind is trapped within the body and thus dreams within the body, and the dream experience cannot be used in any creative way. It may have some sort of physiological function, but the greater potential of the dream experience has not been developed.

When we go from the waking mind into the dream mind, a discernible change takes place: EEG readings change, the psychic structure within which consciousness finds itself is different, the meaning of imagery varies, the time-space dimension alters, rationality gives way to the fantastic, literal meaning becomes symbolic and compensatory. All in all, dream is more fluid than waking, so our experience there is less solid, in the sense that we are not so stuck in the conditioned patterns of thinking, feeling, and reacting that dominate waking. These patterns appear in dream but in a more malleable form.

Because of these differences, dream offers possibilities for change that are not found in the waking state, and therefore training in lucid dream is an attractive proposition. However, the autonomy of dream is not to be underestimated; the path to consistent lucid dreaming can be a long one for some people.

Dreams do seem to be symbolic, and the symbolism pertains, it seems, to the unconscious. For this reason each person's dream language is unique. Understanding dream entails understanding this dimension of oneself.

VAJRAYANA TRAINING

Lucid Dream and the Clear Light of Sleep

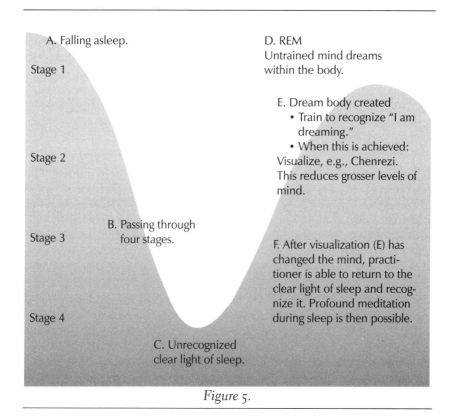

A. Falling asleep.

Stage 1

Stage 2

B. Passing through four stages.

Stage 3

Stage 4

C. Unrecognized clear light of sleep.

D. REM
Untrained mind dreams within the body.

E. Dream body created
• Train to recognize "I am dreaming."
• When this is achieved: Visualize, e.g., Chenrezi. This reduces grosser levels of mind.

F. After visualization (E) has changed the mind, practitioner is able to return to the clear light of sleep and recognize it. Profound meditation during sleep is then possible.

Figure 5.

Vajrayana practitioners describe the stages of falling asleep and entering dream from observation of their own experience. The perspective of Vajrayana is wider than that of neuroscience in that it regards dream as an autonomous mind state within which it is possible to become enlightened. It is not seen as a mere adjunct of consciousness.

Most people dream within their bodies and fail to develop their latent capacity for lucid dream. Their minds remain overwhelmed by what are called gross levels of ignorance—rather as in life—so the opportunity to train for enlightenment in dream passes unexplored.

Lucid dream includes training to fall asleep without losing consciousness. "Waking up" in the dream, or remembering to recognize dream as dream, will obviously be easier if we don't fall unconscious in the first place. Easier said than done.

Because lucid dream is possible for most people, regular methods for developing this ability and then training to meditate within the dream state have been developed. Two areas of training are possible: to fall asleep consciously and to dream lucidly—that is, to awake within the dream.

Falling Asleep Consciously

Falling asleep consciously is more difficult than we might expect. The Dalai Lama describes it as "the highest accomplishment of a yogi."[8] However, there is no harm in trying to do it, and here are concise instructions that you could follow.

PRACTICE: Falling asleep consciously

On a night when you are not so tired that you are likely to fall asleep immediately and your belly is not drum tight with food and drink, lie in bed and relax.

Focus on the flow of images and impressions that come to you as you relax with your eyes closed.

You may find yourself looking at a succession of faces that change as soon as they take form. You may see a series of childlike drawings or photographs, falling as fast as autumn leaves in a high wind.

When you see something that catches your fancy—a face, a scene, a picture barely formed—try to hold it in focus. If you can, hold your attention on the image . . . follow it into full-fledged dream, while retaining awareness that you are dreaming.

Move gently into this sequence—"while delicately observing the mind, lead it gently into the dreamstate, as though you were leading a child by the hand."[9]

Lucid Dreaming

Training to dream lucidly is not so difficult. It begins with the intention to "wake up" in a dream and involves the creation of what is called a special dream body.

The training begins in waking life by repeatedly forming and reinforcing the intention to dream lucidly. Referring to lucid dream, the Dalai Lama says:

> In that state the special dream body is created from the mind and from vital energy (known in Sanskrit as *prana*) within the body. The special dream body is able to disassociate entirely from the gross physical body and travel elsewhere.
>
> One way of developing this special dream body is first of all to recognize the dream as a dream when it occurs. Then, you find that the dream is malleable, and you make efforts to gain control over it. Gradually you become very skilled in this, increasing your ability to control the contents of the dream so that it accords to your own desires. Eventually it is possible to disassociate your dream body from your gross physical body.
>
> In contrast, in the normal dream state, dreaming occurs within the body. But as a result of specific training, the dream body can go elsewhere. This technique is accomplished entirely *by the power of desire or aspiration.*[10] (italics added)

So the first step, while awake, is to concentrate on intention. Repeatedly say to yourself, "Tonight I will dream clear dreams. When I am dreaming I will recognize the dream as a dream." Really focus intention and determination on this aspiration so that it permeates your consciousness to the point of influencing your dream mind. As a consequence of this determined intention, the time will come when you actually wake up in the dream and realize — "Ah, this is a dream!" This is the beginning of lucid dreaming.

We don't have to do something different or more specific to create the dream body. There is, in fact, a dual effect. As we slowly increase our ability to dream lucidly, the special dream body spontaneously begins to grow, like a thought form. As it grows, so does our ability to dream lucidly. The two go together, and when the dream body is fully formed, lucid dreaming is possible on a stable basis.

Once we have created the special dream body and are established in lucid dreaming, serious enlightenment training becomes possible. It goes through two stages: purification in dream and recognition of the clear light of sleep.

Purification in Dream

According to the Dalai Lama, purification occurs when we reduce the grosser level of the mind, to prepare it to recognize the clear light of sleep. "If you can recognize the dream state while you are in it, then you can visualize and deliberately reduce the grosser level of the mind to return again to clear light of sleep. At that point, the subtlest level of mind—the clear light of sleep—is easier to ascertain."[11]

A practitioner who has received Vajrayana training and initiation from a qualified lama would be given a specific visualization for this stage. People who can dream lucidly but have not been initiated could visualize the embodiment of compassion (see picture on page xvi) in the form of four-armed Chenrezi (Sanskrit: Avalokiteshvara) and also recite the associated mantra—OM MANI PADME HUM—in their dreams. It is beneficial to do this even when we are awake.

It is not within the scope of this book to give details of how Vajrayana dream practice is done. Those wishing to pursue this training in detail and who have established themselves in lucid dreaming should seek out a qualified lama and request further instruction. However, anyone can train in lucid dream and then commence visualizing Chenrezi and chanting the mantra. This is a powerful purification practice that could be done every night.

The final stage of training is to return consciously to the clear light of sleep—stage 4 of the cycle—and rest the mind there. This would be a very profound level of meditation.

Purification and Accumulation: Spiritual Energy

Because we are dealing with mind energy at its subtlest levels, dream training must be supported by other forms of training, particularly purification and accumulation. Our energy is affected by everything we do, think, and say. If in life we indulge in negative activity, the consequence will be a disruption or disharmonizing of our energy, and the effects of this will have an adverse impact on the dream state. Our inability to recognize dream is due to negative karmic conditioning that draws veils over our "inner eyes." For this reason the Vajrayana systems introduce practitioners to meditations that purify negative karma, thereby freeing the mind from obscurations. Most of us need to practice these purification meditations for many years, so we are not looking at short-term methods.

Purification meditations are accompanied by accumulation meditations. To attain the deeper meditations, such as the clear light of sleep, it is necessary to have a certain level of spiritual energy within the mind, which accumulation meditations enable us to generate. Regular practice of Chenrezi is a suitable method. Students who train under the guidance of qualified lamas are given more specific practices.

What begins to emerge is that Vajrayana systems contain varieties of highly sophisticated meditation methods that provide the practitioner with a comprehensive discipline. If followed, this discipline will certainly lead to enlightenment. It must be understood that there are many routes, of which dream training is only one. The skillful way of proceeding is for each person to investigate and discover which method works best for him or her.

SLEEPING AND DYING: THE PARALLELS

"A person well trained in Vajrayana can recognize a strict order in the four stages of falling asleep, and is well prepared to ascertain an analogous order in the dying process," says the Dalai Lama.[12]

This parallel emphasizes the value of dream training, and we realize that we can have a trial run at dying and death every time we go to sleep.

If we are able to master any of the methods of dream training, our chances of enlightenment in the death bardos will be improved. We begin to understand that the association between our different minds— waking, dream, meditation, and death—is an integrated one. Death is not some form of psychological guillotine that severs all connection with previous mind states. On the contrary, if we are able to master dream training, the effects are not lost at death but carry over into subsequent bardos and even subsequent lives.

This realization helps us develop a more mature understanding of life, dream, and death, which form an ongoing flow of consciousness that is simply passing through a succession of different states, taking off and donning different garments.

It is significant that there are four stages in falling asleep. They represent the dissolution into one another of the four elements: earth, water, fire, and air. This dissolution happens at death and accompanies the final separation of consciousness from this body and its associated mind. When we fall asleep, a similar dissolution takes place and allows consciousness to float free of the world mind and drift into the mind of dream.

Bokar Rinpoche mentions this: "The energy governing each element ceases to be functional and is absorbed into the energy of the following element. This process of absorption of the four elements into each other does not occur only at death; it also happens in an extremely subtle manner when we fall asleep or when a thought is removed from our mind."[13]

A very profound but simple principle governs the movement of consciousness between our different mind states: the dissolution and reconfiguration of the elements. Knowing this can assist us with our training, because with the development of mindfulness it becomes possible to discern the processes described while we are alive. But it is not something that is controlled by the rational mind. The dissolutions naturally follow shifts of consciousness.

Unrecognized Clear Light

Unrecognized clear light of sleep is what most of us experience as deep unconsciousness after the onset of sleep. It corresponds to the three- or four-day period of unconsciousness following death. It's also the most significant of all the states we experience in life, because it is very close to enlightenment; in the clear light of sleep there are only very slight veils between our mind state and our true nature. Because of the presence of negative karmic energies in our mind, we do not recognize and thus realize this state: We drift unconsciously through it. It is dreamless sleep.

But this is where we need to awaken to become enlightened. The end point of Vajrayana training is to become aware in the clear light of sleep and then meditate there consciously.

Ringu Tulku mentions that in the yogas it is said that dream is a test of how we would do in the bardo. And he continues that if we are able to meditate in the clear light of sleep, we will certainly become enlightened in the bardo of *dharmata.**

This ends our consideration of training for enlightenment in dream. It is an attractive area for those who are interested in dream and its potential for enlightenment, particularly if they have developed some capacity for lucid dream. The Dalai Lama points out that some people naturally have the ability to dream lucidly. This may be a carryover from training in former lives. However, most lucid dreamers I have spoken to don't seem able to exercise the ability consistently, so more training is apparently needed. What is important is to move on from the fascination with astral travel into serious enlightenment training.

---

* In conversation with the author. *Dharmata* is the innate nature of phenomena and mind.

4

The Process of Dying:
Outer and Inner

Of all things in life, what is the most amazing?

The sage Yadhisthira answers: "That a man, seeing others die all around him, never thinks that he
will die."

— Mahabharata

Whatever we have done with our lives makes us
what we are when we die. And everything, absolutely
everything, counts.

— *Sogyal Rinpoche,* The Tibetan Book of Days

THE BARDOS OF DEATH

When we die, we go from the realm of the three living minds into the
death realms. Here we experience the three bardos of death that seem
to be sequential in that we experience each one only once in the death
cycle.

In this chapter we are going to look at the first bardo of death — chikai,
or the mind of the moment of death. This is a highly dynamic time
where a number of things happen in a short period. (The two other death
bardos — the mind of being dead, chonyi, and the mind of re-becoming,
sipa, will be discussed in chapter 6.)

For consciousness to arise, certain conditions must come into place.
For humans, those conditions are the body with its nervous system and
its accompanying subtle energy systems, the latter not yet acknowledged

by neuroscience. The factors all manifest when the five great elements come together (see the next section). The quality of consciousness experienced within any state is determined by the way the elements combine. For example, the consciousness you experience at this moment, while reading these words, differs from what you experienced in your last dream. The way the elements have come together differs now from that of dream.

To pass from one bardo into another, consciousness must be released. This releasing happens, for example, when we fall asleep, when the elements that hold waking consciousness in place dissolve, allowing consciousness to float free. It floats into the sleep/dream bardo, where it associates with and is held in place by the elemental structures that apply there. These structures are different in each of the several bardos, so consciousness is subject to different worlds.

When we are in any one of the bardos, we believe it is reality. This belief traps us and makes us subject to the conditions of that bardo. To clarify this statement, let's look at the elements and their roles.

ABOUT THE ELEMENTS

In Buddhism there is a system of psychology based on an understanding of the five elements, which are earth, air, fire, water, and space. Throughout our existence, from the most superficial physical level to the profoundest spiritual level, our experience is grounded in and determined by the elements.

They are seen as potential building blocks or matrices, capable of existing in free flow as well as being combined in a variety of ways. The bringing together of the combinations is what determines our experiences as humans.

The Physical Level

At the physical level our body is composed of earth, air, fire, water, and space. The characteristics of our body are derived from them. Earth is the solid part, air the breath and energy flow; fire is the body heat, water the liquid that makes up most of the body; and then there is space.

We know that the elements composing our body have come together in a way different from those composing a table, for example. So the experience at the physical level is obvious. The constellations vary and, in doing so, produce different results. They can be destroyed and broken, and what was may cease to be. The elements come together and disintegrate in an endless chain of manifestations and disintegrations.

At a physical level the combinations produce different forms and substances that make up our physical universe. There are corresponding combinations at subtler levels that create forms that we can't see, which constitute the ground for feeling, thinking, and sensing. These forms can be created and dissolved more easily than the physical body, and they make it possible for consciousness to function in different modes.

The Psychological Level

The psychological level is more subtle. Our mind, emotions, and moods are dependent upon the elements and, once again, reflect their characteristics. Our psychological balance is determined by the state of the five elements at a physical level.

Our thinking processes involve a number of different levels of activity. At one level there is the process of specific thoughts coming and going. Then, slightly below that, there is the human mind's ability to create and sustain particular themes. We may work out logically a theme of discussion, follow it through, and hold it in place in our mind. These functions are possible only if the mind is capable of holding the elements together in a certain way, related to the earth element. For example, if a person has a very short attention span, the *earth* element is weak.

The *water* element is the flexibility and creativity within the mind. Do I see an argument coming? Can I handle it, can I change quickly, go around a problem, see other ways? Can I adapt?

Am I easily excited and angered, or am I cold and withdrawn? The *fire* element is the reactive, responsive, warm, consuming quality.

Am I able to grasp concepts swiftly, generalize from specifics, think in the abstract, and see the relationship between ideas? This ability arises out of the *air* element.

The *space* element determines whether my mind is open, relaxed, and spacious or tight and paranoid.

At the psychological level we are intricately involved with the way the elements have come together. In every human being those constellations are different, so that every one of us has a different mental-emotional makeup. And within every one of us those constellations go through rhythms during the day, over a period of days, over a month or a year. There are inner mental-emotional rhythms just as there are biological rhythms, and they affect the condition of the elements and the way they come together and therefore the way we feel and are able to function.

Inner Systems Level

The third level is the inner energy systems, the domain of Buddhist studies and of Oriental medicine. These inner energies move within the body and determine our psychophysical balance. The balance of these systems determines physical and mental health, emotional and spiritual stability, and spiritual capability, which, once again, are entirely composed of the elements.

Archetypal Constellation

The fourth and most profound level is the ultimate archetypal constellation.

In the Buddhist philosophical view, we are all enlightened beings, and at the level of our enlightened reality our state of being is not involved with the elements. But we became confused at some moment in time, and out of that confusion we developed the idea of being separate egocentric entities. The moment that idea came about, either the elements sprang into being in response or we became involved with the elements; perhaps the two happened simultaneously. The moment we decided we were a separate egocentric entity and we became involved with the elements, we concluded that the separate egocentric state was our reality. This is the illusion most of us are experiencing right now. It is what obscures true reality, which is our enlightened nature.

So we lost touch with our fundamental reality, but it remains and will always be present. When we become enlightened, we will realize that our involvement with the elements was an illusion, mere shadows. Until then, our enlightened nature is represented in the form we may call fundamental archetypal expressions. One of these archetypes is the general sense that there is something more to life than this. It might be as general as that. Perhaps we are even participating unconsciously in the archetype that we are not separate fragmented beings; we are part of a whole. These archetypes are primordial organizing forces that enable our consciousness to relate to deeper truths of our reality. At the very deepest level the elements manifest as these ultimate archetypal forms, which allow us to gain access to our true reality. But they are not that reality: They represent it, like a mirror reflecting a rainbow.

These, then, are the subtle levels at which the elements exist and at which we are involved with them. They are woven into our body, making us psychophysical beings. The way we use our minds constantly changes the state of the elements and the systems that depend on them. Simply stated, negative activity of body, speech, or mind harms and throws them out of balance, while positive activity purifies and balances them.

When we grasp with our minds, that action causes the elements to come together and create a form, so it seems solid. When we stop grasping, the form dissolves and we are free once more. Understanding the elements gives us a profound perspective on how we are as human beings.

THE PROCESS OF DYING

The Importance of Recognition

As we die the elements start to dissolve and we leave the body in stages and move into the bardo of dying. If we can recognize what is happening during this process while it is happening, there is a chance for the mind to become liberated.

The reason we're not liberated in life, dream, or death is that we do not recognize the true nature of our existence and experience. In life this means we don't recognize or understand what is happening in our minds, because of our mind's layers of ignorance.

To free ourselves, we need to cultivate within our mind the capacity for recognition. In life we can do that through meditation — training in mindfulness — which enables us to penetrate the immediacy of our thought processes. Through training in mindfulness we bring the mind increasingly into focus in the moment. When that happens, the mind naturally sharpens and gains insight into its own processes. We unmask the most subtle, hidden activities of our minds, and begin to gain an enormous amount of understanding about ourselves: the way we are in the world, what is really going on in our minds.

This process of recognition is enormously beneficial when we start to die, because mindfulness is a faculty that does not disintegrate when the body dies. It is a quality within consciousness. Mindfulness survives into the death experience and provides the basis for being able to recognize what is happening at that time. It enables us to recognize how consciousness passes through definite transits and to take advantage of the opportunities offered by those transits.

Dissolution of the Elements

As we die, consciousness withdraws in a particular way, made possible by the dissolution of the elements. In that withdrawing we experience changes of consciousness that we need to recognize. Every time one of the elements dissolves and collapses, consciousness is exposed to the nakedness of its enlightened reality, like a glimpse of freedom, of clarity. That's the one we try to recognize. If we recognize our enlightened reality, our involvement with the illusion of existence is ended by that single act. We become enlightened. The light comes on and we realize there was no snake, it was a rope all the time. Do you see now why it is called liberation, or realization? We are liberated from the illusion that we are separate egocentric beings and realize that we are enlightened and always have been. If you understand this, you will understand what the *Tibetan Book of the Dead* is all about.

Earth Dissolves

The first element to dissolve is earth. It begins to collapse. This is recognized medically with the weakening of the body. Each element dissolves into the next finer one, so earth dissolves into water. The body seems to lose substance, begins to shrivel. Forms become indistinct; as though the eyesight blurs and fades. Everything seems like a mirage. The body becomes weak; the dying person can't even lift a hand, can't lift the head, perhaps can't even speak or can only whisper.

In the *Tibetan Book of the Dead* it is said that this is accompanied by certain inner visions and sounds. The whole world turns yellow and we hear sounds like great earthquakes. Most people seem to go through these stages so quickly and in such confusion that they don't notice these phenomena. Recognition of these changes depends upon consciousness being clearly focused, sharply present, and aware. The untrained person who lacks mindfulness would probably not notice most of the changes.

As the earth element collapses, there is a letting go within consciousness, and in that moment the enlightened mind is revealed. It's like a tiny window, and if we've got a really well-trained mind, in that moment we can recognize the revealing of our enlightened mind. Here we see the specific application of the training in recognition. The principle is going to repeat itself over and over again during the death process and beyond. The act of recognition enables the dying person to unite with the enlightened mind and thus become enlightened.

Water Dissolves

After earth, the water element dissolves into fire. At this point there is thirst; dying people almost always become thirsty and want water. The bodily fluids are drying, sensations begin to fade, there is numbness, hearing fades, and there's a sense of being surrounded by smoke. Once again the principle applies. As soon as the smokiness begins to permeate our inner environment, we try to recognize: "Now this is the water element going." In the *Tibetan Book of the Dead* it is said that this will be accompanied by a tremendous sound, as though there were a colossal flood, with huge tidal waves overtaking us. Everything becomes white. It is frightening, but despite the fear, try to keep the mind in focus. Try to remain mindful, so that you can recognize.

Fire Dissolves

Next the fire element dissolves into air and the dying person starts to feel cold, from the extremities upward. The ability to think within the body begins to fade, and our physically based thoughts start fading away. It becomes difficult to draw the next breath, we lose the sense of smell, and there's the impression of fireflies or sparks surrounding us. In the *Tibetan Book of the Dead* it is said that this is where it seems that the whole universe is catching fire and becoming a colossal inferno. Everything goes red.

Fear may arise, but despite this, try to remain mindful and recognize the flash of your enlightened nature, which is there when the element collapses and your consciousness is momentarily freed.

Air Dissolves

Then air dissolves into space. This is where breathing stops. Energy circulations are withdrawing into the central nervous system, our volitional functions disappear, the tongue thickens, we lose our sense of taste, the body senses fade, the texture of the skin changes, and this is where the death pallor begins to develop. Inwardly, it's like being enveloped in that last moment when a candle flame flutters, a sense of something flickering, passing out. Everything turns green and there is a sense of a tremendous wind blowing, as though the universe were being blown away. This may cause fear and confusion. Despite this, try to remain mindful so that you can recognize your enlightened nature when it flashes briefly as the element dissolves and your consciousness is momentarily freed.

NOW CLINICALLY DEAD

The dissolution of air is followed by clinical death. We now leave the familiar realm of medical science. According to the *Tibetan Book of the Dead*, a great deal is still going on in the body. That is why it is emphasized that a dead body should not be disturbed, particularly in the period immediately following clinical death. The environment should not be disturbed; rather, it should be kept peaceful and quiet.

At this time the subtler energies begin to withdraw, and they need time to complete the process. What are called the gross physical elements are gone. There is no more electrical activity in the brain. Nothing more is there — no heartbeat, no circulation, no breath. The person is dead.

Inner Energies Dissolve and Powerful Light Experiences Begin

After the gross physical elements that bonded consciousness into the body have dissolved, the dying person moves into the inner channels. Now the inner dissolutions and the brilliant light experiences begin. The first of these is probably the one described by most people who have had near-death experiences. According to the *Tibetan Book of the Dead*, actual death has not yet happened, so if the body is resuscitated, consciousness may still return.

There are three major channels within the body. One goes from the crown of the head to below the navel; a second and a third branch out from below the navel, with one branch coming up on the right-hand side and another on the left-hand side. They pass up behind the eyes and meet in the center of the forehead. The energy systems involved with these channels begin to withdraw.

White Drop Descends — Vast Sky of Moonlight

There is a white life force in the center of the forehead called the white drop, or *bindu*. It was implanted with the father's sperm at conception. This begins to move down toward the heart, and as this happens the whole universe becomes a very clear, bright moonlight color. The mind becomes incredibly blissful, very still, brilliantly clear. In that moment all capacity for anger vanishes. It is not possible to experience anger during this period.

This is one of the most powerful moments for becoming enlightened, because we're face-to-face with our enlightened nature. The light that we experience at this time is our enlightened mind. If we can remember to recognize the light for what it is, we have a chance to dissolve into our enlightened reality. We will attain a level of enlightenment.

So the white bindu comes down toward the heart. The time taken for this to happen varies with the state of consciousness. Somebody who's lived a violent, depraved, selfish, and destructive life would be unlikely to notice this blissful light experience. The moment would be fleeting, like a flash of lightning.

But people who have lived kind, balanced lives and haven't polluted their inner systems can experience this for longer, even as long as six or seven minutes. Most people either become lost in bliss or think the light is a divine being coming to them from somewhere else, so they don't recognize the light as their own enlightened nature. This response is consistent with our tendency in life to project anything we don't understand onto an external idea. If we fail to recognize the white light, it fades and we pass to the next stage.

Red Drop Ascends — Brilliant Sunlike Redness

The second stage is the ascending of the red life force, or red bindu, from below the navel. (The red bindu came into existence at the moment of conception, from the mother's ovum.) At this point the universe takes on a brilliant sunlike redness. Once again we enter an enormously blissful, clear, brilliant state of mind. At this time any possibility of desire ends. It is not possible for that mind to experience desire.

In the *Tibetan Book of the Dead* it is said that even if the most beautiful goddesses appear (and presumably the most beautiful gods), no desire will arise in the mind. Desire does not have the power to blind us to our enlightened existence, our enlightened reality. If the dead person, with enhanced clarity of mind, is able to remember to recognize that the red sunlike light is the enlightened mind, he or she will be able to go toward it, merge with it, and become enlightened. If not, the next stage follows.

Drops Meet in Heart — Sky of Bright-Dark Light

The white and red drops meet in the heart, consciousness becomes enclosed within them, and the sky becomes full of bright-dark light. This concept is difficult to understand, that darkness can be bright light, but this is the experience we have. At this point the third great bliss arises, and it is accompanied by the cessation of all ignorance. The mind now becomes open to its inherent wisdom, again very brilliant, blissful, capable of seeing and understanding. As before, the key is to remember to recognize. The practitioner recognizes that this bright darkness is his or her enlightened mind, goes into and merges with it, and thus attains enlightenment. If not, the next stage occurs.

Deep Unconscious

After the lights, most people fall into a deeply unconscious state. A parallel is the fourth level of sleep, where we go into the deepest unconscious state. During death, this is where the clear light of our enlightened nature can be directly experienced. The *Tibetan Book of the Dead* uses the rather charming image of the child recognizing the mother and joyfully leaping into her lap. It's a very wonderful moment, at which you become enlightened.

Once again, if we do not recognize, we move on.

REAL MOMENT OF DEATH

What I've described may have occupied the twenty or thirty minutes following clinical death. The *Tibetan Book of the Dead* says it may occupy the time it takes to eat a meal. The length of time depends on the individual's state of consciousness. Trained yogis can extend this period for a number of days, producing the phenomenon of the body being clinically dead while the heart remains warm. The consciousness remains within the body, resting in the clear light, which is the profoundest level of meditation. When the Sixteenth Karmapa died, his American physician expressed amazement at encountering this phenomenon more than forty-eight hours after the death.

When Do We Really Die?

According to Khenchen Thrangu Rinpoche:

> As long as we are alive there is a connection between our body and our mind. This connection is kept intact by the so-called royal life-force. This is the life energy that moves for as long as we live between the white aspect which is present at the top of our head and the red aspect which is present at the lower part of the body. The mind coheres with this energy of the royal life-force and is in this way bound by it.
>
> During the process of dying the royal life-force dissolves. The function of this force was to keep the red and white aspects apart. Now, the connection of body and mind collapses and due to the lack of power of the life-force, the white aspect sinks down, while the red aspect moves up. The moment the two meet at the level of the heart the separation of the mind from the body takes place.[1]

This meeting and its consequence mean that although the elements have dissolved during dying (as indeed they do every time we go to sleep, albeit not so profoundly), consciousness can nevertheless return to the body even after the death process is quite far advanced. I have read of cases where revival was successful as long as fifteen minutes after clinical death. But my understanding is that once the red and white aspects meet in the heart, there can be no revival.

WHERE DO WE GO?

Driven by Our Habitual Tendencies

From all the literature it would seem that as death progresses we are increasingly driven by our habitual tendencies, our karmic impetus.

It is said that our last thought is extremely important. "The Buddha compared the last moments of thought to a herd of cows in a barn. When the barn door is opened, the strongest will go out first. If no cow is particularly strong, then the habitual leader will go out first. If no such cow exists, the one nearest the door will go out first. In the absence of any of these, they will all try to get out at once."[2]

The last thought carries through a theme that, combined with other factors, determines where our consciousness leaves. Consciousness leaves by one of several exits, which have corresponding points in the physical body; it could go out the nostrils, or the eyes, the mouth, the navel or lower down, the top of the head, or most important, the Brahma aperture, the top back of the head.* The focus is on learning to eject the consciousness out of this aperture.

The importance of our prevailing mind state at the time of death is much emphasized in Buddhist teachings. For example, the Buddha clearly equated rebirth with grasping at the time of death, pointing out that we are always striving to perpetuate our existence. This, he said, reinforces tendencies we have already established in life. He used the image of throwing a stone—once thrown it continues in the same direction.

George Grimm expands on this teaching:

> According to this, man always becomes what he would like to become, that is, whatever he desires and thirsts after; for whatever we thirst after, that we grasp. Of course this is not to be understood as if it meant that a mere wish would be sufficient; but what has directing force, is the nature of our willing and of our desire in its uttermost depth, that means, our innermost character, as it appears in action as blind impulse, without being guided by the light of knowledge. . . . [E]xactly in this situation is our will at the decisive moment of death, when it determines our grasping of a new germ.[3]

It is our habitual tendencies that determine the direction the mind takes after death, rather than a stray thought that may have drifted through the dying person's mind at the final moment. According to the teaching, there must be some power behind the thought. This understanding is

---

* The Brahma aperture is a point on the top of the head eight finger widths back from the hairline, where the bones forming the skull meet.

confirmed by Ringu Tulku.* Grimm echoes this view in his own rather quaint style:

> To know to what kind of grasping our will may lead us, we must dive into the depths of our animal life, as it reveals itself when the dominating influence of reason is eliminated.
>
> The fundamental condition for the certainty that after death I shall not become attached to a germ in a lower pain-laden world, is therefore this, that I know myself, at latest, in the hour of my death, to be definitively free from all bad inclinations. Indeed, in this decisive and unconscious condition, I can grasp no other germ but the one desired, because every other would be contrary to my innermost nature.[4]

These comments indicate that the direction the mind takes after death is determined not by conscious thought processes but by the powerful habitual tendencies that reflect the deep or real character underlying our superficial personality. This is why so much emphasis is placed on the need to purify these deeper levels of the mind during life. If we do this, the mind will take a beneficial direction when we die. If not, who knows what will happen?

Why Do People Become Unconscious?

After red and white meet, most people become unconscious for three to three and a half days. It is recommended that the body not be moved during that time.

Why do most people stay unconscious during this time? The first reason is that we don't train in life: Every night when we go to sleep we habitually fall unconscious. So we die with an almost irresistible habit that compels us to drift into an unconscious state. We know now that we can avoid that unconsciousness by training in life.

---

* From a personal discussion with Ringu Tulku.

Second, we become very confused about what is happening. Such huge shifts of consciousness, such massive changes, can be very confusing and frightening, so the mind seeks to escape the turmoil and fear. Unconsciousness is an ideal refuge.

Third, there is a residual unconsciousness from the previous stage, the one where the life energies meet in the heart. Every time dissolution happens, energy breaks loose and we fall unconscious; then we regain consciousness, another dissolution happens, energy breaks loose, and we fall unconscious again. It's as though the impact of the brilliance of our enlightened nature overwhelms us. We can see it even in life. People experiencing tremendous input, either negative or positive, reach a point where the mind says, "This is too much," and the person starts becoming unconscious. It's as though the mind wants to withdraw. One of the main lessons is to train ourselves to stay conscious, to face what is happening. When we're training in mindfulness, we have our meditation support, upon which we focus the mind. The mind wants to drift away into distraction, which is the living equivalent of becoming unconscious. The mind that has trained itself to be free from drifting away has already achieved an enormous capacity to face its reality. When we remain present in the moment, we have no option but to see more deeply into our own mind, because our own mind naturally reveals itself if we remain present with it.

Residual states of unconsciousness tend to reassert themselves.

The fourth reason people stay unconscious during this period is the terror at being cut loose. Fear is a big factor in the bardo, because we are going through massive changes. We experience the collapse of all the known and the familiar. The mind that we know in this world starts to disintegrate. The essence of what we've learned withdraws into a deeper level of our consciousness. This is why we experience our whole life as though it were a rerun and the essence is drawn out of it—the main themes of our habitual tendencies, whether positive, neutral, or negative. The mind that was involved with all those experiences disintegrates, collapses, and what we needed to hold ourselves in the world isn't there anymore; it dissolves.

But if we have trained to focus in life, we can take advantage of
the brilliance and clarity that also manifest, and we could well become   ✓
enlightened.

We Can Get an Idea

As we begin to die, new and powerful experiences come upon us. They
arise from within the mind but seem to come from outside. Think of
falling asleep. . . .

When we fall asleep a process occurs. It's not a simple "now you are
awake, now you are asleep" business. No, the mind transits out of waking, through a transition stage, into sleep. A lot happens in that transition. It begins with relaxing physically and becoming drowsy, and there
is a sense of slipping away. This is followed by the appearance of hypnagogic images, the first fragmentary dream-type experiences: voices,
faces, images, scenes. They are usually fairly familiar, so we drift into
sleep, which means that we pass through this phase into the unconsciousness of deep sleep. Because we are familiar with this particular transition, we accept it and float into it—unless, of course, it's a nightmare.
This is interesting because if we began having visions or seeing things
during waking, we would become disturbed and afraid, thinking that
something was wrong. Our conditioning is such that we can accept and
cope with the unusual within small and carefully defined limits, but
when it breaks out of those limits, we panic because we don't know
what is happening.

The unusual, unknown, and unexpected in everyday life are threatening to the average person. Most of us cannot stand being taken by surprise. When this happens in our minds, the fear is magnified, because
we have so little understanding of our minds. If something strange or unusual happens in there, we panic, probably imagining that we are going
mad. Most people have a great fear of losing their sanity.

We are reaching an interesting perspective on ourselves: We *can*
cope with the unusual (the hypnagogic experiences) if it comes at the
right time and place but not otherwise. Furthermore, after the event we

can look back on it and realize it was only a dream. This is easy to do when we wake up.

So Train Yourself

Once we have understood this perspective, we have the basis for very powerful training. We can draw two different perspectives into the same focus: the after-the-event perspective of realizing it was only a dream and the being-in-the-dream-and-thinking-it's-real perspective.

We do this by reflecting repeatedly on our dreams. We see that they seemed real when we were in them, but when we awoke we realized they weren't real. We develop a growing understanding of the insubstantial nature of dream and, incidentally, of thoughts and emotions. The understanding begins in our waking state and gradually filters into dream. Don't make the mistake of thinking that this means we negate dream and dismiss it. No, we are simply learning to see it for what it is: appearance without substance. In doing this we break the grip of the illusion and free ourselves from it. The dream still happens, but our way of being in it changes completely.

It's like Alice in Wonderland. Do you remember what happened at the end of her time in Wonderland? She was in court, attending the trial of the Knave of Hearts, who stole the tarts. All the creatures she had met during her adventures were present, along with the pack of cards, some of whom were court officials. The crazy Queen of Hearts was clearly going to order, "Off with her head!" But Alice began to grow. She got bigger and bigger, so that her head reached the roof of the courtroom, and she looked down on all these funny little creatures. Her perspective changed, and she suddenly realized they were not what she had thought they were. They weren't real. Her fear of the situation evaporated and she challenged the Queen, "Oh, you are nothing but a silly pack of cards!" The Queen screamed, "Off with her head! Off with her head!" but Alice was unimpressed, and the cards all rose up in a flutter about her. At that point she awoke to find a flurry of leaves blowing in her face.

I once had a dream sequence that played out the same principle. I would like to share it because I think it might help you understand the point.

For years I had had dreams of falling off high places. I would find myself climbing a cliff along an easy path, but at a certain point things would begin to change. The path would become narrower and the cliff more precipitous, and then the path would disappear, both behind and before me. The small ledge I was standing on would begin to shrink and vanish, so I would find myself about to plummet into an abyss. Usually I woke up at that point.

After a few years of these dreams I got fed up with them. Cognitively I could understand what they were about, but I wanted to face the issue in the dream. One night I got my chance. I was in a very tall, narrow building. I climbed the stairs to the top and walked through some rooms and out onto a balcony. The drop before me was immense. I turned to reenter the building and couldn't. The door had disappeared, and when I turned back to the balcony it had dwindled to a mere ledge on which I was perched. At this point I remembered. "Bloody hell," I said to myself, "now I'm going to do it!" Whereupon I leaped off the ledge with a great sense of challenge and indignation that the dream should dare to keep treating me thus. The ground was there, way, way below, but I floated in the air, as though buoyed up by some unseen force. I then drifted back onto the now very substantial balcony. "This is not good enough," I thought, and jumped off again, once more with no harmful effect. At that point I was experiencing a feeling of great exhilaration and triumph, and thus I awoke.

We are not dealing with only one simple issue. We are engaging many levels of psychological material. What is important is to realize that we can train in life to develop the state of mind necessary to attain liberation in death.

As this training progresses we develop an enhanced ability to face, accept, and integrate negative emotions, so that they gradually weaken and cease to cause major problems. The fear level in the mind will also diminish. As this happens, our capacity for facing and accepting the unexpected and unknown will also increase, both in life and in our minds. A great deal of transformation, growth, and wisdom will come out of this. But don't imagine it will happen suddenly. I am talking here of a process that could take many years. We are dealing with deeply entrenched habit patterns.

When We Die

So now, back to when we die. . . .

As death commences, powerful psychophysical changes begin. They give rise to profound experiences within the mind, which means we begin to experience them. The *Tibetan Book of the Dead* describes them in detail, in terms of the appearance of buddhas and the universe becoming yellow, white, red, green. It also describes the onset of earth-shaking sounds and sensations.

Most people will not experience the changes in this way. What we will all experience will be our death equivalent of the hypnagogic appearances that accompany the onset of sleep. Our individual psychology will dictate exactly how these appear. There will almost certainly be a loss of contact with the physical body, accompanied by loud sounds and bright lights of various colors. These sounds and lights will seem to be on a universal scale because our consciousness will be overwhelmed by them. Most people do not realize they are dying and think instead that something cataclysmic is happening to the world around them.

It is quite possible that a person could transit this phase without being particularly aware of it, as with falling asleep. Some people go to bed and fall into deep unconscious sleep immediately, without being aware of the hypnagogic appearances. Research on near-death experiences suggests that this might be the experience of most people, because most subjects report the appearance of the luminous white light and the blissful feelings that accompany it—they never talk about earthquakes, floods, infernos, or changing colors.

Detailed assertions as to exactly what will happen would not be accurate or helpful. It seems that very powerful and unusual things will happen. They could trigger confusion, fear, or panic in the mind unless we can see them for what they are: simply appearances. Our ability to do this will depend on our training in life.

Having said this, I think we should bear in mind an important observation. Most people who die, unless they have been especially cruel, greedy, or violent, seem to pass into a very peaceful state upon death. This suggests that they begin to experience the blissful lights almost as the dying process begins to run its course. In addition, many people report the atmosphere of great peace and spiritual power that manifests at death. So although the *Tibetan Book of the Dead* spends some time describing the dissolution of the elements (which is what the colors and great sounds are all about), it seems that this is not such a significant event as the specific light experiences that follow.

The mind has the ability to cut through confusion in moments of crisis and seize upon what it needs in order to cope. In this case it seems there is a strong likelihood that even if we don't feel that our training in life has been particularly successful, the imprints upon deeper memory will be there and will come to our aid. We will have the chance of realizing, "Ah, now I am dying! These are the appearances. They are manifestations of my enlightened mind. I need not fear. Now is my chance to accept, embrace, and go to them rather than attempt to flee. I need not fear."

This principle holds good throughout the time ahead: the process of dying and the experiences that arise in the death bardos. If we commence now a lifelong training of learning to recognize the insubstantial nature of our subjective experiences and dispel the grip they have on our consciousness, we will develop what we need for liberation in life as well as in the death bardos. There is nothing mysterious or obscure about this.

It may not matter if we feel that our efforts have not succeeded. As the mind is freed from the elements, it becomes nine times clearer. This may be difficult to imagine, but it becomes incredibly sharp and perceptive and also, unfortunately, unstable, as in dream. But if we have developed within our stream of consciousness a well-rooted intention and determination to see through subjective experiences and recognize them for what they are, there is a good chance we will be able to do this in death — nine times more powerfully!

The psychological events that accompany dying and death are extensions of principles we already know. When the mind is faced with unfamiliar and unexpected experiences, it feels threatened and usually reacts with fear. This prevents it from relaxing into something new and being able to learn from new experiences. This is true of how we are in life and in dream—the mind seeks instead to retreat and to reestablish familiar patterns. This is the process of retreating into egocentric grasping and delusion.

We can train in life to recognize that dream is insubstantial and thus free ourselves from the grip of dream imagery. This is the basis for recognizing in the death bardos.

So we are able to prepare for death in very powerful, practical ways right now.

Question: Does the manner of death affect the experience of death?

Answer: In principle, apparently not. The dissolutions will still happen, but obviously a peaceful death is preferable, because then the mind won't be disturbed by any form of violence or impact.

Question: If you become enlightened, if you manage just one of these recognitions, what then?

Answer: Well, that's like the jackpot. You've won a thousand million dollars. What now? You know there are millions of possibilities before you, but it may not be full enlightenment. You may not have recognized fully enough for it to lead to enlightenment, but that doesn't matter, because if you've attained any level of recognition, that will lead to a better rebirth. You'll be reborn with a much clearer mind, with a much greater capacity for practicing meditation. This explains why some people are born with unusual spiritual capacities.

If you are able to recognize totally and merge completely with a clear light, you'll become fully enlightened, and then you're an enlightened buddha. And you'll dwell in a nirvana and send countless emanations into samsara. You'll help beings become liberated.

5

Dying Skillfully

> You may view the eternal essence of your existence
> in terms of the impact your every mood and action
> has on those you touch, and then in turn, on those
> they touch, and on and on—even long after your life
> span is completed. You will never know the rippling
> effects of the smile and words of encouragement you
> give to other beings . . .
>
> —*Elisabeth Kübler-Ross,*
> Death: The Final Stage of Growth

Now for the culmination. We've looked at the processes that occur when we die and at some of the factors with which we can work to prepare ourselves for the death experience. Now we will look at how we can die skillfully. To many people this may be a strange concept, because in our culture most people believe that death is a disaster or a tragedy that we should try to avoid.

Through these teachings we receive a different perspective. We learn that when the time comes to die we have a great opportunity for enlightenment, because death is a powerful spiritual moment. When a person dies, if we're at all sensitive to what's going on, we can sense that there's an enormous spiritual event taking place. Intuition is confirmed by teaching: As the mind breaks loose, powerful spiritual forces come into focus.

WE DIE AS WE HAVE LIVED

We can think of death as the irreversible dissolution of the elements, resulting in the final withdrawal of consciousness from the three bardos of life. But this would be to consider only the mechanical aspect of the event. What is most important is the state of that consciousness and its ability to recognize the changes it experiences during death.

The state of consciousness among humans varies enormously and depends on how we have used our energies in this life and previous lives. For example, at one end of the spectrum we find enlightened beings. Their consciousness may be limitless to the point of understanding the universe and more, with no trace of negativity or dualism there. In addition, enlightened qualities such as boundless compassion, wisdom, clarity, and love would be present.

At the other end of the spectrum might be someone who has consistently indulged, over a period of many lifetimes, in highly destructive, harmful, vindictive, egocentric behavior of body, speech, and mind. Such a person's consciousness would be darkly clouded with negativity, confusion, and ignorance. It would be severely conditioned by its negative karmic predispositions and thus have almost no freedom to recognize and respond creatively to inner changes.

When death arrives, the enlightened consciousness floats serenely and effortlessly free of the body and its elements. The darkly clouded consciousness experiences blind, overwhelming terror and confusion and an inability to recognize, even for an instant, what is happening. Its negative karmic forces crush down upon it, producing hell-like appearances and experiences. Yet both experiences are triggered by the same cause—the dissolution of the elements.

What is the point of dying skillfully? If we die skillfully, we can transfer our consciousness into a beneficial state not normally attainable. We can do this because, as the elements dissolve, the enlightened mind is exposed. If we can partially or completely recognize that and identify with it, massive changes within the stream of consciousness are created. They may lead to full enlightenment if the recognition and identification of the enlightened state is complete, or to the mind's being able to reincarnate at a level that would not be attainable otherwise.

Our consciousness passes through time and space, governed by the rolling-on effect of karma. The karma of this life largely determines the immediate circumstances of our next life. Most people, though, have a large amount of unresolved karma from previous lives: negative, positive, and even neutral. So it is a mix of karma that determines what happens in our next life: where, when, and how we are born.

If we do the dying training, we can gain what looks almost like an unfair advantage, even though we have a fair amount of unresolved negative karma. We can achieve, through this training, an auspicious situation in the death bardos and certainly in the rebirth, if there is to be one.

Many lamas say that the easiest method of becoming enlightened is ✓ through bardo training. When compared with other routes, it seems surprisingly easy because we take advantage of those critical moments when we are passing out of this existence. But it does require training.

WHY WE DON'T DIE SKILLFULLY

Skepticism

Why don't more people take advantage of this opportunity? The first, obvious reason is that they don't know about it. It's only since the mid–twentieth century that this teaching has become generally known to the West.

Second, most people tend to be skeptical of views that differ from their own. Skepticism may be valuable in that it enables us to challenge and investigate intelligently. But if our investigation is one-sided, intended simply to disprove rather than discover what's really there, then all we do is reinforce habitual thought patterns.

Ignorance

Ignorance is a mind state that is fundamentally appealing because it seems to be comfortable: Ignorance is bliss. Often when there's something going on inside us or around us and we know it's going to make us uncomfortable, we would rather not know about it. We'd rather not investigate. In terms of our inner state, ignorance manifests as this preferring-to-fall-unconscious. We see this at night when we go to sleep, this lovely, soft drifting into oblivion.

There's a strong tendency in the mind to black out, not to maintain focus, in the face of a very intense psychological or spiritual experience, as during the death process. This tendency is a manifestation of ignorance.

Fear, Anxiety, Panic

We do not realize how extensively fear permeates the human mind. In life it lurks in shadowy corners, and it surfaces under a variety of conditions. This is something most of us understand, even though we may not be conscious of it. What we also may not know is how extensively fear affects our ability to function in the world.

The term *performance anxiety* identifies the arising of fear under certain circumstances, resulting in the reduction of our ability to perform in one way or another. Fear and anxiety reduce intelligence, sometimes radically.

In its extreme manifestation, fear may escalate into panic, at which stage the mind is overwhelmed or swamped and held helpless in the grip of fear. *Blind panic* is a familiar and accurate term for this condition; we become blind mentally and emotionally and lose the power to see and understand what is happening around us.

We develop coping mechanisms for dealing with fear in life. They are generally based on some form of avoidance or substitution. We find ways of covering up the fear when it reveals itself. We distract ourselves and try to remain distracted until the fear subsides.

However, the unconscious doesn't buy into this. Most of us know about being wakened in the small hours of the morning by our anxieties and fears—lying in bed with thoughts whirling and hearts pounding—unable to break the cycle of thinking.

So we know that fear is present in our mind while we are alive.

When we die, much of this mind with its fears finds itself in the death bardos. But now its old stratagems of denial, avoidance, and substitution are not available. In death we are alone with our mind, a bit like the 3:00 A.M. situation but more so. We cannot escape our fears, and when fear is triggered, it makes the task of recognizing in the bardo very difficult, perhaps impossible.

The simple lesson we learn from this is that if we want any chance of recognizing and thus becoming liberated while we are dying and in death, we have to do something about fear while we are alive. This is such an important issue that I am devoting chapter 10 to it.

Unresolved Negativity

Another factor very common in life, but less recognized, is the welling up of unresolved negativity in the mind. What happens with most of us is that we maintain a level of conditioned suppression where the mind creates a smoke screen and denies the existence of negative emotions. The emotions come out in disguised ways. In psychology this is called displacement. They come out in the form of spitefulness or masked and harmful remarks or passive aggression. We recognize these behaviors in people pretending to be nice and kind, but we pick up just below the surface that something else is going on.

Most of us are to some degree untruthful with ourselves, pushing negative and conflicting emotions down and denying their existence. As we die, the mechanisms of suppression disintegrate and the reality of what was always there comes upon us. When this happens, the mind can be overwhelmed, making it impossible for the dying person to recognize. For this reason we need to face and deal with these emotional conditions while we're alive, while we have a chance to come to terms with them and can start transforming them.

Karma

> Karma is not fatalistic or predetermined.
> Karma means *our* ability to create and to change.
> It is creative because we *can* determine how and why we act.
> We *can* change.
> —*Sogyal Rinpoche*, The Tibetan Book of Days[1]

Karma is the controlling force of our existence. In life we do things that are beneficial, neutral, or harmful. If we've done a lot of harmful things, the consequences may not obviously affect our lives while we are living if we have sufficient balance within our karmic stream. For example, I remember reading about all the amazingly awful things a certain dictator of an African country had done. The surprising thing was that he remained wealthy, seemed to have good health (although he went insane later in life), and seemed to escape the consequences of his actions. He seemed to be happy. This was despite having devastated a whole country and having been responsible for ruining the lives of millions.

I questioned a lama about this and asked how it was that this man seemed to be escaping the karmic consequences of his actions. He said two things about it: "The effects will start showing at the end of his life"—which happened, as toward the end of his life he went crazy—and "It's almost certain that he's burning up in this lifetime all the good karma within his stream of consciousness and he's going to have very, very bad news from now on in all his future lives."

This tells us that when we're looking at a living situation, we can't accurately assess the movement of the deeper forces within the mind, because many of them move on much greater, slower cycles and won't start manifesting for a lifetime or so. But certainly at death it seems that the overall tone of that life comes into focus, and if a person has committed many negative actions during life, that karma will appear clearly in the death process. According to the *Tibetan Book of the Dead*, there are certain actions in life that will result in the consciousness immediately being plunged into the most terrible condition at death. The list includes killing parents, killing huge numbers of people, killing a very highly developed spiritual being. These are quite specific actions that have extraordinary and immediate repercussions at the moment of death.

Although karma means that every harmful thing we do to others harms us and harms our subtle system, we can purify the harmful effects within our lifetime. We can even purify the effect of murder.

This is illustrated in the life story of Milarepa (or Mila), the most famous saint in Tibetan Buddhism. In his youth Milarepa, whose father had died, was ill-treated by his uncle. The uncle stole Milarepa's inheritance and reduced him and his mother and sister to poverty and servitude.

As Milarepa grew up, his mother prevailed upon him to learn magic and use his powers to take revenge on the uncle and his family. Milarepa duly set off to train with a teacher of the dark arts, and he soon mastered the training. One glorious evening Milarepa struck. The uncle and his family were gathered in their house (rightfully Milarepa's) dressed in their finery, holding a celebration. Milarepa magically manifested some giant scorpions that converged upon the building. With their great pincers they tore out the supporting pillars of the lower story, and the building crashed to the ground in ruins, crushing all sixteen occupants. Milarepa's mother was jubilant and ran through the village, waving a white flag and proclaiming her triumphant vengeance.

Milarepa then had a change of heart and started seeking spiritual teachings. When he finally found a yogi who would train him, he had to atone for all his harmful behavior. His famous teacher, Marpa, set him to perform years of grueling purification before he would give him any teaching. So it was that one of the most famous episodes in Milarepa's life unfolded: the building and dismantling of towers. Through this great suffering, Milarepa purified the effects of his destructive behavior, became enlightened, and lived to be one of the great yogis and teachers in Tibet.

The issue of karma necessitates being honest with ourselves and looking truthfully at the way we are in the world: how we think, how we communicate, how we behave, how we treat other people, the environment, and other creatures. We discover whether we have a naturally arising benign tendency, a mixture of positive and negative, or a naturally arising malicious tendency. It is these *naturally arising tendencies* that predominate in the death bardos, not our learned, socialized responses, pretences, or self-images.

PREPARATION

How do we best prepare ourselves for our own death? Again a paradox: We do it by focusing on how our life and death may benefit others. The key is to train the mind to move from being self-centered to becoming generous and other-focused. Without the qualities of kindness and generosity, it is difficult to overcome the obstacles to dying skillfully.

We can work in three areas to prepare to die skillfully:

- Generating positive energy
- Counteracting the negative
- Undergoing specific training for death in various ways

GENERATING POSITIVE ENERGY

We can generate positive spiritual or karmic energy during life. This can cover many areas of activity; a few are mentioned here.

We need a certain level of spiritual energy to follow our path. This is not a principle of spiritual growth only; it is also recognized in psychotherapy.

I remember once reading some of Carl Jung's comments on therapy and individuation. He was making the point that some people do not have the energy within the mind to attain individuation in this life. To illustrate this he quoted a patient's dream: The person was in a tall building and wished to reach the top. He entered an elevator, which took him up some distance and then stopped. He stepped out to discover that he had not reached the roof but that the elevator went no farther. Nor were there any stairs. He had no way of reaching the top, which was still some distance above. He woke up.

Jung interpreted this to mean that the person did not possess the necessary psychic energy within his mind to reach individuation.

Practicing Generosity

There are many ways of generating positive energy. All begin with some form of altruistic motivation and activity, because all our difficulties in life and death stem from mental grasping and self-centeredness. These states produce tightness and darkness in the mind, which then becomes increasingly absorbed in its own concerns. As this happens, our problems become inflated and seem bigger than they really are. Eventually they dominate and overwhelm us. In life we call this neurosis.

Someone who is kind, caring, generous, and compassionate, by contrast, sets an entirely different energy field going. It is the energy of love and openness, an essential context for any form of inner or spiritual growth. This energy naturally dispels the grasping, limiting tendencies in the mind, freeing it from the factors that lead to suffering and difficulty in life and death. If this energy is present, the mind will be able to recognize and become liberated in the bardos of death.

This emphasizes a fact that is virtually unknown in our culture: that if the mind is to attain spiritual realization, a certain amount of enriching and expanding is necessary. Without this, growth is not possible. It's like journeying in a car. If we don't fill the tank with gasoline, the engine peters out and stops before we reach our destination. The first and essential step in the process is to cultivate boundless generosity. Without it the mind remains narrow and dark. With it unexpected depths of realization open up. This is true not only while we are alive but also in death, where the beneficial effects will also manifest.

We can begin by consciously practicing generosity. This is something anybody can understand and do: learn to give, not only material things, but psychologically and emotionally.

Start with One Apple . . .

Akong Rinpoche emphasized the importance of practicing generosity and illustrated this with a simple example for first-time givers. Rinpoche suggested a little game: "Get an apple and hold it in your right hand. Then give it away—give it to your left hand. When your left hand has it, give it away again—this time to your right hand. Go on doing this, one hand giving to the other, until you feel comfortable with the idea of giving. Then give the apple to somebody else."*

Precepts and Morality: Spiritual Armor

Keeping precepts and practicing morality are two activities that are not in vogue. In Buddhist training they are seen as entirely practical issues.

---

*From a personal discussion with Akong Rinpoche.

Precepts begin with not killing, not telling lies, not stealing, not shattering our finer systems with drink and drugs, and not harming ourselves or others through our sexual practices.

The reason for morality is not that we can claim moral high ground and look down on others. Avoiding harmful actions sustains and nurtures the finer inner energy systems within our body-mind. *We cannot harm others without harming ourselves*; it is just not possible. Morality is not about being thought well of, being caught or found out, or anything like that; it has entirely to do with our own inner energy system.

In Vajrayana training morality is called the *armor* that protects our inner energy system. As we go into the death process, it is the condition of this system that determines the moment-to-moment experience of what we're going through, so this system is crucial to our chances of recognizing in the bardo.

Precepts and morality are much the same thing. Morality is just a more general way of saying, "What is my orientation in the world? Is there fundamental integrity in the way I handle myself and the world?" Precepts and morality have nothing to do with being the good boy or the good girl. We need never talk to anybody about them. If we want to take precepts, we don't need to tell anybody. We just develop this deeper integrity in our own minds.

Dream Training

We do dream training to familiarize ourselves with the disintegration of the elements as we fall asleep. Then we familiarize ourselves with lucid dreaming, because these are parallels to death and the death state (see chapter 3).

Taking and Sending: Tonglen

For someone who is not a serious meditation practitioner, the most powerful way of practicing while we are alive and when we are dying is taking and sending, or tonglen. It develops a mind and heart that are naturally open to others. The method of practicing tonglen is fully explained in chapter 16.

COUNTERACTING THE NEGATIVE

Meditation and Mindfulness

How do we counteract the negative? The first and most powerfully bene-ficial method is to stabilize the mind through meditation—training in mindfulness. Negative energy destabilizes the mind, so we learn to master the two stages of training: settling and stabilizing the mind. The stable mind is able to let go of its negative tendencies and to observe the arising of every tendency, whether negative, neutral, or positive. The rea-son many well-disposed people become caught in the negative is that they don't see the cycles of the mind that lead to engaging negative thoughts.

The engaging of thoughts naturally happens if our mind is not sta-ble, because we don't understand that it's not necessary to engage every thought or emotion that presents itself on our inner screen. As a result we incessantly engage, engage, engage, making it possible for negative cycles to keep running. Bad habits are difficult to break because the mind is engaging at a subliminal level: By the time we're conscious of the arising of the emotion or the thought, it has already been seized by the mind and entrenched as "me, my thought, my feeling."

When the mind is stabilized and able to develop a sharp level of in-sight, the person becomes fully aware of this process. The mind sees the moment when a choice is made to engage. It discovers something we usually don't realize: that when we are angry, for example, the experi-ence of anger or other emotion is preceded by a half-seen decision to give way to that emotion. Most people either ignore this moment of de-cision or aren't even aware of it because their minds are too turbulent.

If the mind is stabilized, we are able to see the mechanism by which we engage, and then we are able not to engage. We can let go and free the mind. We develop a deeper understanding and insight into our psy-chological processes and begin to free the mind from habitual negative states. This results in a much clearer and calmer mind in life and also when passing into death.

Training in mindfulness is the most comprehensive method of coun-teracting negativity.

Don't Feed the Negative

We need to begin training, in all dimensions of our lives, to turn away from and not feed negative predispositions. For example, many of us gossip, criticize, and find fault with others, often in a self-righteous way. This sort of behavior reinforces judgmental criticism, anger, and hatred, and it corrodes the mind. We don't have to be this way.

In Buddhism there is the concept of a practitioner. This person is not only training in meditation but is also rigorously alert to all the mind's tendencies to reinforce negativity of any kind. A practitioner honestly acknowledges and faces the existence of these tendencies when they arise and simply does not feed new energy into them. It is important that this be done without suppressing or denying. This is a fine line to tread and is not at all satisfying to our egocentric way of being in the world. It's also uncomfortable and demanding because there is no space for self-indulgence. But it is worthwhile.

SPECIFIC TRAINING FOR DEATH

Purification Meditations

Several meditations that use visualization and mantra have the specific purpose of connecting with karmic tendencies—habitual patterning—and purifying them. This is the domain of Vajrayana. The most commonly known practice is Chenrezi, which purifies the mind and generates compassion.

Serious practitioners would do Dorje Sempa practice (Vajrasattva in Sanskrit).

Attachment and Resentment

As attachment and resentment are two big pots of glue that keep us stuck in samsara, they are addressed in chapter 8.

Transference of Consciousness

Specific training for death, called *phowa*, is widely taught by lamas. Anyone who is seriously interested in training in this meditation should have no difficulty locating a properly qualified teacher.* The meditation involves a specialized visualization that enables one to eject one's consciousness at the moment of death so as to assure a rebirth in a very spiritual realm.

AT THE MOMENT OF DEATH

Tonglen

If one has trained in tonglen, it would be ideal to die while practicing it.

Last Thought

Our last thought is important. Think about a red-hot iron in the forge: It's malleable. We can bend it this way; if it's not right we can bend it another way. When we die, the iron is taken out of the forge and plunged into water and the angle of the iron is set. Our last thought is like that, so that last thought is very important. We should try to control our environment while we're approaching death and have harmonious things around us. We deal with any negative or disturbing issues that might come up. We settle everything so that nothing can suddenly come up and disturb the equilibrium of our mind as we're approaching that moment. (For a more detailed discussion on the importance of the last thought, see chapter 4.)

---

*A properly qualified teacher is one who has received transmission and training in this method and has mastered it. Before taking on a teacher in this field, it is essential to ensure that the teacher is part of an authentic and pure lineage and has authority to teach.

Visualization

If we've done any visualization meditation, we can focus now on our visualization and even have a picture of the deity, the archetype, close by, so that we see it every time we open our eyes. I had a friend who was dying of multiple sclerosis and considered himself fortunate because he had about two years to prepare. He used to lie and look at a huge picture of Chenrezi at the foot of his bed.

I asked him one day how he was getting on with his visualization, and he said in a very matter-of-fact way, "I can now manifest it in my dream." It was wonderful, because here was this poor man withering away in a situation we normally think of as dreadful, and he was so joyful. He knew that when he died he was going to be able to manifest this very beneficial image in his mind. He was quite certain that his dying mind would focus in the best possible way.

Anybody can do this. Every night when you go to bed, do whatever visualization you have been practicing and fall asleep with it in your mind. When you die, your inherent capacity to visualize will arise very strongly. So even if you think you're no good at it, just think of the deity, of whatever it is that this transformation means to you. Just think about it.

Question: Who are the archetypal deities?
Answer: Different religions have different archetypal deities. I would say in Christianity it would be God, however a person may relate to that concept; or Jesus or the Virgin Mary; or one of the saints or even an angel. Tibetans say that within a religious system like Christianity, there are certain power points that manifest the spiritual energy of that system. We might find one that works for us according to our beliefs. In Tibetan Buddhism a deity like Chenrezi is the archetype of compassion; there are quite a few other archetypal deities of compassion, and we would focus on one of them.

Question: The *Book of the Dead* was written by Tibetans for Tibetans. To what extent might the bardo experiences of people raised in other cultural and religious climates be altered or colored by their beliefs and conditioning?

Answer: It seems that they would probably see according to their cultural conditioning—bright lights, angels, a saint, or the focal figure of their religion.

The most important thing to understand is the connection between living and dying. The mind that dies is the mind we know now. When we realize this, we feel empowered to face death in a positive way, as we would any other event in life for which we have prepared. There are many ways of preparing, and they are all central to spiritual practice in life as well as in death. We can get ready now for the last great adventure of this lifetime!

6

Now We Are Dead

Gone
Gone
Gone beyond
Gone beyond "beyond."
Hail the goer!
— Heart Sutra

Once the process of dying is complete, we regain consciousness and find ourselves in the second of the death bardos. As Ringu Tulku observes in the appendix, "Death is not the end of life." Life goes on, but now it is different, like a dream from which we do not wake when dawn breaks.

We wake in the death bardo, the bardo of being dead, regaining consciousness as we do after fainting. But now there is no physical body. People feel disoriented and even frightened, so they may attempt to reenter their body, which they can see.

In terms of the great cycle of six bardos, we have now left the three bardos of life and cannot return to them until we are reborn. The bardo of dying, chikai, has also been left behind and will not be revisited until the death of the next body. So now we are to experience the next two bardos of death: chonyi, in which we awaken about three days after losing consciousness, and sipa, the bardo of becoming, which we enter when the previous one (chonyi) ends and leave when we are born.

It is said that death lasts forty-nine days, but I doubt the value of this time computation for two reasons. First, as far as I can ascertain, time does not run in the death bardos as it does here. For instance, I was once talking to Akong Rinpoche about a story circulating in Samye Ling that a Roman soldier was frequently sighted wandering the hills of Eskdale-muir. Being averse to boredom myself, I felt rather sorry for this two-thousand-year-old wanderer. I expressed my concern, and Rinpoche said, "Oh, no, he probably thinks he has been here for only a day." So we experience time in the death bardos differently, like Rip Van Winkle.

Second, the texts describing the bardos give only a very general picture that is subject to countless variations according to individual circumstances.

The attribution of days may be little more than a symbolic division of time, and I have long since given up expecting dead friends to reappear punctually after seven weeks.

For a long time I wondered at the value of amassing information about these bardos. It is interesting and fascinating to know about them, but to what end? Bokar Rinpoche answered this question when he pointed out that unless we know about the bardos, we cannot be liberated from them.[1] The reason we study them is practical—so that while we are alive we can train and prepare our minds to become liberated when the unique conditions arise. For most people, liberation in the death bardos is impossible, because they have not prepared. Who could pass an examination in a subject he or she had never studied?

When we regain consciousness in the chonyi bardo, we experience the projections of our minds, appearing in the form of deities or bright lights.

PROJECTION

As in life, so in death. Our experience is governed by projection. This topic is dealt with in chapter 9, so this summary is simply to help us understand the nature of experience in the death bardos.

Our human condition is more complex than we realize. Most of us focus only on our consciousness of the world and think that's all there is. It isn't. We are made up of fathomless depths that extend into the unconscious and beyond. These realms are beyond our normal ken, so we do not know about them consciously. We may think they do not exist, but they do. The energies within them are enormously powerful and determine the experience of the conscious mind all the time, without our realizing it.

Think of a movie, of watching images flickering on a screen. This is where we focus, and we attribute to it a certain reality. But if we think about it, we realize the images are a product of bright light shining through celluloid back there in the projection room. That is the source. We almost never consider the source and are absorbed instead in the effect, the appearance. That is projection.

Projection in Life

Projection is an unconscious process. All our unconscious feelings and impulses are constantly imposed on the world around us and act as filters through which we experience the world. If the filter is negative, we experience the outer situation as negative. If the filter is positive, the experience is positive.

Because we do not realize that the energy is coming from within ourselves, we think it is coming to us from outside. Thus, for example, ten different people could attend a movie and each come away with a different view of it. We might even wonder if they were indeed at the same event. Why? Because each experienced the movie in terms of his or her own projections, and each experience was different. Each person's reality is determined by inner feelings, attitudes, and beliefs that are projected onto the outer situation or event.

In life there is a certain objective content that mitigates the effect of our projections, because outer situations and events can force a measure of objectivity upon us. Furthermore, if we are a bit intelligent, we can reflect on our experiences and gain new perspectives, freeing ourselves to some degree from the effect of projections. Inner growth and change are about freeing ourselves from our projections. While we are in their grip, we are trapped in delusion and held in bondage by our unconscious processes.

Projection in Dream

When we fall asleep and dream, we experience a further step away from freedom into deeper subjective bondage. Dream is a more intense experience of projection, where our unconscious energies manifest as people, places, and events. We find ourselves in the power of the dream, and few of us realize that monsters or horrors are no more than a manifestation of our own mind. In dream we cannot blame our projections on outer sources: We are forced to experience them directly.

Freedom from the dream bardo begins with recognition of the nature of the dream. The dream is me. It's my mind manifesting its projection as an appearance, which seems to be external and objective but in fact is not. See how powerful and convincing the projective mechanism is. It's the same with hallucination.

This point was illustrated in the life of a cave-dwelling yogi. His cave was high in a cliff, and there he meditated day and night. Each night he heard a scratching noise at the foot of the cliff. It drew closer, until by dawn it was at the lip of his cave. One dawn it was closer yet and the legs of a huge spider appeared over the ledge. Next dawn, not only the legs but also mandibles and two big eyes came into view. This was scary stuff, even for a hardened Himalayan yogi. He decided that drastic action was called for and armed himself with a knife.

As chance would have it, his guru paid his monthly call that day and scaled the cliff. He asked the yogi how things were going.

"Not too bad, but there's just a little problem with a nocturnal visitor. Not a big deal. It's an inquisitive spider that climbs the cliff. Tonight I am expecting him to make it into the cave, but I will be ready with my knife."

"Ah, stab him in the tummy, will you?"

"Yes, I reckon so."

"Hmm, not a bad solution for a nonviolent Buddhist. But before you do that, maybe you'd like to try something a little gentler. As it happens, I have a piece of chalk in my pocket. Take it and keep it by you. When the spider appears, instead of stabbing it, draw a cross on its tummy."

"Well, it doesn't sound like a good idea to me, but you are my guru, so I guess I should follow your suggestion."

"Quite so." And the guru left.

Next dawn the spider made it into the cave and reared up for the kill. Quick as a flash the yogi grabbed the guru's chalk and made a cross. Yo! The spider vanished.

"Whew! The old guy knew what he was talking about after all."

When the sun's rays brought the light of day, the yogi happened to glance down. There on his stomach was a large chalked cross.

In life we believe our projections and thus turn them into reality. In dream our projections force themselves upon us as reality.

Projection in Death

When we die, a further level of intensity is manifested. Not only do our inner states take form and create our environment, they do so with colossal power and a vividness that may be overwhelming. Now there is nothing left to intervene and interrupt our experience of our projections. In death we are on our own, alone with ourself, the projections of our own mind.

What Determines the Nature of our Projections?

What determines the nature of our projections is a crucial question.

In life we lie to ourselves about ourselves. I may present myself to myself and to the world as a good guy—kind, caring, generous, and so on. In my heart the story may be different—selfish, angry, vindictive, destructive. I may succeed in convincing myself, at a conscious level, that I am the good guy. But that's as far as it will go. The deeper levels of my being do not lie. They are what I truly am, and it's from these deeper levels that projections arise. When we die, this deeper level dominates our experience. The projections that now determine our reality arise in this place.

Karmic Patterning

The law of karma governs everything in life—a little like gravity. Is gravity good or bad? Does it reward or punish? The answer to both questions is no.

So, if I choose to step off the top of a tall building, will I fall to the ground below?

Yes.

But what if I'm a really good, kind, generous person? Surely I shouldn't be punished in such a way?

It's not punishment; it's consequence.

Well then, what if I'm the most awful serial murderer and am being pursued. I find a hang glider, leap off, and fly to safety. Did gravity spare me? Was I being rewarded in some obscure way?

No, it was consequence.

Okay, so karma is purely a law of consequence. We create causes, and consequences follow. Unfortunately most of the consequences we experience in this life manifest actions we performed in former lives, as we have forgotten what we did then or how we were.

With karma, everything we do, think, or say represents use of energy. When we use energy, karmically conditioned patterns are formed within our stream of consciousness. The patterns faithfully reflect the nature of the action, thought, word.

If I deliberately kill with hatred and rejoice in the act, a powerful negative karmic pattern will be imprinted with two potential consequences in life. First, I will have created within my stream of consciousness a tendency toward killing: This is conditioning. Second, I will have planted within my stream of consciousness the cause for being killed myself at some time in the future. This is cause and effect. It is not possible for me to experience an effect if I have not previously created the cause.

This is the law of karma and it applies to everything, whether good, bad, or indifferent. It places responsibility for our lives firmly in our own hands.

In life we experience the ripening of karma.

In death we still experience our karma, but differently. Negative karma darkens the mind and makes it turbulent, confused, and full of fear. Positive karma makes it light, joyful, full of peace and happiness.

In death our projections are a manifestation of our karmic conditioning. Bokar Rinpoche calls it latent conditioning, presumably because it is not objective experience but determines the nature of the world we experience now, and also because we are unable to remember it. Nevertheless, it determines the nature of the world we experience in the chonyi bardo.

Carl Jung puts it slightly differently: "The reality experienced in the Chonyid state is . . . the reality of thought. The thought-forms appear as realities, fantasy takes on real form, and the terrifying dream evoked by karma and played out by the *unconscious dominants* begins."[2] (italics added)

Jung's "unconscious dominants" may be what Bokar Rinpoche calls latent conditioning.

Karma and My Death

Bokar Rinpoche says, "At death, the individual consciousness has no freedom of choice. It is subjected to karma."[3]

Now We Can Discuss the Death Bardos

Now that we can understand how they work, let's look more closely at the death bardos.

- They are realms where we experience the unmitigated manifestation of our own projections.

- Our projections always express the state of our karmic conditioning, whether positive, negative, or neutral.

- Because our projections are an unconscious process that we don't understand or recognize, we believe that they come to us from external sources; they have separate, objective reality; they are not part of ourselves and therefore can harm or benefit; and we are *subject* to them.

We are disempowered in these bardos by our unconscious projections, as we are in dream. Terrifying apparitions may paralyze us with fear to the point of our becoming unconscious. The absurdity, which we don't recognize, is that what we are in fear of is our own mind.

Now we see why all the forms of training place overwhelming emphasis on developing recognition. In life we develop recognition by training in mindfulness. Mindfulness leads to insight. Insight pierces the veils of ignorance and delusion, laying bare our projections. We come face-to-face with our own mind and so understand and free ourselves from projection.

In dream we train ourselves to recognize, "Ah, this is a dream," and so we learn lucid dreaming.

These two forms of training can lead to liberation or enlightenment while we are alive. They are the basis of enlightenment in death through liberation from the death bardos—they make recognition possible.

THE SECOND OF THE DEATH BARDOS: CHONYI

After death we wake in chonyi, the second of the death bardos. The five elements of functioning are gone and we find ourselves in a new, finer "mental" body, highly mobile and with a consciousness of great power. If we think of a place, we will be there in an instant. For people who have trained to think of Dewachen, this is a fine moment, because if they remember to focus, they will immediately find themselves there and thus be liberated.* Ringu Tulku says that this is the time of greatest potential. Enlightenment is comparatively easy.[4]

This information is very encouraging and on the face of it may give the impression that enlightenment in this bardo is as easy as falling out of bed. Unfortunately this may not be so. We still have karma to contend with. Ringu Tulku points out that although this is a time when liberation could easily occur, the force of karma withholds it from most beings.[5]

Sogyal Rinpoche says, "Now previous negative deeds harm you; positive deeds help." He also emphasizes that "whatever we have done with our lives makes us what we are when we die. And everything, absolutely everything, counts."[6]

Our habitual tendencies now take control and blow consciousness through the bardo like feathers on the wind. Most people find their

---

*Dewachen is a "pure land" (rather like heaven) where we can be born if we train appropriately. Once there, we are easily able to practice meditation or other forms of training and become enlightened. From there we can effectively help many beings who are still bound to the wheel of life.

mind in the grip of fear, sorrow, and negative feelings. These are so powerful that the mind is unable to remember or focus in a positive way. All of which brings us back to the emphasis on training during life.

The Lights

When we wake in the chonyi bardo, there unfolds an inner movie of very powerful projections, presenting us with a sequence of experiences, different from the projections of the personal unconscious discussed above, since they arise from our enlightened nature. Each one holds the potential for enlightenment.

These projections arise from the depths of our enlightened nature and reflect five aspects of wisdom—our wisdom nature—that are present in our minds: discriminating wisdom, the wisdom of equanimity, all-accomplishing wisdom, the wisdom of the *dharmadhatu*, and mirrorlike wisdom.

If in life we could allow the complete expression of any one of these wisdoms in our mind, we would, by that action, become enlightened.

If now, in death, we recognize the bright lights that are about to manifest as our wisdom nature, we will, by that fact, become enlightened.

So simple.

If we undertook any of the trainings during life, they would bear fruit now.

In the *Tibetan Book of the Dead*, the experiences that come to us now are described as following one after another on successive days.

On the first day, dazzling blue lights manifest out of our wisdom nature and appear as a projection that fills the entire universe. At the same time a soft, grayish white light appears, which corresponds to one of the six deluded psychological orientations that make up samsaric existence. That is the existence we know and to which we are bound by karma.

Consciousness in this bardo is not shrouded in a body, so it is very clear. It is said that our minds are nine times sharper and clearer. So if we were to recognize the dazzling light as our own wisdom nature, this act of recognition would be intensely powerful. We would merge with it and become enlightened.

But as Bokar Rinpoche says, "If a person seeing this has no idea of what is happening, the sheer brightness . . . is somehow terrifying and the person will turn away from it. One will be more inclined to follow the light of the world of the gods* (the soft, grayish white light), as it is soft and pleasant."[7]

He then states the two attitudes we should adopt when the dazzling appearance comes upon us. First, recognize that the blinding blue light manifests the presence of our wisdom nature and pray that this enlightened form, which we may see in the form of a buddha or simply as a brilliant light, will dispel the suffering of the bardo.† The second attitude requires more profound knowledge: it involves recognizing that the light has no external existence and is the manifestation of one of the five buddhas (wisdoms) present in our mind from time without beginning. It is the luminosity of our own mind.[8]

The *Tibetan Book of the Dead* consists largely of detailed descriptions of these appearances and, in some instances, was read aloud by a lama sitting beside the corpse, as an offering of guidance. The dead person would be reminded repeatedly, "Today you will see such and such lights, deities. Do not fear. Although they seem to arise and come from outside you, they are simply manifestations of your own mind. Recognize them as such, merge with them, and you will become liberated."

Bokar Rinpoche concludes, "If we are not afraid and recognize these deities and their lights for what they really are, we are freed from the second bardo and do not enter into the third bardo of death. If we have not recognized them, the bardo of becoming begins."[9]

So this accounts for the first fourteen days or so. Each day brings a new appearance, arising out of a different aspect of the mind. The first group will be peaceful, but those that come later are fierce and make

---

* The gods are the devas of Indian mythology. They are superior to humans in terms of life span and the pleasures they enjoy but are nevertheless prisoners in the cycle of existence and can fall into the lower worlds. These gods have nothing to do with the God of Christianity, Islam, or Judaism.

† This approach accommodates the belief that the light exists as an outside separate entity, so it is prayed to as such.

frightening sounds. No matter—even those arise out of our wisdom nature, and the instruction is always the same: Have no fear: Recognize and you will be liberated. So there are many chances for liberation.

I would like to offer another way of understanding how our habitual ways of being in life carry over and make recognition of the bright lights difficult. Because we carry with us from life into death the habit of attributing external existence and identity to our projections, we perceive the appearances as external and believe that they are coming from some outside source. They are so big and so brilliant that there is an instinctive tendency to shrink away and escape. At this point the dull grayish light offers solace. It's soft, familiar, and comfortable. Psychologically it reflects what most of us do in life: go for the comfortable psychological options. Thus we opt to return to the endlessly turning wheel of life and death; we miss yet again a chance to become enlightened and free ourselves forever.

What emerges from the teachings is that our nonrational, noncognitive forces are immensely powerful. We experience them in life as habitual tendencies and projections, both of which can be ignored and not faced for what they are. Most of us do this and thus get out of touch with ourselves. In this bardo our habit of avoidance compels us yet again to turn away from the bright light, unless we have trained in life to come to terms with what is happening in our minds.

While I was studying psychology I read about projection but couldn't really understand what it was all about, until one night in the mountains of Zimbabwe. A group of us were staying in a cabin overlooking a high valley with towering peaks beyond. I went to sleep on the veranda but was soon awakened by a rumbling roar that shook the universe. I was so terrified that I couldn't move. The ground quaked and shook and I expected the stone walls of the cabin to tumble at any moment. Then a brilliant, silver-white light bloomed in the sky high above the valley, illuminating the distant peaks and valleys with a brightness beyond daylight. I knew these mountains well and recognized the details of the buttresses, ravines, and cliffs. The light was sharp and bright, casting vivid, clear-cut shadows that sliced the landscape with darkness. The experience was beyond anything I had known, and I was overwhelmed. My rational mind raced to find an explanation, but nothing made sense.

Then I realized that one of my companions who was sleeping nearby had not stirred. I called out, "Sally, look what's happening!" She snuffled, turned in her sleeping bag, and looked in my direction. I suddenly realized that to her it was normal darkness. She muttered something about my keeping my dreams to myself and drifted back to sleep.

Slowly the rumbling subsided, the light faded, and the crickets chirped on in the warm African night. I lay trembling for an hour or so before sleep finally took me again.

Now I know about projection. It is much more powerful than conscious, rational thought. And when we are caught in it, the reality it creates overwhelms other realities, even when it defies all logic. That is what we are dealing with.

Every Time You Argue, You Are Following the Dim Light

Carl Jung gives us a good insight into why it is so difficult to go to the bright lights and not be seduced by the dull lights when they appear in the chonyi bardo: "According to the teachings of the *Bardo Thodol*, it is still possible for him [the dead person], in each of the Bardo states, to reach enlightenment. Provided that he does not yield to his desire to follow the 'dim lights.' This is as much as to say that the dead man must desperately resist the dictates of reason, as we understand it, and give up the supremacy of egohood, regarded by reason as sacrosanct."[10]

Jung recognizes the extent to which reason in daily life is subverted to become an ally of the egocentric action of the mind. This is evidenced by our reactions when our egocentricity feels assaulted or threatened: for example, if we are falsely accused of doing something wrong, or if our opinions are questioned. Our natural and perhaps instinctive response is to stand up for ourselves by offering reasons, rationalizations, and arguments. There is a part of us that insists, "This is how it should be," or "I must," or declares: "How dare they!" There may be a sense of outrage and injustice: "I must put forward my point of view," "I must have my say," "This is not right," and so on.

This area is difficult to deal with because *objectively* we can easily *justify* defending ourselves by whatever means we choose: perhaps argument. In some situations it is appropriate to stand one's ground, but we need wisdom and discrimination to discern the difference between the practical situation and the situation driven by egocentricity.

Liberation from egocentricity is not necessarily a logical or even reasonable business. Nothing except egocentricity itself says it should be. There may be times when it looks like madness, because we don't do what others expect of us. We no longer conform to the norm. Jung also points this out when he says, "the Chonyid state is equivalent to a deliberately induced psychosis."[11]

This doesn't mean we have to make ourselves psychotic to become enlightened, here or in the death bardos, but it does emphasize that the situation is radical. If we want to be liberated, we must be prepared to do something radical. Why? Because egocentric grasping is totally unrelenting. It has no concern for logic, rationality, or sanity. It is simply a mad, blind, inward-looking force that asserts itself all the time, without any intelligent reflection or pause. It cares nothing for anything except preservation and perpetuation of self, self, self.

We cannot break free from a force like this by polite, genteel, or reasonable means. We must meet fire with fire. So the situation may become a bit crazy.

Here is an exercise to give context to what we are dealing with. (*Warning:* Do not play this game if you are not in a light, fairly easy frame of mind. It might even be a good idea to do it in a group so that you can support one another and see how we are all the same. If we are not enlightened, egocentricity will be there. *Definitely* do not play the game if you are feeling depressed, self-critical, insecure, or in any way down. Remember—the point of all this is to help yourself, not punish yourself.)

A GAME: Liberation through intensification

Here is an interesting and amusing way of finding out what chance you have of recognition in the bardo. Call it the "game of liberation from ego grasping through intensification." The game embodies two principles. First we have difficulty recognizing ego grasping for what it is. That is understandable, since almost everything we do, think, or say is egocentric, so that it is invisible to us. To free ourselves, we must progressively expose egocentricity, enabling ourselves to recognize and see it for what it really is, and then be prepared to let it go. Second, egocentric grasping is most apparent (and easily recognized by others) when we are in the grip of intense mind states, such as strong emotions, or delusions—that is, we are carried away by our own ideas and opinions.

The game is to catch ourselves out. Try to keep a sense of humor about it!

Sit down comfortably where you won't be disturbed for a half hour or so. Unplug your telephone and switch off your mobile. Relax and allow your mind to go free: Don't try to focus or think about anything for a while. Equally, don't try to get rid of thoughts. Just let yourself be there.

After a few minutes, go back in memory to the last time you had a strong emotional experience, such as being angry, insulted, afraid, or jealous. Reflect on that time; play with the feelings that manifested; allow yourself to taste the memory. You will begin to get a sense of how things got out of perspective, out of proportion to the cause. Just observe this; don't judge or condemn yourself. Be an objective witness to your own past, without criticism or justification, almost as though you were reviewing someone else's life.

Keep doing this until you begin to see how your whole mind state got puffed up or inflated. Small things took on great significance. Innocent events, comments, or actions were interpreted as being aimed directly at you with harmful intent. See how this became a roller-coaster scenario that intensified under its own momentum.

Then step back in your mind and look at it. What was really there? A big ego! Try to get a *feel* for that sense of *self* and how inflated it became.

An excellent way of testing the strength of egocentricity is to see where your sense of humor is or was. If you have lost it, you can be pretty sure egocentricity has replaced it.

Now get up, walk around, have a break. Have some refreshment. . . .

Sit down again. Relax and let your mind be free. This time, reflect on the last time you saw someone else in the grip of a strong mind state. It could have been an emotion or a strong idea, opinion, or point of view.

Once again, get a sense of what was there. It's often easier to see strong egocentricity manifesting in others than in ourselves. See how blind and self-absorbed the person became. See how inaccessible he or

she became to others' points of view—how out of perspective, unrea-
sonable, stubborn, and insistent. These are all hallmarks of ego grasping.
See them for what they are: They are training for the dim light, training
for failure in the death bardo!

Now you are beginning to understand how egocentricity permeates
life—not just your life but everyone's life. Play this game a few times
until you feel confident that you have begun to recognize the signs. Another good focus, by the way, is self-pity, which is very prevalent in our
guilt-ridden culture. See if you have a dose of it.

Once this level of recognition is established, there will be a natural
growth of perception in your mind. Without trying, you will begin to
recognize how egocentricity maintains itself. This recognition will introduce space and the beginnings of freedom. As this happens, you will
find your mind maturing, so that little by little you will find yourself
able to let go. What does that mean? It means to stand back and look at
your own reactivity in the same way you were able to look at the reactivity of others. (When we look at the intensification of mind states, we
are essentially looking at reactivity.) There is no repression or suppression in this looking; it's an objectivity that we need in order to be free.
As this grows, your power to resist the dim lights in life will strengthen.
And this is not fanciful. If you look at the descriptions of what these
lights represent, the connections become obvious. They represent the
major negative mind states that blind us in life and cause our minds to
gravitate to fixed thought patterns and miss the chance to become enlightened in the bardo. Do you begin to see how training in life is training for freedom in death?

Now for Arguments

When we argue, we are locked into egocentricity. I am not referring to a
situation where, for example, a good lawyer is presenting a reasoned argument without being emotionally involved. No, I am referring to the
situation in which people are going at one another because their opinions or points of view differ. Both sides are convinced they are right and

that everyone else is wrong—others must listen to and agree with them. I'm sure you understand what I mean.

The game is to catch yourself arguing, even in the smallest, mildest way: "No dear, you go that way, not this way. I always go that way because it is better. . . ."

First you catch yourself at it. As soon as you realize you are arguing, stop. Just stop. And see what happens in your mind: rationalizations, justifications, resentment, a sense of "I have lost out," and many other things. "They must be told" is a favorite perspective, especially when the telling is "for their benefit, so I really should."

If you can do this it will be the beginning of liberation in the bardo, because the mind impulse that drove you to argue is precisely the one that will drive you to avoid the bright lights in favor of the dim. If you can break free from it now, you have the beginning of a chance.

This is a life's work!

Another warning about these exercises: Try to approach them in a lighthearted way—as games. Remember, by uncovering egocentric grasping, you are not making things worse. You are simply revealing what has always been there, standing in the way of your enlightenment. Like a doctor discovering what is wrong with a sick patient—it's the beginning of the cure. If you can look at it in this way, you will be able to rejoice in your discoveries.

Making these discoveries does not imply that you have to fly into immediate action of some kind, like trying to force yourself to change or thinking you have to become a universal doormat because you have such a big ego. That sort of approach doesn't work and leads to suppression, guilt, and neurosis. Remember what Krishnamurti so often said, "The seeing is the doing." This is a profound truth of psychological growth. Unlike objective life situations, when we are working with the mind, the act of gaining insight is the most essential element, because our psychological problems depend for their survival on anonymity. They exert their influence in secret. When we see them for what they are, their power is stripped from them and a spontaneous process of change commences. We have now done our work, and time will reveal the outcome.

Apart from laziness, a factor that prevents us from being able to explore our enlightenment potential is fear. We fear change and we fear the unknown. As a consequence we seek psychological safety, which usually means staying with the familiar and refusing to reach beyond our habitual patterns of thinking and believing. So we protect ourselves, which means we entrench ourselves in our cocoon of egocentricity. Protection is limiting and enclosing. The enlightened mind is open and boundless. It is free and joyful. It has nothing to protect.

So safety and security are the path of the dim lights. Arguing is a form of self-justification and thus self-protection. We learn to give them up.

THE BARDO OF BECOMING: SIPA

Sipa is the last of the death bardos, and it may not be until this bardo that we begin to realize that we have died. Apparently some people don't realize it even here and may go on for a long time thinking they are still alive.

In the beginning days there will be a strong tendency in the mind to return to the former life. The world we have left is visible and audible. We may try to communicate with people, but they can neither see nor hear us because the body we now have is mental, not physical. It is a thought body. Much of the personality we had in the last life has disintegrated and fallen away with the dissolution of the elements. We go where we think: "This mental body can move at the speed of thought and in an instant reach out anywhere in the universe."[12]

In this bardo we continue to experience powerful phenomena that arise from within our minds. In this instance they actually reflect the five elements and therefore manifest as elemental forces—sounds of earthquakes, crashing waves and great floods, tornadoes and infernos. The nature of these appearances depends upon our karma.

During this bardo the conditioning of our former life begins to fade away, largely because of the overwhelming experiences the mind undergoes. It is here that we begin losing memory of the former life.

· If one has mastered one of the trainings during life and can remember to apply it during this time, enlightenment is still possible — right up until the moment before the mind enters the womb, egg, or other reproductive method of the realm into which it is going to be born. If not, the mind is driven by the winds of karma, constantly experiencing the consequences of its past deeds, words, and thoughts.

A great longing to be anchored again in some manifest form develops during this bardo. The mind becomes increasingly distressed by its inability to come to rest anywhere and starts searching for a new birth. Its focus into one of the six realms begins to intensify (the six realms are discussed in the following chapter).

For the average person, rebirth is not a matter of conscious, rational choice. Rather, it follows the predominant state of the consciousness, which of course comes down again to karma and habitual tendencies.

If, in the former life, a person developed and strengthened positive human qualities, the energy related to this would produce a strong tendency in the mind to be attracted to an appropriate human birth. If, by contrast, the former life had been one of greed, violence, and harm, the karmic energy associated with that would not predispose the person to seek human birth. Its tendencies would be more compatible with one of the "lower realms," and that is where the mind would gravitate, resulting in birth in a painful place. It follows that there is no punishing or reward involved in this process: It is pure cause and effect. We simply reap the harvest of our former actions, and none other than ourselves will determine the harvest. "As ye sow, so shall ye reap."

As our days stretch out in the bardo of becoming, we are drawn closer and closer to rebirth. Eventually a connection will be made, let us suppose with a human birth. We see our future parents, and at the moment of conception the mind enters the womb and becomes unconscious. This is the moment of birth. It is the moment we leave the bardo of becoming and enter into one of the six realms of the bardo of life. The wheel turns and the cycle continues; we pass out of the realms of death back into living.

7

The Six Psychological Orientations

The six realms are not purely mythical stories or concepts of heaven and hell; they are also psychological pictures. As long as there is a physical body involved with life, that automatically brings pain and pleasure. Physical and spiritual. All six realms are characterized by this continual process of striving, the continual process of trying to reach some kind of ultimate answer, to achieve permanent pleasure.

—*Chögyam Trungpa*, Transcending Madness

While we are in the death bardos, all our options are open, in the sense that highly beneficial rebirths and, as we now know, even enlightenment are possible.

But our options are not as wide as we may hope because during the first two death bardos there is a contest afoot. It is the contest between the effects of training to recognize, on the one hand, and our inclination to follow habitual tendencies, on the other. Force of habit favors habitual tendencies and prompts us to drift back into compulsive rebirth, which is what we have done countless times in the past.

There's no guarantee that our next birth will be human, so it's worth knowing the other options so that we can recognize the tendencies that lead to rebirth in other realms.

Remember when reading the descriptions of the realms that it's generally the fixed, settled, and compulsive mind state that leads to birth in another realm, not the occasional passing thought, feeling, or mood.

When we die, the underlying tendencies that have developed in life through the way we've used our energy will naturally assert themselves. Our experience in the death bardos is governed by that underlying orientation and will largely determine the choice we make.

To say we "make a choice" does not mean it's a cognitively determined choice. Rather, it's a choice we make through inclination—how we are drawn by our habitual tendencies to act, think, and feel in certain ways. We do this in life all the time. If we have an inclination to meet every situation, let's say, with anger and aggression, every time we do that we strengthen that inclination. It will arise more readily in the next situation and we will become more and more aggressive.

Conversely, if we train ourselves to meet situations with patience, kindness, intelligence, and reserve, a change will come about in the mind. First it will be at superficial levels, and then it will slowly penetrate so that our personality changes from, let's say, being impulsive and angry to being tolerant and patient.

Habitual mind states are primary issues. We learn to train the mind, to free it from the habitual tendencies and strengthen the wholesome, liberating ones. In life we have a chance to change our energy orientation. Once we've died it's virtually impossible to do so because the underlying tendencies break loose and assert themselves, as they do in dream. Our power to redirect our energy is lost, and we find ourselves almost completely at the mercy of the winds of karma. Everything we did in our lives now comes into play. It's as though we've set all the causes in motion and now feel the effects. We've lost the power to generate new causes until we have another birth. Now the big issue is, "Will I be able to recognize and be liberated, and if not, what sort of rebirth am I going to get?"

THE REALMS

Existence plays out in what we call six realms, presented in the *Tibetan Book of the Dead* as locations in time and space. We can think of them in that way, or we can think of them as primary psychological orientations that dominate our outlook. Our mind has come from one of these six realms—the human realm. Right now, while we are alive, our primary orientation is human, although some humans lose that even while they're alive.

We look at the six possibilities and check out which realm reflects our mind state and is thus where we're likely to be going. But remember, we are human, so it is to be hoped that most of us are manifesting primarily the positive human qualities. These are to be kind, intelligent, compassionate, wise, and able to curb our natural tendency to give way to desire in everything we do, because the human realm is primarily driven by desire. The extent to which we are able to work creatively with our tendencies determines the extent to which we realize the potential of the human realm. Although we are human, we also manifest characteristics from the five other realms, and this is why we can experience them. In any one lifetime, or even in a day, we as human beings can experience the six different characteristics, the six different personality types, the six different realms.

The realms are divided into three higher and three lower.

The higher realms:

The god realm—characterized by pleasure, bliss, and pride

The warring gods—jealousy

The human realm—desire, also called thirst

The lower realms:

The animal realm—instinct and impulse

The hungry ghosts—craving and greed

The hell realm—anger and hatred

THE THREE HIGHER REALMS

The God Realm: Pleasure, Bliss, and Pride

The highest realm is the god realm, the person oriented mainly to pleasure and bliss. The personality is primarily caught in pride, the overriding negative characteristic of the person. If we're in the god realm, we think we're better, we need to feel we're better. We want things to go wonderfully, blissfully, peacefully, calmly. We want to look beautiful, want people to admire us and confirm the fact that we're better than everybody else. If that has been our primary orientation in life, it will come up strongly in this new world into which we emerge. It will prompt our consciousness to drift toward the dull light of the god realm because that feels comfortable and familiar. The situation is not so simple, because the god realm is one of the "higher realms." To be born in it, one needs to generate a specific type of energy produced mainly in meditation. Very few people manage birth in this realm. It's like a country club for the rich and powerful: That's also difficult to get into!

Warring Gods: Jealousy

Second is the realm of the warring gods. The Sanskrit word for it is *asura*. This is fundamentally the political mentality, typified by jealousy in the sense of being highly competitive. In every situation, we check out the place to identify our main antagonist, the one we're going to watch out for, and then the one whom we can draw into an alliance and manipulate. This is asura thinking: always in competitive mode and ready to manipulate every situation in terms of it. It's almost a fighting mode. Asuras can't help thinking politically. They're always aware of the strengths and weaknesses in any situation. If they're unrestrained, they're a nuisance because they're always fighting, manipulating, causing trouble unnecessarily, but every organization needs an asura because they make excellent administrators. They want to know every detail because this is essential to strategizing and aids in protecting them and their charges.

Asuras are also jealous in that they are never content. They look to see what others have, especially the gods, and they want it. Their jealousy prevents them from enjoying what they have.

The Human Realm: Desire or Thirst

Humans are driven by desire in one form or another, often described as thirst: forever wanting what we do not have and not wanting what we get.

So we swing between these two moods: desire and aversion, endlessly self-referring, obsessing about what we want or lack or can't bear.

But the human has the greatest intelligence. Even though beings in the two god realms are more powerful, humans are more intelligent. This is why, in the fairy stories where there are powerful giants and powerful gods, the human hero eventually gets the better of them because the human works out how to trick them or get around them.

THE THREE LOWER REALMS

Then there are what are called the three lower realms, which are pretty well unrelieved bad news, and we try very hard not to end up in one of them. Remember that we are also describing different mentalities, so one doesn't have to view them as specific locations into which we are born. We can experience these states while we are human.

The Animal Realm: Instinct and Impulse

In the animal realm instinct and impulse are the driving forces. "Everything is put into practice in an instinctive way rather than by applying intellectual or emotional frustrations as a way of getting or possessing something."[1] In life we may see this quality in people who might be nice, good, hardworking, but there's a kind of dull, not very self-aware quality about them. They go for habitual comfort and convenience, like curling up to sleep in the coziest chair. We're talking here about a spiritual unawareness, an ignorance and inability to recognize the buddha nature inherent in all sentient beings.

Hungry Ghosts: Craving and Greed

Hungry ghosts, or *pretas*, are beings who are driven by greed. It's a craving greed, an insatiable need characterized by a sense of lack: "a state where everything that appears in one's life is regarded as something to be consumed or collected."[2] The dynamic component of greed is a sense of lacking, that no matter how much we get, it's not enough. It could be a material thing such as money or possessions: We must have more. It might be love: Some people have this emotional black hole of needing love, and no matter how much they get, it's not enough. The more they get, the less they can give. The hungry ghost realm is described as the height of poverty, there is such insatiable hunger and thirst.

The Hell Realm: Anger and Hatred

The last realm is the anger, hatred, malice realm, which is characterized as a hell state. People's minds are so tormented by anger and hatred that they don't find relief. We meet people whose minds are stuck in anger and hatred, people who suffer. Birth in a hell realm results from sustained malicious harmfulness, usually affecting many victims.

HOW LITERAL ARE THE SIX REALMS?

It's up to us to consider whether we look at these realms as actual places or as psychological conditions. If we look around in life we see people who have these predominant characteristics manifesting in their stream of consciousness.

Question: Must we understand all this on a literal or a metaphorical level?

Answer: I don't think we have to try to figure out too much because, what is metaphor? It simply enables the mind to present itself with another reference point that will give it a deeper or alternative perspective on something when we don't understand it directly. When we're dead, the underlying principles operating in the mind now will still operate then. There's no reason for principles that are manifesting in our life now not to continue there, even though their focus and their form may be different.

One of the aspects of human intelligence is the capacity to understand principles, to extrapolate the deeper sense of meaning, not just be stuck with detail. The more we develop our intelligence, the more we are able to work with principles and abstractions, and as we get into these realms, they increasingly become our reality. We probably don't need to work it out too much, but the principle we need to understand is that the mind states can lead us to fixate in one of the six primary modes or realms. If we remain obsessively fixated in one of them, that will become our habitual mode until the karma fueling it is exhausted. A strong and sustained fixation causes us to "take birth," either in the sense of literally manifesting in the realm concerned or by being trapped in the mind state reminiscent of that realm—as in obsessive-compulsive mind states.

While we have a body, external events can help jolt us out of obsessive states, but when we die this is no longer the case. In the death bardos our tendencies dominate and dictate the directions the mind is likely to take. This is why when the brilliant lights manifest we will instinctively shy away from them and find ourselves naturally drawn to the soft, dull lights. As in life, it's really not easy to resist this tendency toward the known and comfortable—hence the need to train now.

The *Tibetan Book of the Dead* seems to me to contain a lot of symbolic imagery, and some sections contain exhaustive descriptions of what happens in the death bardos. I am not qualified to analyze or comment on this material, which makes up the bulk of what we read in the formal texts. If you are fascinated by it, I suggest you read one of the good translations. I recommend the Shambhala Publications edition, which I have personally found most useful.

As to how we should relate to or understand the information, I have found Bokar Rinpoche's comment very helpful and illuminating: "The teachings in the texts, of course, are very general and the experiences of the bardos are as numerous as the karmic patterns of the mind. Basically what you experience in the bardos is your experience of the imprints of karma, it is nothing else. The different bardos that each individual experiences are considerable, just as the difference of the karmas of beings."[3]

Question: If you are born in a lower realm, how do you get out of it?

Answer: Every being carries an enormous cometlike trail of karma, only a minute portion of which manifests in any one lifetime. Between lives there's a kind of returning to the melting pot, and although the predominant theme of the next life will be determined by the former life, other karmic forces from former lives will also come to fruition. It is to be hoped that some will be positive enough to take you out of an animal birth. It is said that animals that have positive contact with humans have a very good chance of rebirth as humans. People can do special practices for animals and that can help them out, so there are many options for rebirth from a lower realm.

Question: Can dead people read our minds?

Answer: Kalu Rinpoche says, when referring to the time in the sipa bardo, "During this period in the bardo, there is a certain kind of clairvoyance, very rudimentary and not really under conscious control, but nevertheless an ability to perceive the thoughts of others. There is also a certain new sense of the mind's power, although this power is also not consciously or intelligently controlled."[4]

So it doesn't seem that they have the power to check up on us. From what I can understand, thinking about them is a bit like calling them — it draws them to us.

Question: What happens if the body has been cremated?

Answer: Once the death process is complete, consciousness has finished with the body and is occupying a mental body that has no dependence on the old physical body. If you call the person, in your mind or in any other way, he or she will hear you.

Question: What if the person didn't have three days before cremation?

Answer: Consciousness may not have ideal conditions, but the person will still wake up after three or four days.

Question: Do you have to be in the presence of the body when you are helping a person who has died?

Answer: You don't have to be in the presence of the body, but it would be a good idea to call the person by name. The dead are in a place where the power of thought works very strongly, and thinking of somebody draws that person to you.

Question: Do we meet up with other streams of consciousness?

Answer: They are there, but mostly we're so caught in our own experience that we don't see them. It's like dreaming: Other consciousnesses are around us, but mostly we are swamped by our own mind states. But there are beings who can help us, and they do try to do so where necessary.

Question: What happens if you get it right and become enlightened?

Answer: You will be finished with the whole cycle of birth and death. You preempt any karma that can force you to rebirth and you go to what is called a pure realm, a pure land. This is one of the options. Then you are able to send your consciousness back into a chosen form to help beings on one or many planets. This is the situation with the lamas who come back, known as *tulkus.* They are recognized reincarnations and have freed themselves; they've purified and cut free from all negative karma that compels rebirth. They then manifest purely to help others. That's what we are training for.

Question: I'm not so convinced that the pure realm is that great. I'd be more than happy to experience a good few more human births before I eventually get there. I think there's a lot of good consciousness in human form.

Answer: You don't want to go to a pure realm? Carry on being human? The only problem is that you don't know what unresolved karma is going to pop up in your next life.

Question: If you become enlightened, would you see God?

Answer: You would become one with God—that's the Buddhist view. I don't know how others would view it.

Question: If there's an end point with enlightenment, did we have a beginning?

Answer: The Buddha says we've been doing what we've been doing since beginningless time. If you can understand that, it will answer your question!

SOME THOUGHTS AT THE END OF PART ONE

Can we see now that the *Tibetan Book of the Dead* depicts a definite connection between what we do with our lives, what we dream, and what we will experience in the death bardos?

First, happiness and suffering, liberation and bondage, are not arbitrary experiences that come upon us. They are simply consequences of past actions, in life as in death. So we can train now to ensure that our death experience is a positive one. This is a great comfort.

Second, enlightenment in the bardo is a real possibility and in relative terms is easier than when we are alive. Our chances there depend entirely on our training here. And it's not as though the training entails some postponement of living. It's the same as the basic training for enlightenment in life, with a few added extras.

This ends our consideration of the greater scheme: being born, living, dreaming, meditating, dying, being dead, re-becoming. No wonder the Buddha called it the wheel of life; it just keeps on turning. As Joseph Goldstein once remarked in a lecture, the wheel of life is "not too bad when you are at the top but painful when it turns over and you find yourself beneath it." We may be experiencing a relative happiness and comfort in our lives now, but the wheel is turning, and it seems that in all the options that life offers, most are painful, more so than this one.

The real option is awakening to recognize and experience the absolute: our enlightened reality. We do not have to remain in bondage to our own creation of clouds of negative karma. One of the ways of liberation is through the bardos of death.

That's what we're training for—in life, dream, and death.

Death yantra.

Making Friends with Our Mind

Some of us are at war with ourselves without realizing it: We repress feelings, deny the existence of unwelcome mind states, and refuse to accept ourselves as we are. As a result we experience inner conflict, anxiety, depressive states, and fear; we are unhappy in life and fearful of death.

It is possible to change this state by making friends with our own mind, learning to be kind and gentle with it. You can do this if you follow the steps given here and in part 4.

8

Mindfulness

Mindfulness is a mind state that combines our
sharpest intelligence with a stable openness to
our deepest inner states and processes.

This is a short chapter to introduce a very simple method of training the
mind. It is training to develop a faculty that, once it manifests, will penetrate the waking mind, the dreaming mind, and the mind we experience during and after death. It is the one training that changes the mind
at all levels.

THE JOURNEY BEYOND INTELLECT

When we do not understand our own minds, the habitual tendencies remain unseen and, therefore, in control. This we now know.

But simply knowing about the habitual tendencies is not enough. It
doesn't change them, because they are rooted in our mind's deepest levels of conditioning, where they are untouched by intellect. Superficial
habits, such as smoking, are easier to change than our habitual tendencies. So we can't expect to bring about change through devices such as
analysis or intellectual understanding. In fact, even working to achieve a
conceptualized goal may present an obstacle, because the deep change
we require arises not from attacking the perceived problem but from letting go of its cause. To do this we develop a faculty that most people neglect: mindfulness. Mindfulness is the essential element of all Buddhist
meditation and mind training.

When we are mindful we experience being present with ourselves in a way more complete and profound than when we are thinking, concentrating, or analyzing. All these are activities of the mind that prevent its coming to rest and being still, whereas mindfulness is a state of being in which the mind is simply left alone. This allows it to reveal itself fully, to its furthest depths.

It's a bit like studying an animal. If it constantly moves in and out of sight, not much can be learned. But if it remains fairly still, the observer can examine it thoroughly and learn about it.

Mindfulness is a deceptive condition. It's not dramatic. It doesn't produce immediate, spectacular experiences—and we are addicted to dramatic, spectacular experiences. Mindfulness is a subtle process of learning to be ourselves at an increasingly real, profound, and simple level. It may be embarrassing, but it may also be inspiring, because it starts revealing our childishness, our weakness, shame, and silly foibles and also our marvelous wisdom and amazing capacity for love and compassion and clarity. It may reveal everything.

Mindfulness brings the mind out of fragmentation into its natural center—out of its usual state of being scattered and distracted and blown by the wind, where it can't know anything about anything, let alone itself. The true nature of the mind is total clarity, complete wisdom, and boundless compassion. So there's this paradox: We yearn to be happy, kind, loving, and wise, and we look for these qualities in all sorts of strange places, while they are in our hearts all the time. The trouble is that it's a slow, boring process getting to it. That is what we have to face first of all.

Mindfulness brings the mind out of distraction because it involves the cultivation of a faculty, and the more you train, the more that faculty develops. In the beginning we may think that not much is happening. It's like starting to learn a language. We master only a few words at the beginning, but as time goes by, slowly it changes. Ten, fifteen, twenty years later, we look back and realize, "Yes, my mind has changed." The interesting thing is that the mind changes on its own. We don't have to introduce new ideas of how our minds should be tomorrow; the mind does it for itself. That's what happens.

If we develop mindfulness, we develop the essential ingredient that carries through into dream and into death.

Mindfulness is the quality of the mind that does not disintegrate at death. When we die, the essence of what we have learned is distilled into a deeper stream of consciousness, which is the one where mindfulness is embedded. So if we've developed mindfulness, we've developed the basis for recognition, because we've trained ourselves to recognize our own mind. We're recognizing now what sort of person we are, what we're doing with our life, what we do to others, how we work with our psychological states.

Mindfulness is a state of being fully present with ourselves, without distraction. When we are mindful, the mind naturally opens up and reveals itself, so that hidden mechanisms and mind states are seen. This is not easy for a beginner to experience, because often much of what is revealed is not very nice. It is often the opposite of what one would like to be. If our attitude to ourselves is critical or one of rejection, this may lead to turmoil and depression. So we develop mindfulness within a specific context.

The Context for Mindfulness

The context is one of honesty and open acceptance of ourselves as we are. This means we have to examine attitude. What is my attitude to myself? Most of us don't realize how critical and judgmental we are about ourselves. Attitude reveals itself in all the "shoulds" we have about ourselves, and also in any underlying sense of impatience, inadequacy, or failure. All these are products of expecting ourselves to be something we are not and cannot reasonably expect to be—perfect.

If we train in mindfulness, the mind will automatically have its depths revealed to itself, and there will be a steady process of inner discovery. To sustain and integrate the effects of this, the meditator develops an attitude of tolerant acceptance of self as revealed.

For example, if I think I am a kind, patient, and tolerant person, it could come as a nasty surprise to discover that just below the surface I am really quite unkind and even inclined to be vindictive. This discovery might tip me into morbid introspection, self-criticism, and depression if I define it as some ghastly failure or fault.

However, if I have a healthy attitude of openness and self-acceptance, the situation will be different. I would simply say to myself, "This is the human condition. Humans are not perfect, so we naturally find imperfections in the form of negative tendencies in the mind." In this instance it is possible to accept our mind states without praise or blame and just allow the mind to continue revealing itself. It does not, though, mean we endorse, approve, or act out the negative condition. Discovery does not imply approval. It's like the medical situation: A doctor may discover that we have a disease. We don't try to pretend this is not the case, but neither do we say, "Oh, that's great." Instead, we realize that what is there has been revealed, and whether we like it or not, that's the fact of the matter. We are now in a position to do something about it. It's the same with the mind.

MAKING FRIENDS: PEACE OF MIND

As we progressively accept ourselves as we are, we are making friends with ourselves and coming to terms with the totality of our inner reality. This is powerful because it permits the deeper forces of the mind to be revealed to awareness and integrated into consciousness. The process leads to what is called insight—a penetrating and accurate seeing into our own depths and understanding of what we see.

This is how we begin preparing in life. It should be obvious that this training will transform the mind during life. It is the path to enlightenment.

More important, mindfulness brings us increasingly into the experience of that part of our consciousness that flows through the gates of death. Growth will soon be evidenced by changes in our dream world. People who are training intensively in mindfulness typically report an intensification of dream activity, with better recall and more vivid and meaningful dreams with more profound themes.

This is the start in our training for living, dreaming, dying: training in mindfulness and the development of an attitude of honest, kind self-acceptance. This is the ground for getting to know the forces within our minds that we will experience during death and in the bardos of death.

HOW TO BECOME MINDFUL

Mindfulness is knowing what's happening while it's happening. Knowing what's happening while it's happening, that's all: training to have the mind in the moment, present with whatever is taking place. This is surprisingly difficult to do, because our mind is so busy and geared to doing things that it has difficulty simply observing our inner environment without thinking we've got to do something about it.

Beginner meditators frequently come up with the following remarks and questions.

Oh, I couldn't get rid of that feeling. Mindfulness is not about getting rid of feelings.

I couldn't get rid of that thought. It is not about getting rid of thoughts.

I couldn't make my mind go blank. It is not about making the mind go blank.

I couldn't empty my mind. It is not about emptying the mind.

This is what's so difficult for us to understand. Mindfulness is not about doing anything to the mind we observe. We leave that mind as it is. We do not intervene or interfere in any way. It's like sitting beside a river, watching the water flow by. We don't jump in, we don't throw things into it, we don't build a dam. We don't do anything: We simply observe the river flowing and let it go by.

If we can learn to do this with our mind, we develop "bare attention." Bare attention is movie-camera consciousness. The movie camera observes without comment, without judgment, without evaluation, without intervention—but it takes a lot of training for us to be able to do that.

The basic exercise in mindfulness is working with what we call the meditation support. We support the mind's focus, because in the beginning the mind cannot remain stable without some point of focus. If we try to observe our mind's activity without some sort of anchor, the mind will simply keep drifting away. It will go into its normal thinking patterns: daydreams, analyzes, mulling over the past, so we won't be able to keep it in focus.

It's a subtle training because the meditation support is not an object of concentration. It's a place to rest the mind—like a butterfly, very light. When it lands, it lands very lightly, then it flutters away and lands again. We use the meditation support like that. We just touch it very lightly with our mind. We don't grasp, don't seize hold of it, don't try to use it in any way. Often people try to use the meditation support as a way of forcing the mind into one or other way of being, like trying to force the mind to be calm or to stop thinking. So they grab the support and try to bludgeon the mind into silence. That's missing the point. We don't have to make the mind silent. When we stop churning the mind, it will fall silent on its own. Every time we engage thought we disturb the mind, like wind blowing on water; it ruffles the surface.

So it's this amazingly simple but difficult process of just learning to be present without intervention. The meditation support facilitates this.

If you want to begin training in mindfulness, try this simple exercise.

EXERCISE: Training in mindfulness using sound

Sit quietly; simply be aware of your auditory consciousness but don't try to find a sound. Soon sounds will come to you. Let your mind rest with whatever sound commands your attention.

Notice how sounds keep changing: A sound arises, then another, and so on. Our minds can be quite rigid; we want to hold a particular sound so as to experience a sense of continuity, because this makes us feel secure.

We don't have to do that. We can relax, allowing sounds to come and go. From time to time a particular sound commands our attention; the mind will naturally go to it. Then it may fade and another sound will replace it. We naturally hear the call of a dove. When it stops there's traffic, then the rustle of the leaves; when that stops, something else: The door's creaking. So sounds come to us all the time. We don't have to look for them.

In this way the mind learns to relax, be open, and receive in a simple, easy, nonjudging, nonseeking, nongrasping way.

Then it will drift into thinking. That's okay; it's not wrong or a failure, it's not a disaster. It's normal.

Our minds have been thinking all our lives. It's not reasonable to expect them to stop now, just because we've decided to meditate. So the mind thinks. This means we've lost our mindfulness, either partially or completely. When we realize we're thinking, we don't chastise ourselves; we very gently refocus on sound. No need to do anything to the thought the mind had engaged. No need to push it away, to analyze it, to seek meaning in it; just leave it where it is and go back to the support. This is a very simple outline of how we train in mindfulness.

Practice for five or ten minutes a day for a week. Then you can extend the periods to fifteen and twenty minutes. Increase the time gradually and in manageable increments.

If you are serious about developing mindfulness, read more about it in my two previous books: *What Is Meditation?* (also published in South Africa as *Tranquil Mind*) and *Diamond Mind*.

This is your basic training, and you can keep doing it for the rest of your life. If you persevere with it in a gentle, self-accepting, noncritical way, the inherent tranquillity and wisdom of the mind will manifest spontaneously to take you further on your inner journey. You will read more about this in chapter 14.

> We do not need to be religious to see the benefits of mindfulness. It can lead to an increase in worldly as well as spiritual happiness. We can practice it anywhere and at all times while working, eating, riding in a car or enjoying ourselves in the sunshine. The aim is to integrate it within whatever we are doing, wherever we happen to be.
> —*Akong Rinpoche*, Taming the Tiger

9
Breaking the Cycle of Illusion

As long as we project we cannot see the nature
of mind.
—*Kalu Rinpoche*

Successful dying is related to successful living. The liberating principles
that work in life also work in death.

PROJECTION

Let's look at a key to these liberating principles: projection. Of all the
mind's activities, projection is the most profound, the most difficult to
understand and identify. It is an unconscious process and thus by its very
nature eludes us. Yet projection pervades everything we do on the relative level. It affects most of our other psychological processes, such as attachment and resentment. We learn from Carl Jung that projection is "a
natural process whereby an unconscious quality, characteristic or talent
of one's own is perceived and reacted to in an outer person or thing."[1]

"A natural process": Because of the way we are put together as human
beings, projection happens. We don't consciously decide to project. We
are usually unaware of its operation, yet it comes into play all the time
and subverts many levels of our psychological process.

"Unconscious": Projection is an autonomous function independent
of consciousness. It is the shadow we don't want to know about that hi-
jacks us through our emotions.

"Quality, characteristic or talent": We are often unaware of our potential, whether positive or negative.

"Perceived and reacted to in an outer person or thing": We attribute our unresolved psychological states to the external world: We attach them to another person, an event, the environment, and then we relate to them as though they originated outside. Projection involves both negative and positive mind states.

How do we recognize our projections? We see them reflected in things we do, think, and say. The world is our mirror, and the mirror reflects those aspects of ourselves that we fail to see or to know: our shadow. We all have a shadow. When we walk in the sun, it appears. When we walk in the realm of the psyche, it hides.

Our ego or rational mind is involved in its own ambitions and image management, so it represses all the aspects of ourself that we find unacceptable. Our cultural conditioning rejects them. And through this cultural leveling process, we similarly banish our greatest qualities, including the spiritual, to the shadow.

Positive projection happens when we feel too unworthy to have positive qualities or prefer not to face the responsibility of realizing our positive potential. We put it onto others. And through the media and market manipulators we are encouraged to idolize other people— until, of course, they exhibit normal human weaknesses and come crashing down.

One classic indicator of negative projection is blame. When we find ourselves blaming, it is almost certain that we are projecting. Blame often carries a strong emotional and moral backup force of self-righteousness.

At times there is validity, but when we see an emotional component out of proportion to the situation, that is an indication of projection. We may then ask ourselves where this comes from. Where, emotionally, does it arise? It might be from fear, anger, insecurity. It is more creative to look at what is in our own mind than to thoughtlessly give vent to habitual impulses and reactions.

During our four-year retreat at Samye Ling in Scotland, the lama in charge, Lama Yeshe Losal, said one day, "You don't need to spend time pointing out other people's faults. If you identify and face your own faults, you will be so busy that you won't have any time to point out other people's faults."

The classic positive projection is the romantic notion of falling in love. "To fall in love is to project the most noble and infinitely valuable part of one's being onto another human being."[2] A whole explosion happens out of our psyche and onto the other person. We don't get to know the other person; we want the beloved to be only what we've put on him or her. It's the basis of so many disastrous relationships. When the projections wear off, the "love" can easily turn to "hate," which is just another projection.

Complete human beings have integrated their fundamental systems of masculine and feminine energy. Tantric pictures symbolically present the union of male and female, which is the ultimate integration of the human personality: the androgynous state of being not one or the other but both.

Mature relationships are not shadow projections but potentials for mature love.

We cannot liberate our mind until we have broken the grip of projection. Projection dislocates our energy systems at many levels, beginning with focus. While we are caught in projection, it is not possible to focus the mind to recognize its own experience, and we know now that recognition is a fundamental issue in life, dream, and death.

The principle of projection goes right down to the most fundamental issue of the human condition: belief in the idea of a separate ego. The whole egocentric cycle is sustained and maintained by projection. So while that is going on, we don't know what's happening in our own mind.

As we are dying, the pattern is repeated with the arising of the powerful inner experiences: If we don't recognize them for what they are, we experience them as external. The chance for enlightenment is missed because instead of identifying with the clear light, or whatever it is that's arising, we see it as something out there; we fear it and fall unconscious. This is the consequence of not seeing or knowing or understanding the nature of our own mind, even at a preliminary level. When it presents itself to us, even with a fraction of its true power, we're overwhelmed and become unconscious. This is the cycle of our existence.

I saw a funny film a while ago called *Beautiful People:* It was about humanlike traits in animals. There was a baboon who pulled up a rock looking for juicy, edible insects. To his dismay he found a snake, and baboons are terrified of snakes. This one just fell over backward and fainted. It was such a funny scene that they replayed it three times. I've always remembered that because it's what we do. All through our existence we're presented with our own reality, and like this baboon, we fall over backward and faint: Instead of being able to face the enlightened moment, we go unconscious.

When we die, the same thing happens. The enlightened potential is there, but we fall unconscious. When the new body arises in the post-death condition, the mental projections arise, day after day, in vivid, dramatic form. Because they are so powerful, we keep falling unconscious in the face of the nakedness of our own mind.

The principle we're working with is not complicated. In essence it's very simple: It's this whole issue of projection and refusing to face what is there. When we realize this, it's important not to become critical of ourselves. We are simply discovering the fundamental ignorance of the human condition: We can't face the real issue, we can't bring our minds into focus, so our minds are fragmented. That's why we're not enlightened.

The first step toward piercing projection is training in mindfulness. Mindfulness will also equip us to see through some of our other psychological obstacles, two of the most formidable being attachment and resentment.

LEARNING TO LET GO

Over and over again we read that attachment and resentment prevent peaceful death and make recognition difficult in the bardos of death.

Attachment, or *grasping,* may involve people, possessions, situations, ideas, beliefs. We try right to the end to hold on to something that has been important to us during life. When we're alive we're so involved with our grasping that we don't really see it for what it is. Everybody's grasping. We're all being encouraged to grasp. It's the whole matrix in which our existence happens. We don't realize the psychological depths to which it penetrates and how it is at the root of our being. When this is revealed through mindfulness and meditation, it surprises a lot of people.

And so to *resentment*. We don't understand the extent of our resentment either, because it's one of those masked emotional states that don't often flare up in discernible form. It's more of a background wash in the mind. It is the accumulated consequence of unresolved hurts, angers, rejections, and disappointments. When we die it has a vengeful quality. Our energy is no longer directed outward, as it is in life, and it starts to fall inward. As this happens the underlying mind patterns become vividly active and overwhelming because they are no longer masked by projection.

We need to look at these two in more detail.

ATTACHMENT, OR GRASPING

> It is one of the great lies propagated by our culture that
> getting more and more physical and material prosperity
> will lead to greater and greater happiness. This simply is
> not true. Genuine happiness lies in not wanting. Endless
> wanting is such a burden to the mind. If we really wish to
> be happy and create happiness for those around us, our
> task is to clean, aerate and order our minds.
>
> — *Tenzin Palmo*, www.tenzinpalmo.com

Because we usually do not recognize our attachments, we may need to reflect awhile to find out what is really going on in our minds.

We are always thinking, so the first thing to find out is what sort of thought patterns our mind follows. After we've meditated for a while, our mind moves according to specific patterns caused by underlying tendencies. One person's mind goes this way, another person's mind goes that way. Just as in life we have personality characteristics, so in meditation these characteristics reveal themselves in thought patterns. These thought patterns tell us a great deal about ourselves. They tell us what sort of person we are, what sort of fundamental tendencies are carrying us through life. This is important, because everything we do in life is an expression of the kind of person we are. It's like a light that shines: It's direction is determined by the way it's aimed.

Our kind of personality is revealed by the underlying tendencies in our minds, and within those tendencies is the way we grasp and what we grasp. Do we grasp at money? At people? At emotions? At sensations? At events? Experiences? Possessions? Reputation? Lifestyle? What dominates in your grasping pattern? Discovering this is essential because it will manifest as we approach death, when we don't want to let go of this life, don't want to be parted from the known: my identity, my partner, my child, my home, my new car, my bank balance. The mind says, "I don't want to lose you, I don't want to lose it." Woody Allen has quipped, "If I can't take it with me, I ain't going." But we don't have that option.

There's a kind of madness in all this, because we haven't got it anyway. We don't own that person. The house may be registered in our name, but we haven't really got it. It's not enmeshed in our personalities except through our ideas. The mind nevertheless believes that it *has* got them and thus clings to the *idea* of ownership. This is the psychological factor that causes problems.

So we have this idea of ownership, which arises out of grasping. There are interesting stories told by the *delogs* who meet or observe people who have died.* It may happen that when people wake up in the death state, they see others taking their possessions—their boots, their money, their favorite wine, whatever it is—and they fly into great anger. This is tremendously harmful for the mind in the death bardos, and it is thrown off balance quite powerfully.

In 1982, when Akong Rinpoche first visited South Africa and was speaking in Johannesburg, attendance had become a bit of a social event

---

* A delog is a person with the ability to go into suspended animation and, while in that state, enter into the death bardos, meet people there, and help them and do a lot of work.

among a stratum of wealthy matriarchs. One in particular was notice-able because she wore a different outfit for each event. At the end of the day Rinpoche said, "If you want to take refuge, you've got to take a vow not to kill anything for twenty-four hours." An exclamation of horror es-caped this lady: "What about the moths?" Everybody looked up in some surprise. Rinpoche inquired, "The moths?" She replied, "Yes, the moths in my wardrobe. Can't I kill the moths in my clothes?" He was silent for fully a minute, digesting this piece of information, and then—his Eng-lish wasn't great in those days—he said, "Better you throw away all your clothes." He paused and then said, "Better you throw away your wardrobe as well!"

Often we are attached at surprisingly simple levels, and this grasping causes grief and pain when we die, all because other people are going to have our possessions. They're going to invade our most personal spaces and they're going to take what is there, and it will no longer be ours. And if we are observing that, as we can from the other side, it can become a source of great suffering. Grasping is such a powerful factor that it can even prevent us from dying.

So, to pass peacefully out of this realm we need an intelligent under-standing about our relationship to our possessions. They are here, we use them, they're for our benefit, for the benefit of others. We can help people with them, they can be valuable, they can be useful, but that's all. My money has no mystic significance, nor have my possessions. We also need to examine grasping or clinging tendencies in our relationship to the people in our life, because we will be leaving them behind too.

Because this is such an important issue, I have devised a little exer-cise to help you identify and weaken your grasping tendencies. Let's look at attachment and see how we relate to all the things we think we pos-sess. There are three parts to this exercise:

Step 1: Identify my grasping

Step 2: Imagine losing or giving away

Step 3: Now give it away

Certain questions seem to crop up regularly, so I have included feed-back from workshops that may answer some of your own queries.

EXERCISE: Where is the important attachment in my life?

STEP 1: Identify my grasping

Sit comfortably in a quiet place where you won't be disturbed. You will need thirty to forty minutes. Have a pen and paper handy.

Begin reviewing your possessions by looking at your life. See where your sense of ownership, or your sense of possessing, is most intensely focused. Just see where your mind goes, and then write down what comes to mind. Don't try to analyze; just write. If you like, you can grade things according to importance: 10 = very important; 1 = little importance.

Note not only tangible things but any attachment: It could be attachment to people, to objects, to symbols, to ideas, to knowledge. It could even be attachment to attachment!

When you have made your list, put it aside; don't read through it.

The following day, repeat the exercise, again putting the list aside without reading it.

After a week, do the exercise a third time. Now go through all three lists and analyze the items or themes that crop up most often. If you like, count your scores; see by your scoring how intensely you grasp.

This should begin to give you a pretty good idea of how your mind grasps and how much importance you attach to objects of grasping. It will spill over into daily life and sensitize you to how your mind works in grasping mode.

Ask yourself the big question: Do I see the consequences of my grasping? Particularly, do I see how it causes difficulties (in my mind and externally) and even suffering and conflict?

This is where we can learn.

The exercise is not over yet. Here are some questions that came up when I did a workshop in Cape Town. See if any resonate with you.

Question: Do I have to give up things I am very attached to?

Answer: No, we don't need to let go of the physical things. It's the psychological attachment that's the issue. It's that part of the mind that says, "This is an all-important thing." What we're looking at is how a simple, practical thing can become enmeshed with our psychological grasping issues.

Question: What I'm struggling with is how can we learn to be compassionate if we have to let go of the people we love?

Answer: The question comes from the assumption that loving means holding on to, whereas really, loving is letting go.

Question: Grasping too tightly seems to destroy?

Answer: Yes, so you see that when you grasp the thing, you actually smother it; you destroy it.

Question: The disturbing part of the exercise was realizing that at some level I was attached to being attached.

Answer: Maybe that was getting closer to seeing pure grasping that is in the mind even when our object of grasping is not there.

Question: The first thing on my list was the attachment I have about knowing things.

Answer: Attachment to knowledge, to being "the first to know," is a big one. Especially in our culture.

Question: I'm not so attached to my books as to the ideas in them.

Answer: Our ultimate attachment is to the *idea* of self.

STEP 2: Imagine losing or giving away

Relax in the same way as before, with pen and paper on hand.

Go through all the things that have come up in the initial attachment list and imagine losing the important ones. Lose them in the sense that they are taken away from you or you have to give them away. If it's your reputation, you lose it; if it's your good looks, you lose them; if it's your knowledge, you lose it—whatever it is.

Imagine going through a situation where suddenly, in one hour's time, you have to catch a plane out of the country, leave everything behind, and never come back. That's happening to people all the time. So just see what happens in your mind.

Question: Isn't it like a monster: Once you cut its head off, it grows two back? If you consider giving away what you're attached to, your natural response is to grasp.

Answer: Is it? We'll have to find out. Don't make it into a theory. You know this is a real experiential thing.

Question: I enjoy what I have; I enjoy who I am and the life I have, and right now while I'm alive I don't want to give that up or let that go. When I die, that will be fine.

Answer: Okay, but what if you walk out this front door in an hour's time and get struck by lightning and you're dead, what will your mind be doing? Is it still going to want to go on living and therefore suffer because its body has been reduced to a charred heap? Or will it have developed the power to let go and enter the death experience mindfully? That's the issue we're dealing with, isn't it? You don't become morbid about life — it's good to enjoy life, but attachment to living becomes a problem.

Question: But is it wrong to want to enjoy these things?

Answer: It's not wrong; it's fine. Enjoy them fully. But discover your relationship to them. This is what we're trying to do. We're not trying to make ourselves feel bad about what we've got. We're trying to find out whether we can be free at the same time, in which case we enjoy things much more. Curious, that: The less possessive we are, the more we enjoy.

Question: What about the things I need?

Answer: That's practical, isn't it, needing things? So it's seeing that we do have needs, but the need can become an excuse for attachment, and that's the one we're trying to work loose.

Question: Losing the teachings and the practices in a material sense: That's hard to imagine. It would feel like losing direction or getting lost.

Answer: Yes, but the essence won't be destroyed, because that essence becomes you; that's your inner wisdom that remains. It's the external things that go.

STEP 3: Now give it away

Finally, you actually give away one of your possessions: something you are attached to. Just do it and see what happens. This exercise challenges grasping in a very direct and practical way. See how it affects your mind. Be sure to actually give something away. Go on doing that until the giving becomes easier. You will begin to understand generosity and its liberating power.

The following real story happened at Godwin Samararatne's retreat center in Nilambé, Sri Lanka. Godwin had talked on generosity, about giving away what we find precious. One of the retreatants had bought herself one luxury at Harrods in London for this rather rigorous retreat: a beige cashmere stole. Morning after morning as she sat in her *kuti* (meditation hut) during the monsoon, she saw a little stick woman aged about seventy years, a tea picker, shivering in her traditional cotton dress. She had to give her the stole. Then morning after morning she saw the stole, not around the shoulders but on top of the head of this tea picker, folded like a pancake. Next thing she saw her washing the precious cashmere stole in the river, beating it on the rocks!

What a lesson in learning to let go!

RESENTMENT

Like many of our most disturbing mind states, resentment is often masked and not seen for what it is. The result is that most people think they are free of it. Sadly, this is often not the case. It festers in the depths of the mind and poisons us in life. In death it manifests as a major karmic obstacle that disturbs the mind and prevents recognition. If we look into the anatomy of resentment, we will see why it is such a powerfully negative emotion. It's a blend of anger, hurt, hatred, grief, pride, rejection, shame, vengeance—and grasping. What a mixture! For me the most striking feature is how pointless it is. We carry resentment, very often with a sense that we should, as though we were thereby getting revenge on the object of our resentment, particularly if it has arisen out of a wrong done to us by someone. What we miss is the fact that the only person being harmed by our resentment is ourself. The psychology is a bit along the lines of "I am angry with you, therefore I will drink poison every time I think of you."

The great antidote is *forgiveness*. It's difficult for most of us but easier if we realize that we are learning to forgive ourselves. Odd paradox. Forgiving the object of our resentment heals our hearts. Refusing to forgive tightens the cord of egocentricity until we become strangled, miserable wretches resenting the whole world. In a novel I was reading the other day, the author commented, "My father had a highly developed sense of grievance." This comes from resentment. What a mind to take into the death bardos! It reminds me of a wonderful comment by a meditator at a recent retreat.

We had been doing an exercise that was designed to help meditators develop insight. In the feedback session someone said, "When I watch my thoughts and I realize what's coming up, I think, 'Jeez, it's not safe to let this mind of mine out on the streets!'"

So if our mind is not fit to be let out onto the streets, whatever will we do when we are in the death bardos with nothing but our mind?

Let's look at our own resentment and how much of it is masked and how much accepted. There are two parts to this exercise.

Step 1: Identify and recognize it

Step 2: Heal the wound

Step 1 is an exercise you do only once, and only when you are in a good space psychologically. Preferably do it with another person or with a group. If you are a bit fragile, have a counselor or therapist handy, because you don't want to land yourself in a neurotic turmoil.

EXERCISE: Freedom from resentment

STEP 1: Identify and recognize it

Sit comfortably as before, and relax. Have a pen and paper handy.

Now allow your mind to drift to a memory of something that upset you and caused you to feel resentful. Maybe a memory of feeling wronged. Allow your mind to touch that painful spot, feel the resentment, even allow it to grow a bit. See how there is a tendency to get in there and develop the feeling; see how many feelings come up, how you want revenge and to prove that you were right. Really allow yourself to recognize and acknowledge, "Yes, this is resentment, pure and simple."

This is necessary because the mind will tend to rationalize and thus obscure the reality of what is there. We can easily justify the feeling and convince ourselves that we *should* feel it.

Now, do this only once, when your mind is in an okay state, so that you understand where your mind can instinctively go, and then let go of it. While we're alive we're able to cover these feelings over with sugar, but when we die they come up, so we need to know about them.

You may find that resentment is often interwoven with other feelings, such as jealousy, hurt, expectations, guilt. Don't dwell on them. Do this exercise just long enough to reveal to yourself the fact of this emotional state in you. Write brief notes. Then have a break: Chat with people, have tea, go for a run. Break the thought cycle.

Question: I felt a lot of regret while doing it.
Answer: Regrets and resentments, yes. One of the big things in the *Tibetan Book of the Dead* is to live your life so that when you die, you die without regrets. You live your life so that you do what's really valuable; you practice kindness, generosity, forgiveness, you train yourself, so that when it comes to dying, you don't suddenly think, "Oh, if only . . ."

Question: The resentment seems to go on and on?
Answer: Well, when you're really into resentment, you can sustain it all your life. Some people do, because it's got a lot of energy and there's a kind of self-righteousness in it, which is the most corrosive part.

Question: I feel I should not be jealous.
Answer: If there's a "should not," this could be the basis of suppression or repression. We have to deal with those, because they add guilt to the underlying condition. So this is why one of the first things we emphasize in meditation is to accept and come to terms with the way we are, which means accepting and coming to terms with the fact that negative emotionality is there. It's part of the unenlightened state. Then change becomes possible.

Question: So we come to terms with our feelings?

Answer: Yes, we really accept and come to terms with ourselves and our feelings. From there the underlying state unravels itself.

Question: How do we deal with other people being resentful toward us?

Answer: If they can't forgive, then maybe just keep clear of them. Keep away from them until something can be done creatively. You know there are times when it's wise and skillful just to keep away from certain people until things shift enough for the issue to be dealt with.

Question: What I've found is that letting go is a long and slow healing process. I would think that it was done, then suddenly out of the blue a surge of anger comes up in me.

Answer: Yes, and along the way it's important not to feel guilty about this anger. What you've just described is an honest mind. You're frankly acknowledging what's going on, and that is the start, as you say, of the healing.

Don't try to analyze too much. What's important is to identify the fact that resentment is there, see what it's doing, and see that we need to let it go. So we take those steps.

This ends step 1 of the resentment exercise. What we have done is enable ourselves to recognize the existence of resentment and prepare the ground for coming to terms with it and accepting it.

Step 2 is learning to heal the wound. That is where we free the mind.

This is something we probably need to do for ourselves, and we can also help those who are approaching death to do it. By now we are clear in our minds about the existence of this emotion.

Next we will discover that we feel resentful toward certain people — people who we feel have harmed us or whatever. We hold them accountable for our pain, misfortunes, suffering. They are the targets of our resentment, and when we think of them, strong feelings arise in us, which we project onto them. This is the poisonous situation we need to heal.

STEP 2: Heal the wound

Sit as before and relax. Have pen and paper ready.

Allow your mind to go to the resentment, this time being specific: "I feel resentful toward that particular person." What would normally happen when this feeling comes is that we become trapped in it and the mind begins to go around and around in a circle, constantly recycling the same thoughts, feelings, stories, memories, without resolving anything. Simply mulling over memories in this way is a dead end that has no value. Now we learn to break out.

Begin to write: Write all your feelings, hurts, and complaints as though you were writing a letter to the person.

Question: Are you going to send the letter to the person?
Answer: No. This is an exercise. Often the person is dead or very old or has gone out of one's life. It's not necessary to communicate directly.

Question: Should you never do that?
Answer: If the situation is one where you can speak honestly to the person without causing hurt or dumping your unresolved issues, then maybe it could come to this. But complete this exercise first.

Once you have written all and expressed all your feelings, you need to be heard. You do this in one of two ways. If you have a patient friend whom you trust and who is prepared to help you, read the letter to that person so that you can hear your own voice saying the words. Otherwise simply sit in a private place and read your letter aloud to yourself.

When you have done this, swap places with the person who is the target of your resentment. Be that person and write a reply to yourself. But here you introduce a new ingredient. When that person replies, the response is not aggressive or defensive or whatever you remember that made it impossible for you to communicate in the past. This time the person is open, caring, honest, wanting to help and heal the situation. So communication becomes much easier and more positive than it ever was in reality.

Suppose the person was your mother. You are angry and resentful because she neglected you when you were very young. She abandoned you; she didn't give you the love you needed. Now you put yourself in her position, and she begins to tell you what her life was about, her hardships and problems. Suddenly you start to get another perspective from your mother, or your father, or your older brother, or whoever it was.

When the person has replied fully and you have written everything you can remember or think of, go back to being yourself, to your catalog of complaints in the light of this new information, because you're still resentful. You say, "I don't care what you were experiencing, I'm still angry and hurt, and my life's still a ruin." Whatever it is, say it all again. Then go back to being your mother again. So she says, "Well, I'm really very sorry, but I loved you and I did my best, and I managed to get enough money together to educate you, and you know, the reason you're able to be so eloquently destructive of me now is that I gave you the education you needed." Go through this as many times as you need to, backward and forward, backward and forward. Each time you write, remember to hear yourself.

While you're doing this you may need to draw pictures. Sometimes the material gets so deeply emotionally obscure and overwhelming that it is difficult to articulate. Draw in whatever form your mind chooses, any way of expressing what you felt.

You're giving yourself two ways of dealing with your emotional issues: writing and drawing. In doing this, you break the tendency to go around in circles of endlessly embellished ideas. You give yourself a straight line, where you can go straight through facts. You start to see the bigger picture, a fuller perspective. And what is important, you also start hearing yourself: hearing this three-year-old child endlessly whining because life didn't give it what it wanted. Now this may sound a bit critical, but I don't mean to be, because we've all got that unresolved, infantile material in our minds. It's very painful, and to relieve the pain we need to give it a chance to release its bond in the infantile mode and come into some sort of maturity. The way to free ourselves is to face the issues fully. Usually there are only a few emotional issues involved, but until we deal with them we carry that underlying material through life. Every time anything goes wrong in life, it gets drawn into this underlying, unresolved place. So our resentment finds endless reasons to be sparked off. Now we're getting right to the core of it.

Writing breaks the pattern of compulsive, repetitive thinking, because as you write you begin to see what is actually there. The lamas call this a letter of blame.

Question: Is it important to get to the truth?

Answer: If possible, get to the truth, but what's more important is to see the other person's point of view. Put yourself in his or her position, because with resentment issues, what we tend to do is disempower ourselves and excessively empower others, and that becomes the pattern in our lives.

Question: What if the issue is that the person is not honest and caring?

Answer: You can be creative here, I think. Remember that what you're doing is freeing yourself, so you can either invent honest and caring or see that if the person is not honest and caring, she is in trouble psychologically. She must be quite damaged, so try not to make judgments about her. Just begin to see what a painful mind state she must be experiencing. It's like a person who's got only one leg and cannot run in an Olympic race, so you can't reasonably expect that of the person. What you're trying to do is remove the basis of thinking that the person was deliberately setting out to destroy and harm you.

Now, unhappily, there may be instances in life where a person did do that. Then you look behind that, to what a painful, damaged sort of personality would need to do that, particularly to a child, so that eventually you can find compassion for the person instead of regarding him or her as this all-powerful monster or whatever.

Question: Should the friend I am reading to give feedback?

Answer: Preferably not. The friend is just there to enable you to voice the issues.

Question: I seem to turn my anger and resentment against myself.

Answer: That usually arises when you don't feel free or confident enough to express it to the other person, when, for example, as a child it was not possible to express your anger without being crushed. So the child will turn anger back against itself and blame itself.

So, as you do this exercise you could well bring out the fact that the anger or the resentment, or whatever it is, is a double-edged sword: It's against the other person, and it's being driven back into one's own heart. The exercise should help you free both directions, because now you are free to voice it and express the hurt and blame, and the other person is giving you a sympathetic hearing.

Question: Life didn't turn out the way I wanted it.

Answer: Well, you face that: "I wanted it this way," and it wasn't this way. So you state it and you keep bringing it out until you see that wanting it my way is actually infantile, not coming to terms with reality.

Question: So it's very egocentric?

Answer: You're surmising that the problem arises from the egocentric, infantile grasping aspect of the personality. Yes, and through the exercise we're introducing an element of maturity. As the mind matures, it releases, because in this context our suffering comes from these unresolved, infantile attitudes.

Go through this cycle now, with all its permutations. We need to get right to the core of it, because that is what will arise at the moment of dying. It is this deep, hidden, psychological energy that wells up. It's not rational; it's not cleverly, intellectually formulated; it doesn't structure itself particularly in accordance with the political or economic system that surrounds us. It is just an age-old welling up of deep, unresolved, endless grief, misery, anger, pain, disempowerment, all those things that have emerged in our discussion.

Carry on with the writing until you know you have said all you need to say and heard all that the other person has to say in response. Fully exhaust the situation so that there is nothing left unsaid, nothing left that still tugs at your mind. You have said it all and heard it all.

Now you are ready to conclude.

Sit, relax, and visualize the person you felt resentment toward. Maybe she walks into the room and stands before you. All the issues between you have been resolved. You look at her and feel kindly toward her. Whoever it is looks at you in the same way. This has possibly never happened before. You look at each other with caring and friendship; a freshness and joyful freedom dawns between you.

In your mind you say, "I forgive you." Then say it out loud: "I forgive you." It's all over—finished. All that remains between you is love and caring. Finally, say good-bye.

With a last glance the person turns away and leaves the room. You are done. You are free.

Go through this process of writing as often as you need to. Let's suppose the object of your resentment is a person: you saying, the person responding; you saying, the person responding, until eventually you know that you've completely worked it out, exhausted it. You know the other person's situation and you really have been able to forgive him and yourself. You are ready to accept him as another suffering human being. He is not different from you, not all-powerful. This person is also a human being, wounded, being crushed by life, struggling to do his best, and he just could not do for you what you thought you needed.

The principle is to break our one-sided way of looking at life, to look at both sides of the picture.

You can also do the exercise with somebody you're helping, somebody who is approaching death: Talk to the person. Don't say to him or her: "Now, what are you resenting?" You talk to the person, and slowly, if resentment is the major issue in the person's mind, it will start coming out, because as people approach death, they often know it, and these issues will start surfacing in their minds, and then in whatever way you can, you help them.

This ends the resentment exercise.

Most of this book has looked at fairly abstract areas of our existence, in the sense that we have focused on states of consciousness and how they change as we flow through the six bardos. We have looked at ourselves as streams of consciousness experiencing the endless play of illusion that the Buddha called samsara—going around in circles.

Throughout, my concern has been to help clarify a few simple things. First, we are already enlightened beings, but somehow we are out of touch with that fact, even though it is our ultimate reality. Second, because we have missed the point, we have created an alternative reality for ourselves, one dominated by egocentricity. This we call relative or conventional. Where there is egocentricity there will be confused and unskillful behavior. This will generate negative and conflicting emotions, and when these states arise, we have a hard time. This is what the Buddha called duhkha—stress, or not-what-we-want.

It is possible to extricate ourselves from this situation, but it requires a bit of work. We have to do the work. Buddhism is sometimes called a do-it-yourself religion; I think there is some truth in that.

I must share with you a charming story: In years past we had a retreat center in a tiny village in northern Cape Province in South Africa. There was a dwindling Afrikaans Calvinist population and us, a small group of Buddhists. With a bit of careful effort on both sides, we got along okay.

The matriarch in the village was a charming old Afrikaans lady—Aunt Jaapie—a retired schoolteacher. One day Aunt Jaapie was overheard in conversation with a visitor to the village.

"How many people are living here?" he asked.

"Well," replied Aunt Jaapie, with firm authority in her voice, "there are twenty-five of us who believe in Christ and are going to heaven; then there are fourteen others who have decided to make their own arrangements."

That's us. Here we are making our own arrangements.

These arrangements, as far as preparing for death is concerned, are both general and specific. At a general level we address the all-important matter of projection: This is a life's work. In specific we focus on attachment and resentment, identified by lamas as especially important because if we don't begin freeing ourselves from them they will complicate matters in death. So it makes a lot of sense to deal with them while we can.

I included material from workshops in this chapter because I think this helps give an idea of how many of life's issues are involved when we address attachment and resentment. Dealing with them really leaves us much happier and freer in life. This is the basis of breaking the cycle in which we are caught—the cycle of illusion.

10

Fear

If there is sufficient reason to fear, then fear is good!
Fear creates preventive measures, so that's good. Yet
if there is no basis for fear, then when you meditate
analytically the fear will be reduced. That's the
proper way.

— *The Dalai Lama*, The Power of Compassion

During my early discussions with Ringu Tulku about the *Tibetan Book of the Dead*, he stopped me and asked, "What about fear?" He emphasized, "Fear is the biggest problem in the bardos of death. Help people to understand this."

I delved into the main texts again and there it was. When we are in the bardos of death, the unusual experiences will tend to frighten us, as nightmares do. We all know how fear cripples the mind and reduces our ability to understand what is happening. This is as true in death as in life.

SEEING THROUGH ILLUSION

The Buddhist view of life as twofold — relative and ultimate — gives an interesting perspective on fear.

Fear arises in the relative world because of ignorance of our true nature. The ultimate perspective is that each of us is an enlightened being. But our clouds of obscurations have caused us to lose sight of the sun of our enlightened nature. Like a sleeper, we are caught in a dream that we believe is real. For as long as we believe this, we will experience the dream as real, and we will suffer the terrors of nightmare. While we are in dream, our reality—the waking state—is forgotten. But though it may be forgotten, it's still there, tucked up in bed. Tai Situ Rinpoche remarked during a teaching at Samye Ling, "A dream is the dream of one night. From birth to death is the dream of one lifetime." The relative condition is like the dream. It's an illusion. Our enlightened reality is always present, but we forget it because we believe so strongly in the illusory or relative state. It is our fundamental ignorance or misunderstanding that gives this relative state its power over us.

So it's all about breaking free from the illusion, from the illusory state of bondage, limitation, fear, and endless stress. Freedom seems to dawn gradually for most people. With training we learn to dream lucidly, to recognize the dream as dream and not reality. So we dispel the illusion in its own territory, that is, dream time. With training we can learn to dispel the illusion of this lifetime.

This is very powerful psychologically and spiritually because it echoes what will happen when we become enlightened. We can strengthen our power to see through illusion in all bardos: life, dream, and death.

When we work with fear, we use the same principle as in dream: we learn to recognize that fear is an insubstantial illusion. But in the beginning the illusion is strong and our minds are weak, so even if we remind ourselves that fear is an illusion, it won't help—we remain in the grip of fear. So a graduated approach is needed.

We acknowledge that for us, trapped in the relative, fear is a very real problem that will not vanish just because we remind ourselves that it's an illusion. So our first step is to train ourselves to deal with fear as though it were a reality. We employ skillful methods of facing fear and freeing ourselves from its crippling effects at the relative level. As we progress, a little light enters the picture. We experience a little freedom, gain some confidence in our ability to work successfully at freeing our minds from fear. Once we have done the work with the relative, we will be in a position to start with the ultimate perspective.

What follows is a graduated approach to dealing with fear using the relative and the absolute.

FEAR: THE RELATIVE PERSPECTIVE

In the conventional sense, fear may be an appropriate response to a situation fraught with danger on a physical or a psychological level. As the Dalai Lama remarked, "If there is sufficient reason to fear, then fear is good! Fear creates preventive measures, so that's good."[1]

He was asked how we could overcome fear as a habitual state, especially when there was no apparent cause. "I think that the kind of outlook you have and the way you think makes a big difference. Often we find ourselves being hit by a sudden thought or feeling, such as fear, which, if we leave it to itself, or give in without paying much attention, can begin to work in its own cause and begin to affect us. It is crucial that when such things arise one must apply one's faculty of reasoning so that one does not fall under the sway of these thoughts and feelings."[2]

What follows is not about the kind of fear that warns us of danger. We will look at fear as a mind state, as the thoughts and feelings that tend to overpower us. We will look at fearfulness as a habitual state, especially where there is no apparent cause.

Come to Terms with the Situation

When we understand projection, we are able to come to terms with the fact of fear as an ingredient of the personality. Until we do this, we will believe that fear does not belong and should not arise unless there is some specific external reason. While this attitude prevails, fear will be a problem and we will try in vain to get rid of it or escape it. We may feel trapped, convinced that something has gone wrong. When we are not able or prepared to accept ourselves as we are, we are indeed trapped with a monster, and we panic.

In this situation, fear lurks constantly by the door and feeds a host of low-grade neurotic conditions such as anxiety, tension, stress, and insecurity. These compound one another.

This cycle happens for two reasons. First, most of us have fixed ideas about ourselves and how we should be, not only in the outer world but particularly in the inner world of our feelings, thoughts, mind states. As a consequence, if some state arises that does not fit this image, we refuse to accept it and deny its existence. Psychologically, this is like trying to drive your car with the brakes on. Something's going to burn out.

When we refuse to accept something inwardly, we project it onto external targets. More important, the state we don't want will stay with us because our inner resistance holds it in place.

Second, once the cycle gets going, it operates at an unconscious level; we are unaware of it, so we don't understand what is happening. We assume there must be some external cause and blame our job, a relationship, the environment, or the stock market. These may be triggers, but they aren't the real thing.

The real thing is simple. It's my refusal to accept my inner situation and my failure to recognize that this throws up a range of painful mind states that won't go away. The escape from this torture chamber is to accept the situation. This is easier said than done because fear is such a strong emotion and we may be conditioned to reject it. We need a graduated approach, learning to cope when fear strikes.

If we can come to terms with fear in life, we will be well on the way to being able to face the death bardos. More important, if we are able to understand the *anatomy* of fear, we will discover that it is a paper tiger.

Before looking at practical fear management, I would like to mention a novel antidote to fear in the death bardo that I came upon some years ago.

In Tibet, about forty miles from Lhasa, a high valley lies among peaks that abut the northern slopes of the mighty Himalayas. Emerald green streams cascade to a river that flows on to the distant Brahmaputra, and thence to many holy places.

In the heart of this valley is Tsurphu Monastery, the ancient seat of the great Karmapa, the Black Hat Lama of Tibet—an important place of pilgrimage. Above the monastery is a special place. A path winds among mountain buttresses until it reaches a small ravine. The drop is more than nine hundred feet. At some time in the past a boulder rolled into this cleft and became wedged, creating a precarious bridge. It is a unique bridge: Those who cross it, I was told, become, by that act, liberated from fear in the death bardo. Imagine that!

"I must do it," I thought, and for years this intention lay in my mind.

Finally, on my second pilgrimage to Tsurphu, the chance arose, and together with thirty or so fellow pilgrims from South Africa and Zimbabwe I set forth, puffing up the path more than eleven thousand feet above sea level. We skirted a sky burial site where the last vultures were completing their meal.

"A good reminder," I thought, and plodded on. I looked up and saw the cleft high above. At its topmost point I spied the rock resting impossibly between what looked like two vertical walls. The slightest jolt must surely send it plunging to the valley floor hundreds of feet below.

"I don't know about fear in the bardo," I thought, "what about right now!"

We reached the rock within an hour. Rain had swept the mountains the night before, and the rocks were still wet. Slippery. I looked at our rock. It hung about nine feet below the lip of the ravine and from above looked even more unlikely to support weight. The drop to the right was breathtaking. Quickly, before fear paralyzed my resolve, I slithered down, slipped, landed with a jolt on the rock. It felt firm. I looked down. Not a good idea. Two narrow tips rested against the walls, and it bellied out to about three feet in the middle. There I stood. To my left the mountains. On the right, space. No handrail. Over the years Tibetans had attached prayer flags across the space, and these have accumulated to form a comforting wall of fluttering cloth. Another illusion of security. A picture flashed through my mind of me hurtling through space like a meteor, streaming prayer flags on my way to the bardo.

So up the other side I clambered and was finally helped to level ground by one of the party.

With that ordeal safely behind me, I am now anticipating my arrival in the bardo with interest.

But we can't all traipse off to Tibet to seek magical cures, so let's look at some more-practical means of dealing with ourselves.

Dealing with Fear

When fear strikes, remind yourself: Fear is no different in essence from other emotions. If we refuse to accept it, if we suppress or repress it when it manifests, we will hold it in place and it will go on and on. If we accept it and come to terms with it, it will still manifest, but it will pass just like every other emotion. Acceptance releases us from the terrifying specter of fear going on and on forever.

That is your starting point: Put the situation into perspective so that you don't collapse every time a hint of fear wafts through your mind.

It Doesn't Have to Paralyze You

We allow fear to paralyze us, to make us seize up psychologically and physically. After a few times down that road, we feel helpless in the face of fear. Action is needed. Do something to break the cycle.

Physical work can give temporary relief, so develop a policy of action. If you don't, you will be like a mouse hypnotized by a snake, and the fear cycle will be strong and long. If you can do heavy manual work like digging the garden, do it until you are exhausted. Do housework, wash dishes, scrub floors—anything.

Activity alone won't get rid of the fear, but it will break the cycle of fear and panic. Activity lets you focus your attention outwardly, away from the fear, instead of inwardly and into the fear. You're helping yourself to focus away from the fear without repressing it and are thus giving your mind a chance to settle down and let the fear subside.

Relaxation

Fear and anxiety create tension in the mind. This communicates itself to the body. The body becomes tense, and this makes the mind more tense. And so the cycle goes, tighter and tighter. You need to break this cycle. Relax your body and it will help relax your mind.

Take time to relax completely at least once a day, for an hour if possible. If you are a tense, anxious, fearful person, you are probably also hyperactive. You fill your life with a host of unnecessary activities that you tell yourself are essential, so you can't possibly find an hour for relaxation. You can, and you must. This is important: You are dealing with your long-term welfare, which takes precedence over the short-term playing out of neuroses.

If possible, go to a relaxation group or have regular massage. Read up on relaxation. I can recommend an excellent book by Edie Irwin entitled *Healing Relaxation.** She has also produced wonderful tapes that have helped many people. Nowadays there are many ways to find help in this area, so make the effort.

Therapy

There is a Tibetan word for therapy that sounds like "sowa": using what is there to help yourself, no matter what the problem. If you have a stomach problem, eat suitable food to effect a cure. That's sowa. If you have an illness, take the appropriate treatment. If you have a difficulty with your mind or emotions, consider psychotherapy.

Much of our fear is hidden, repressed, and masked by other mental or emotional states. If we want to begin dealing with it, we probably need help accessing it in a safe and supportive way. Most forms of therapy will do this and more, so help is at hand. Reach for it.

Meditation

Meditation and the effects of mindfulness on body and mind are now accepted in our society. Meditation enables us to create the conditions for the most profound changes in body, mind, and emotions.

Most of us have little self-knowledge because we tend to be so externally focused on objects, events, or situations. We've been able to walk on the moon but not to find peace in our hearts, because we don't know how to work creatively with our thoughts and feelings.

Training in meditation changes this and enables us to explore and unfold our inner potential in a safe and creative way. In doing so we learn to face, come to terms with, and integrate our emotional issues. This matures the mind and prepares it for the greater journey into spiritual realms.

We begin meditation by making friends—with ourself, our mind, our emotions, our fears. We accept what is there and relax in its presence, free from the sense of having to get rid of anything or fight with negative states. This is a huge relief and brings great strength and stability to the mind. It allows the growth of a new kind of mind, one that is tolerant, compassionate, able to free itself from fear forever, both here and in the bardos of death. We learn to accept ourselves.

---

* Edie Irwin, *Healing Relaxation* (London: Rider, 1999).

This is long-term training, but the effects will carry over into the death bardos, so it's training for life as well as for death.

Fear and the Human Condition

In an address to members of a cancer center in Zimbabwe, Akong Rinpoche said that fear arises in the mind mainly because of unresolved psychological states and repressed emotion—and then there is the fear of death:

> Birth, aging, sickness, and death characterize the human state. If there is birth, the other three follow. Many of our problems arise because we don't understand this and thus may wish to avoid sickness and death. Nobody has ever escaped these, so how can we? When we realize this, we learn to accept the human condition.
>
> Every day, appreciate the things you enjoy and be grateful for them. Try not to focus on your problems.
>
> Cancer and AIDS are products of our imbalance—imbalance in the way we live that has caused imbalance in our body-mind system. This leaves us vulnerable to diseases. Even if cancer were cured, other diseases would appear to take its place. So rather than worry about your condition, try to enjoy your life while you have it. Appreciate your life and rejoice.
>
> *Death isn't a big deal*—it's like changing house. Train your mind to prepare for changes. Some training you can start includes loving-kindness, compassion, meditation. These help overcome fear.
>
> Fear is a waste of time, so enjoy life.*

When the lama gave this talk, I sensed a feeling of shock in the audience; I don't think they had anticipated quite such a blunt approach. But as Akong Rinpoche went on, the mood changed to one of almost lightness and joy. Someone had at last given them permission to be okay about dying. Imagine telling a group of people who are approaching death, "Death isn't a big deal." What a contrast to the attitude, ingrained

---

* Addressed to members of the Harare Cancer Centre, Zimbabwe, in 1999.

in our culture, that death is such an awful big deal that we don't even dare talk about it.

The meeting ended on a note of liberation and bubbling relief. This is not to say that the death issue was avoided at this center, because it's an excellently and compassionately run place, where people are helped to come to terms with their mortality. I think, rather, it was a case of surprise that a lama and a guest would thrust so directly to the heart of the issue.

I would like to share a story, also about Akong Rinpoche and death.

A friend of mine in Ireland was spending time with a woman, also a student of Akong Rinpoche. She was dying and had got into quite a state about it. She pleaded with my friend to phone Rinpoche for advice, encouragement, or some form of reassurance. Rather reluctantly, because he knows how Rinpoche can be in these situations, my friend called Samye Ling. Without hesitation Rinpoche said: "Tell her not to take herself so seriously."

With great trepidation my friend returned to the frightened, dying woman, sat on her bed, and took her hand.

"What did Rinpoche say? Did he send any message?'

"Ah, well, yes. Yes, he did say something."

"Well, what? What? Tell me!"

"Oh, he said, I mean, he told me to tell you . . . not to take yourself so seriously."

There was a moment of shocked silence, and then she burst into gales of laughter. The two of them laughed and laughed and laughed.

Her fear was gone. With compassionate insight, Rinpoche knew exactly what was needed to shift this dying student from the mental turmoil of the relative to the calm of the absolute.

Don't Delve into Fear

It's tempting. There's a line of logic that says, "If I get to the root of the problem, I will be able to root it out and be rid of it forever." This is a medical model and a working-in-the-outside-world model. It is founded on the assumption that things have single causes that come from outside us, like a virus. Find it, kill it, and you will be cured. This may work in the outside world but not in our minds.

Unless you are in the hands of a skilled therapist, delving will not work. In fact, it is certain to make matters worse, because the act of delving into fear to get rid of it (which is why we delve) will make it stronger. Why? Because this type of delving has an aggressive component that will feed the fear. Also, it's a psychological truth that we feed energy into whatever we focus on. Any neurotic will confirm this. In fact, you can confirm it from your own experience. Think back to the last time you had a major problem that became a preoccupation. After a while you found yourself thinking about it most of the time, didn't you? Even when you didn't want to, your mind kept going back to it, sucked in by powerful emotional content. A vicious cycle ensued. This is the basis of obsessive-compulsive thinking and behavior. We are all subject to it, but few of us become trapped in it.

Now do you understand why you don't tackle fear head-on? If you do, you get sucked into it, and that intensifies it.

By contrast, if you do therapy or meditate, gentle resolving energy enters the mind. This allows the source of the fear to reveal itself in its own time and way. Then we are able to understand fear, and the energy is integrated. We grow in wisdom, peace, and understanding.

If we can begin to master fear in life, that ability will carry through into the death bardos, where it will enable us to face and recognize the projections of our minds.

FEAR: THE ULTIMATE PERSPECTIVE

> A star at dawn
> A bubble in a stream
> A flash of lightning in a summer cloud
> A flickering lamp
> A phantom and a dream
> Thus shall you view all conditioned existence.*

---

*From the Diamond Sutra.

This is the Buddha's teaching on the nature of our existence: It flickers, seems to be there, and then vanishes without a trace.

The truth of this is easier to understand in relation to psychological states and experiences than physical ones. For example, something frightening happens and we feel threatened. Fear flickers into existence and grips the mind. It seems very real and solid. We suffer.

The threat passes. Our perception of danger subsides; the fear drains away and vanishes, no trace left behind. This tells us two things:

First, fear is temporary. It does not have the power to last forever, because that is not its nature. Nothing we experience can last forever. All things have their time and then vanish.

Second, it has no substance or solidity. Once it passes, there is no trace left behind, only memory. Nothing else.

When we reflect on this we can understand intellectually the truth of the teaching that all conditioned phenomena are impermanent and without substance. But this is only a beginning. The important part is to understand in a *real* way, at gut level, so that when fear does arise we can relax in its presence, not take it too seriously, and say instead, "It's okay. It won't last; and anyway, it's not real or substantial. It's like a mirage. It doesn't have the power to harm me."

This level of understanding transforms our experience and allows the mind to go free. It admits a feeling of spaciousness to the mind so that when painful thoughts or feelings grip us, we don't immediately fly into panic or reactive behavior. Instead we develop the power to relax in their presence, knowing that in time they will fade and pass.

To reach this state of mind, we need to deepen our understanding about how the mind works, and we need to embark on systematic training.

Factual Truth and Psychological Truth

In life it often makes sense to deal with facts. They keep us in touch with reality. But in our psychological life this principle can change, and the fact-bound mind can keep us trapped. This is because psychological realities are fluid, whereas facts are bound up with time and what we know through repeated experience.

For example, if I am faced with an unpleasant or painful experience that I know will last only a short while, I can usually endure it—like having an injection or getting a tooth filled. I say to myself, "It will soon be over, so it's not so bad," and I can cope with it.

But if the painful experience becomes long-term or if we think it's permanent, powerful negative states such as depression, stress, anxiety, or even suicidal feelings creep into the mind.

Factually, what changes is not the experience but the length of time associated with it. This makes all the difference between bearable and unbearable. The idea that "this will go on forever" traps us into suffering. We give this idea the status of fact, and although our assumption may not be correct, we make it our reality.

The subtlety of this mind trick is not easy to spot until we have it laid out before us. Even then we cannot easily free ourselves. If we could stand back and review the experience, we would be able to change the facts, because psychological facts of this sort are only as factual and solid as we make them. For example, we might reflect, "I could bear that sound for a short while, so why has it become an issue? It has become an issue because the mind has decided it will go on forever. This changes my experience of it. I have redefined the experience, and deep inner resistance has developed. The idea of time and the resistance have combined to produce an unbearable situation. So now I am in great suffering."

If we do this we make an interesting discovery: The objective factual situation has not changed. What has changed is the way we have defined it and are relating to it.

Under one definition it was bearable.

Under another it became unbearable.

So it's the definition, or the way we view it, that determines the experience.

How interesting; here lies a realization that can free us! Psychological facts are always changing, but if they can change, they are not solid, fixed, real. Like a star at dawn fades and is gone, like a bubble in a stream: Now you see it, now you don't. If we can truly understand this, not just intellectually, we will loosen up and relax in relation to thoughts and feelings that enter our minds. We will be more ready to release them to go their way. The mind will be freed to experience real joy, freedom, inner lightness, even when things are difficult outwardly. We will realize that we can transform negative psychological facts into neutral or even positive ones.

Here is a Zen story that illustrates the point.

The Zen Monk Who Was Tortured

It's said that during the Second World War the emperor of Japan decreed that all Japanese should support the war effort. Some people refused, and a number were tortured to force them to comply. Among these was a Zen monk.

The monk was subjected to water torture. He was strapped to a bed with his head clamped so that movement was impossible. Water was dripped at steady intervals onto his forehead. Most people can bear this for a little while, but after some time they go mad or will do anything that is asked of them.

The monk lay there without any apparent distress. At length the torturers gave up and he went his way.

Many years later he was walking down a street in Tokyo when a stranger stopped him.

"Excuse me, sir, but were you not subjected to the water torture during the war?"

"Yes," said the monk, "I was."

"Well, I was the one who tortured you, and I have never forgotten you, because of all the people who were subjected to the torture, you were the only one who seemed unaffected by it. How did you do it?"

The monk reflected for a moment.

"Ah, now I remember. Every drop was the first drop!"

It's a Matter of Training

It's easy to describe how to change our experience; being able to do it is another matter. But that's okay. We start where we are and take small steps. A journey of a thousand miles begins with the first step, so we can proceed step-by-step. Here are three steps:

Step 1: Catch the mind defining
Step 2: It does not matter
Step 3: Gain an overview

STEP 1: Catch the mind defining

When a situation upsets you, try to trace the process of becoming upset. How did your mind define the event and its consequences? The key to your emotional reaction is here rather than in the actual event.

For example, you are settling down to read a book. You become aware of sound—the neighbors' dog barking. You realize it has been barking for ten minutes, but only now has it fully come to your notice.

So you go back to your book.

But now, in the back of your mind, you are listening for the barking. This intermittent noise sets up a reaction in your mind. The first time it stopped, your mind said, "Ah, at last it's stopped," and there was a sense of relief.

Now your mind is more focused on the dog than on your book. You are becoming increasingly angry, agitated, and disturbed. Plans and comments develop in your mind. Your afternoon is now ruined.

What happened? A common event—a barking dog. The noise could have been accepted and ignored, which in fact the mind had done for the first ten minutes. If the mind had continued in this mode, the afternoon would have remained enjoyable. But the mind took hold of the event, defined it as an invasion and a violation of your peace and therefore a threat. Once that had happened, it was a problem that got bigger and more acute every time the dog barked. And so there was upset and suffering instead of a peaceful afternoon. All because of how the mind defined it.

We do this all the time without realizing it. So we alert ourselves to this defining action of the mind, see if we can catch it early and free ourselves from it by simply not allowing ourselves to develop the story. One spin-off of this is that we will begin to discover our own underlying emotions and attitudes that we are normally not aware of. Usually we project them onto others.

You do this little exercise many times, and you don't need a special time for it. Once you have begun to familiarize yourself with the workings of your mind, you will be able to do it wherever you are and whatever you are doing. Start with small events, because when the big ones come along, the amount of emotion that boils up usually overwhelms the mind and prevents objective reflecting. Although, even with these, you can usually look back on them when you have settled down and then see what went on.

Quite soon you will begin noticing the patterns your mind follows, and this will further deepen your understanding and insight.

STEP 2: It does not matter

Begin to change perspective with small, insignificant things that cause minor upsets in daily life.

Godwin Samararatne had a wonderful way of turning around our tendency to define and then react. When, for example, neighbors to a retreat center somehow always either mowed their lawns or played loud sports commentaries when a retreat was in progress, he said, "So let's call this our lawn mower meditation." With this gentle humor he turned the situation around and people experienced that it really didn't matter.

I once heard of a marvelous example of *It does not matter*.

When I first went to Samye Ling many years ago, I noticed a small table in the dining room. It was quaint and not very well shaped and had obviously been painstakingly carved out of a single log of wood. Round the thick rim of the table had been carved the words IT DOES NOT MATTER.

This intrigued me, so I asked one of the inhabitants if he knew the story of the table.

"Yes," he said with a chuckle, "I carved it!" And so the story unfolded.

In the very early days the carver used to be in charge of Akong Rinpoche's interview schedule.

A young man in his late teens turned up at the center, obviously greatly distressed. He said he would like to see the lama, and the carver arranged an interview. In conversation the carver learned that this visitor was seeking peace after a disaster in his life. He used to live with his parents in Kent, where they had a very beautiful, original Tudor house. The parents went on holiday and left him in charge.

By accident he burned the house down. The insurance had lapsed. He felt that his life was in ruins and he was suicidally depressed. In the hope of finding solace, he had come to talk to the lama.

With a long face and in this terrible state he entered the lama's office. Minutes passed. Then the door opened, and out stepped a radiantly beaming young man who had shed his cares and was shining with joy.

The carver was amazed and thought the lama must have worked some magic, so he asked the young man what had happened.

"Nothing; he listened to my story. When I had finished he just said, 'It doesn't matter.'"

The moment was right, the lama's compassion came into focus, and facing ultimate reality had freed this young man's mind from suffering.

Relatively, everything is happening to everything and it does matter, because we have to understand cause and effect, our karma, but ultimately nothing is happening to anything and it doesn't matter.

These stories demonstrate powerfully how often our minds hold on to suffering just because we think it has to be that way. "Terrible" things can happen to us in life, but does that mean we have to crush ourselves under the sense of "terribleness"? No, we can let go if we really want to. And a good way of letting go is to get things into perspective. Once it's happened, that's it. We can release it and move on.

If we begin applying the principle in small ways, the mind gradually changes and becomes more robust, more able to free itself and not burden itself with endless small worries. Gradually it becomes able to look through bigger experiences. We become stronger.

So we learn to challenge the mind's false assumptions by unmasking the hidden defining process. Once we have done this, "we" take control and correct the situation by letting go of unnecessary and destructive assumptions about how we have to be. It is the basis for learning to live in the moment, free from grasping and aversion.

STEP 3: Gain an overview

It is informative to gain an overview of the situations you have dealt with. List them and add details such as how you felt when the thing happened and then how you felt once you had reflected. An important part of this training is to do it often enough in relation to small situations to begin getting positive feedback. This will happen in the form of small changes of attitude, when you realize that small things that used to bother you no longer do so. You become less reactive and more intelligently reflective. You are able to let go of things you would formerly have held on to.

As you begin noticing these changes, you will gain the confidence that it works. Then, as the exercise goes on, a profounder change sets in. You start really knowing that things are not what they seem to be. Particularly, they are not what your mind would have you believe they are. This leads to a deep shift in the way you relate to your thoughts and emotions. Formerly you may have taken them at face value, believing they were real, important, powerful, permanent, solid. Now you begin to discover they are none of those things. They are just bubbles in a stream. As this realization deepens, you find you can face and free yourself from more and more emotional states, including fear.

The Training Is for Life

Many of the exercises we do will help us integrate and deal with psychological issues that arise out of experiences of this lifetime. But that unfortunately does not mean we will be free from negative and conflicting emotions. Because of karmic factors, deep-rooted negative tendencies will continue to arise in the mind and prompt us to think and feel in ways that are harmful. But they will not have the disabling effects of this life's neuroses. They are the underlying bedrock of one aspect of our humanity: We have to accept it, come to terms and work with it. This is why, in Vajrayana, purification meditations are constantly emphasized. Dealing with these habitual tendencies is an ongoing aspect of spiritual practice, and it is not reasonable to expect them to disappear quickly.

The aspect of training we are looking at here is for the rest of life. In fact, it becomes the basis of how we become in the world and embodies one of the profoundest trainings in Buddhism: that of learning to see everything as illusory and empty of egocentric existence. But we don't try to work that one out right now.

The point is to recognize the need for profound permanent change in the way we view and relate to our experiences and to the world. By taking little steps, we avoid crippling ourselves by attempting to realize impossible philosophical feats at once. We work instead at our immediate level of understanding and capability. But we don't do it for just a few days or months: We keep at it.

If you have difficulty with this approach, reflect on your life. Most of us spend at least sixteen years being educated. We accept this and more as a necessity if we are to make it in the world. But what does it really amount to? Usually survival and perhaps job satisfaction. We invest huge effort in mastering information, attitude, and skills. But when we die, they die. In the next life we do the same again . . . and again . . . and again. These areas contribute little or nothing to our ultimate liberation and happiness, but we put our greatest effort into them.

But here we are looking at something more. We are looking at a system of training that will yield long-term benefits to truly help us at a deep and significant level in this and future lives. We will become freer, happier, more able to help others; and most important, we will set our feet on the path to ultimate liberation. There is nothing more important.

From the perspective of our present study, the training equips us to face and deal skillfully with all emotional states that may arise, including fear. If we can manage this, we will have overcome one of the biggest obstacles to liberation in the death bardo: We will have overcome fear.

The principle we work with is a simple one. We understand that the task facing us is huge: learning to free ourselves from reactive involvement with negative and conflicting emotions and thoughts. We don't attempt to tackle the giant. We begin with small issues that we can cope with, and we develop our skills in relation to them. It's like bodybuilding: In the beginning we are not strong, so we lift only light weights. We build our strength.

This is important with our mind states because by practicing with small issues when we are not under pressure, we learn the principle of freeing ourselves. We gain confidence and skill. Then, when big emotions come along, we know what to do. We have equipped ourselves through training to deal with them, and so we can.

There is nothing mysterious about this approach. We do it in many areas of daily life; why not in relation to the mind?

"This Too Will Pass"

Fear—like all our emotions—is like a dream or a phantom. If we take it seriously and focus on it, we feed it and give it the status of reality. We make it seem solid. We give it power that it does not intrinsically have. Fear is no more than a projection of our own mind.

We train ourselves in life to see that it is not substantial. We begin by exposing and challenging the mind's defining process that lies at the root of fear. Most of us are so locked into our belief in the reality and substance of fear that we cannot break free immediately.

Changes will manifest first in your dreams. When this happens, take heart, because you will have achieved something that will bear fruit in death. How wonderful!

Gradually your relationship to fear will begin to change, and then you can try adopting the absolute perspective. When fear or any other emotion arises, simply let it be and remind yourself, "It has no substance. It's like a dream, a star at dawn, a bubble in a stream," after which it fades and passes.

Remember the Buddha's words: "This too will pass."

11

Impulse Arising and the Furies

This chapter was written for meditators, yet I hope that nonmeditators may also glean some insight into the mind's subtle activities.

IMPULSE AND GRASPING

There is a certain, quite easily accessible stage in meditation when the mind has begun to settle and a little mindfulness has been established. The mind is no longer rushing off after every thought. Although thoughts continue to arise, they do not have the power of urgency that immediately prompts one to catch up with them and rush off into thinking (this is called "following thoughts" in the texts). Nor is one suppressing or repressing.

When you are in this state, you begin to notice a pattern. You are no longer carried away by thoughts that arise from association with sounds. Instead you begin to notice that impulses arise in the mind—like bubbles forming on the bottom of a glass of soda pop. These are impulses to engage in a particular line of thinking or feeling. Normally we are not aware of an impulse because acting upon it (thinking) is almost instantaneous; we don't even realize it's there. So in a literal sense it's constantly carrying us away into habitual reactive thinking or emotions.

Now that the impulse is revealed, we see and know that there are two stages:

The first stage is that of impulse arising (from within the unconscious and therefore out of habitual tendency). The second stage is reactive grasping of impulse and acting out by embarking on a line of habitual thinking or reacting emotionally. When we do this we don't recognize that we are reactively repeating and therefore reinforcing habitual patterns that disturb the mind and prevent mindfulness, clarity, tranquillity, peace of mind. These reactive cycles are the basis of being carried away by our thoughts and emotions.

"Judgment" in the Bardo

In the bardo of becoming there is a time of "judgment" when this tendency to be carried away happens quite literally: The Furies put ropes around our necks and drag us off to be smitten and tormented by our conscience.*

What we learn from this is that in life, every time we yield to the allure of impulse arising, we are reinforcing a habitual thought pattern of not following our deeper intelligence or conscience. The moral element is relevant because thinking and giving way to emotion are the lifeblood of egocentricity, which gives rise to negative and conflicting emotions. When we give way incessantly to impulses, we are overriding an inherent moral sense. Most of us are so conditioned to engaging thought in this way that we don't even realize there is a moral sense in us that knows this is not skillful and that we shouldn't do it.

The consequence is that we live with an almost irresistible tendency toward following the impulse. So it has power. When we are in the bardo it's this *tendency* that manifests in the symbolic guise of a Fury and simply does again what we allowed it to do throughout life: It carries us away. "Seize on him, Furies, take him to your torments!" said Shakespeare.† But now the experience is more dramatic and total because we experience nakedly and completely the mind's impulses. What we think, that we become.

---

* The Furies in Greek mythology were three female spirits who punished evildoers. They had to guard the entrance to the underworld to ensure that those who entered had atoned for their sins. They were known as punishers of those who offended the gods. Yet in Greece they were called Eumenides, or "kindly ones."
†*Richard III*, act 1, scene 4.

If we train in life to see impulse arising, understand what it is, and know that we don't have to engage or follow, we will have prepared for freedom through recognition when we stand in the presence of the Lord of Death. This is the symbolic moment in the death bardo when all our positive and negative actions of the former life are balanced and we begin to experience the consequences of both.

WHAT WE CAN DO NOW

What should I be doing now? How do I prepare in this life? How can I equate my present psychological conditions with the events that await me?

It seems to me that these questions are answered if we understand that no magic changes enter our stream of consciousness just because we die.

Immature Minds

Our underlying tendencies, which we have generally not seen or have ignored in life, will surface and manifest more obviously and powerfully in the bardos. This we already know.

If we have not trained or disciplined our minds in life in any way, and particularly if we have not developed any mindfulness or insight, we will die with minds that are immature. The immature mind is one that has not resolved and integrated its infantile complexes. It has not faced the existence of underlying habitual tendencies. This mind will have lived a life of more or less unconscious acting out and projecting of all its unresolved negative and conflicting tendencies. Living this way reinforces the negative in the mind.

The sense of being helplessly under the control of great external forces in the bardos arises not because there are in fact external forces bearing down on us but because we have lived lives of allowing our habitual tendencies to control us. When we dream, it is these tendencies that shape and color the dream. When we die, it is these tendencies that dictate our reactions to the deep projections in the chikai and chonyi bardos. It is these tendencies that cause us to flee helplessly through the sipa bardo and plunge once again into inappropriate births. It is these tendencies that manifest as seemingly external forces.

If we understand this, our life strategy and course of action become compellingly obvious: Do something now to free the mind from the grip of habitual tendencies. Above all, develop mindfulness, gain insight, stabilize the mind. These are within the reach of most of us.

Causation: We Reap What We Sow

> I say: take no thought of the harvest,
> But only of proper sowing.
> —T. S. Eliot, "Choruses from 'The Rock'"

Many people live their lives in a childish and irresponsible way. They exploit and harm others or the environment regardless of the suffering they cause, if they think they can get away with it. Often they maintain a facade as decent, law-abiding citizens and feel satisfied as long as their social appearance remains intact. This is a tragic mistake, because in the bardo *all* our chickens come home to roost and there is no escape. Appearance no longer exists. Realities arise.

The consequences of our actions manifest as powerful experiences and determine our ability to recognize. So the way we use our body, speech, and mind while in life is crucially important to the bardo experience. Consequences of negative actions will rebound upon us with terrible and devastating force. Consequences of positive actions will produce extremely harmonious and beneficial experiences and enhance our chances of enlightenment.

This is something many people cannot understand because it differs from life experience. Here we often do harmful things and move on, forgetting about them because the consequences don't manifest in discernible ways. Some people even go through life being remarkably destructive and harmful and yet seem to be happy, successful, and prosperous to the end of their days. This is a fool's paradise, because we never escape the consequences of any of our actions. In Buddhist and Hindu teachings it is emphasized that by the law of karma we inevitably experience the consequences of our actions—negative and positive. The same truth is recognized in Christianity: "Do not be deceived; God is not mocked, for you reap whatever you sow. If you sow to your own flesh, you will reap corruption from the flesh; but if you sow to the Spirit, you will reap eternal life from the Spirit. So let us not grow weary in doing what is right, for we will reap at harvest time, if we do not give up."*

In the bardos we experience in a raw and naked way the results of our behavior at all levels.

If we understand this, we certainly have the basis for knowing how to train *now*: Learn to live compassionate, kind lives. Develop mindfulness and integrate the deeper energies of the mind. Train to diminish grasping. Definitely avoid harmful behavior. If we don't do these things, there is absolutely no point in learning any of the bardo meditations because we won't be able to practice them. Their success depends entirely on a favorable preparation of the mind in these other areas.

Illusion Is Like Mist over Water

Why is this training so powerful and important?

Because if we do it, we directly affect and cause the dismantling of the psychological mechanisms that are perpetually operating to keep our minds trapped in ignorance. I will try to illustrate without using Tibetan or Sanskrit terms.

Think of your true nature as an ocean of light: perfectly still, brilliantly clear, luminous, not needing to *do* anything at all.

Although your true nature is like this, there is a potential for anything to arise out of it, like mist drifting up out of an ocean. Now think magically for a moment. This mist, if left alone, will eventually condense and vanish back into the ocean. But somehow instead of doing this it gets the idea that it is something different, separate and unique. The idea draws more mist to itself until a vortex of swirling mist energy is created. The

---

* Galatians 6:7–9.

vortex begins to whirl and move across the face of the ocean, creating quite a spectacle and constantly growing. Thus its sense of separate existence is reinforced and enhanced.

Soon the mist forgets it ever had a connection with the ocean and whirls away like a tornado. But there is an interesting thing about this tornado: It can survive only as long as it keeps thinking, particularly thinking that it is separate, and then thinking grasping thoughts in relation to that separateness. These particular thoughts are very powerful and create a black hole effect: More and more mist gets sucked into it faster and faster with increasing intensity until the appearance of something very solid comes about. But this apparent solidity is entirely dependent upon the continuation of thinking. A very solid sense of identity has now emerged, an identity that fears one thing above all others: cessation of thinking.

This is an oversimplified analogy of our human egocentric existence, but it will do if it isn't pushed too far.

In terms of our experience as humans, the mist is our emotions, thoughts, and concepts. They arise out of the ocean in the form of *impulses*—to feel, think, conceptualize. Our normal way of being is to take hold of the impulse and feed or energize it, that is, to develop emotions, pursue thinking, construct concepts. We don't normally know about the connection between the arising of an impulse and the subsequent thinking because the connection happens at a subliminal level. We discover it only when our self-awareness is enhanced through mindfulness.

This is the normal human cycle: constantly thinking and feeling, and believing we *have* to think and feel. So much so that even if we tried, we would find ourselves unable to stop the process. A self-perpetuating cycle is in place, embedded in habitual tendencies. These are the deep ocean currents of the unconscious that constantly shape the impulses and float them into consciousness. There we engage them, develop them, make them ours (*my* feelings, *my* thoughts, *my* ideas), and thus feed and strengthen them. We reinforce the tendencies and the all-pervasive sense of self. This is why meditation, although simple, is difficult: It directly challenges a deep-rooted and well-established regime that is older than time itself.

Relax and Let It Be

"The most important practice in life as well as when we die is to relax in our own emotions, thoughts, concepts," Ringu Tulku says, and then elaborates upon this comment:

> The real purpose of any meditation is not to have good experiences. When we meditate, sometimes we feel peaceful, light, relaxed; not many thoughts arise; we feel nice afterward, sometimes even joyful; sometimes we even have thought-free states. All this is not considered important because if you experience these states you want to keep them and hold on to them. Then they go, you lose them and feel bad and frustrated because you want to get them back and cannot.
>
> These experiences are all right and it's nice to have them. They belong to the stages of practice, but they are not the real goal.
>
> What is the real goal? The real experience? It is not whether you have a good or bad experience but to learn to take whatever comes and not be bothered by it. When you have bad thoughts, lots of thoughts, lots of emotions, you learn to take them as they come and relax in that. When you have good experiences, you take them as they come and relax in them. Meditation is learning that whatever arises—whether good or bad, nice or not—*we can relax in it and let it be.* If we learn this, then whatever comes won't be able to overcome us and make us panic; it won't be able to take over all our power and make us be this or that way. Learning this is the essence of meditation. When we are able to do it, we develop confidence in meditation and know how to deal with our thoughts and emotions as they arise.[1]

This can be the basis for training for freedom in life as well as in death.

A Deeper Perspective on Meditation

The most important principle: Meditation does not involve *doing* anything. The moment there is any sense of doing in the mind (particularly of *me* doing), there is no meditation. People who try to achieve particular mind states or induce chosen emotional states or moods are not meditating: They are playing with the mist.

Now we are ready to look again at Ringu Tulku's advice: "relax in our own emotions, thoughts, concepts." In other words, learn to be in the presence of these phenomena without *doing* anything about them. Like sitting in a bath of hot water. For most of us this instruction might as well be in Greek for all the good it does us, because we are not aware of the mechanism of engaging (which is the grasping process). It happens subliminally, outside conscious awareness. In the normal way of being we *never* relax in our emotions. Instead we compulsively engage them in one way or another and only become aware of them once we have engaged them.

This is a conundrum. We can't begin to understand even *how* to do this relaxing, let alone actually do it. We also begin to realize why recognizing the wisdom lights in the bardo isn't such an easy business, despite the fact that they are so dramatic and obvious. These subliminal mechanisms that fool us in life translate into the bardo: They manifest as an inclination to fear and avoid the manifestations of our wisdom nature.

Still, the situation isn't hopeless. We can train in life. But we have to understand that there is a step before the "relaxing in our own emotions." That step is the simple but essential development of mindfulness.

Mindfulness leads to expanded awareness and also begins to train the mind in the simple but all-important ability to observe one's mind processes without intervening—that is, engaging. Awareness penetrates the secrets of subliminal activity and reveals the actual mechanisms of grasping at emotions, thoughts, concepts.

Now We Understand Grasping

Only when we really understand through this direct insight how the mind perpetually grasps are we ready not to grasp. This is the beginning. In terms of our meditation experience it means we are learning to observe the arising of emotions and feelings without engaging them. But we haven't gotten there yet, because there is still the sense of an observer—me watching my thoughts—so we haven't fully relaxed in the thoughts. That ability comes with training: first, letting go of the idea of doing anything, then letting go of the idea of there being anyone doing it. This means the observer. When this level of meditation arises, there is no sense of meditation happening, because there is just the relaxed experience of emotions, thoughts, concepts, without any sense of anyone's experiencing them.

Here is the power of the meditation: Now the mist drifts up out of the ocean and no longer thinks about itself; it simply experiences itself nonverbally and nonconceptually. This is bad news for the tornado because it means its power source has been disconnected. It now has no option but to subside. If one meditates long enough in this way, the process whereby the tornado came into existence is reversed and all the drama subsides and fades away. *Nirodha!**

Of course, there are many other factors involved, so it's not quite so simple, but this is a fair exposition of the principle of liberation in life and in the bardo.

We can train to do it in life, but we may have limited success because of the strength of our negative and conflicting emotionality and the weakness of our understanding. This is largely due to the density and grossness of the elements that constitute our psychophysical organism here in the bardo of life.

The good news is that in the bardos of death the bodies we inhabit are subtler and afford much stronger powers of comprehension. So if we can remember to focus on the wisdom lights and recognize them (that is, relax in our emotions, thoughts, concepts), or if someone reminds us to do so, we will have a far greater chance of success. Thus we can attain liberation in the bardo as a consequence of training undertaken in life, even though we were unable to attain liberation in life.

---

* Tibetan for "cessation."

COMMENT ON INSIGHT

In Buddhist psychology (*abhidharma*) we learn that there is both mind and impulses of mind. I have been referring to the latter as "impulse arising" because in our experience that is what happens—the impulses arise within our minds and lead to thinking. This constitutes one of the basic structures of all our thinking processes, and we have seen how the tendency to act it out carries over into the death bardos and leads to difficulties with the Furies.

We keep following impulses because we don't know about them: They arise outside the range of our normal awareness and have us in their grip before we know they are there. So we have to learn to spot them at their first appearance. We can train ourselves to do this and thus free our minds from compulsive thinking, but it's doubtful that this can be done unless a person has established a reasonable level of mindfulness. Be that as it may, in meditation watch impulses come and go, and be alert for their various characteristics described below. If you can't do it, return to it in a year or so when your mindfulness is stronger.

When an impulse arises, there is a feeling component that precedes specific thought. Thought follows when we hook into the feeling impulse and thus provide the ground needed for thought to come into being. When we understand this we will understand what I call "content." Everything that goes on in the mind is content. It's constantly coming and going, arising and changing. When it has gone, there is nothing left to show for it—no trace. At most a memory.

Impulses arise at a subliminal level, so we need to rest in awareness to observe them. The reason for this is that awareness accesses subliminal activity in a way that is not possible while we are thinking or reasoning.

Arising Impulses

During meditation, when impulses arise within the subliminal, they manifest characteristics you can be alert for:

- They are usually not associated with preceding thoughts or external stimuli.

- They are inchoate: They have not yet taken specific form, so there is more a sense of moving toward a particular emotional condition or experience.

- They precede and determine the nature of subsequent thinking activity, becoming the emotional or feeling content of specific thoughts that follow, so it is the force within the thought.

- As impulses arise they are like bubbles pushing up through mud: shapeless, containing feeling energy but not yet focused and not yet hooked into our actual thinking process. They are a subliminal force within the mind that has not yet fully taken root. To enter fully into the field of distracting thoughts, they need hooks. They find them when mindfulness is weak.

This hooking is what we call "identifying with thought" (in this sense, to be strictly accurate, it is "thought potential"). It is the moment when content and observer merge and the meditator moves from observing thought arising to being the thought and thus getting carried away into thinking.

Bare Attention and Engaging

If we see and understand all this we are in a position to practice bare attention. Awareness of the thought process at this moment of arising is what makes freedom from thought possible, because when the mind is only at the stage of impulse arising, the energies haven't fully engaged. There is an almost impartial quality about the energy of the impulse. When it is driven into specific thought, the situation changes and it becomes "*my* thought with *my* feeling, therefore *me*." This is what is meant by being caught in the thought. The inner energy has transmuted from being something relatively neutral and therefore not very important or compelling into something entirely personal and therefore extremely important and compelling.

The image of a car's gearbox may help us understand.

Imagine the car is static and in neutral. You start the engine and it begins to run. Because you are not in gear, nothing more happens. It remains where it is, but because the engine is running, the potential has arisen for things to happen. This is the moment of impulse arising. It is the motive force for all that could follow, but nothing more has happened yet.

Then you engage the engine by putting in the clutch and selecting a gear. This changes the situation because the energy is being directed into motion and many possible consequences arise. The car could go forward, backward, fast, slow, and into any of a number of situations all because you used the gearbox to engage the source of energy (impulse arising).

The analogy can be taken further. The driver controls the accelerator. This is the amount of energy and focus you decide to put into the thought. The person could, for example, immediately release the accelerator and allow the engine to stall. This is one way of ending a thought: not feeding any more energy into it. But what usually happens is that we remain in gear and travel until the vehicle runs out of gas. Only then do we get relief and come to rest.

What we can learn from this analogy is that the easiest way to free the mind from thinking is to learn not to engage at the impulse-arising state. This is what experienced meditators do. But it's difficult for beginners because (1) impulse arising manifests subliminally and is therefore not seen or recognized unless the mind is relatively tranquil and mindfulness is strong, and (2) the emotional force driving one to hook in (that is, identify with) immediately is enormously strong and instinctive; there is a strong emotional energy of habit urging one to do it.

We are talking here of the essence of conditioning. We are conditioned to identify with and therefore get carried away in thought. The mechanism of conditioning comes into operation at this precise moment in the subliminal. Now we can see why conditioning is so powerful and difficult to break. It is motivated by two forces: (1) impulse arising, which always carries powerful emotional energy, and (2) compulsion to hook in (identify with), which is the habitual mode of the human mind.

Most of us have great difficulty standing up against the alliance between these two. That is why in the normal human mind habits are very difficult to break and it is almost impossible to break free of conditioning. Both of these usually require the intervention of some outside force.

Where mindfulness is present, freeing the mind can be absurdly easy because the meditator has developed the mind qualities needed to be present and to *know*, through *direct observation*, impulse arising. This is a state of *awareness*, which we can now see arises from mindfulness.

With this direct observation, the tendency to *engage* impulse arising (that is, put the car in gear and release the clutch) is seen clearly for what it is. The meditator is simply able not to do it. The result is that the impulse is felt within the mind for what it is, and sooner or later it passes, leaving the thinking mind undisturbed. This is why the mind becomes increasingly calm and tranquil: It is no longer being whipped up by the disruptive emotional force contained in impulse arising.

The process of impulse arising happens in a flash — maybe a few nanoseconds — so unless the mind is relaxed and clearly aware, it will be missed. But even though the process is rapid, it is a complex psychological happening:

- It is rooted ultimately in one of the mind's habitual tendencies, so it draws its deepest power from karmic habit that may have been reinforced over millions of lifetimes and arises from there. The energy motivating it is therefore not limited to the psychology of a particular personality of this lifetime.

- This deeper energy flow will mix with and become incorporated into the psychology of this life's personality, particularly negative and neurotic potentials. Both of these factors give it enormous power.

- As it nudges up through the subliminal, it broadcasts emotional messages ahead of itself. These are picked up by the thinking mind at a nonverbal level, which activates its scanning/preference mechanism.

If what is arising is a preferred emotion, it triggers a powerful impulse in the mind to engage. This is why engaging pleasurable impulses is so difficult to resist. If it is negative and not preferred, it triggers instinctive repressive impulses that instantaneously block it from conscious awareness.

In this instance the meditator knows that something is going on but is unable to know what it is because the mind has blocked it. This is why insight cannot arise in a mind that is suppressing its negative feelings.

By the same token, insight is unable to arise in a mind that is addicted only to "nice" feelings and thinks that meditation should be only blissful or positive. This attitude also produces suppression by fixating on the preferred state and thus blocking out awareness of all else.

MINDFULNESS LEADS TO LIBERATION

When mindfulness is strong enough, the meditator can remain quietly still with impulse arising. This is the beginning of true liberation because impulse arising carries not only the superficial emotion but also the secret of its cause and the key to freedom from it. Both of these are missed if we repress. This is why training in meditation includes the essential training in an attitude of acceptance of whatever mental or emotional state arises in the mind. When we learn to accept ourselves (this includes accepting impulse arising), we learn to become impartial observers at the moment of impulse arising. So we don't hook in. This is what is meant by remaining quietly still — calm abiding.

When we are able to do this, a totally new experience arises in the mind: Impulse arises. The meditator simply observes it impartially, that is, without hooking in via any reactive tendencies. This is classical *bare attention*, mentioned in so many books as something easy. Now we can see that bare attention is not so easy and is in fact possible only in a mind that has developed a considerable degree of mindfulness.

This act of observing without hooking in is very powerful. A new quality of sharpness and broad openness arises in the mind as a result. This quality is like a brilliant light. It dispels the darkness of our normal reactive confusion. When this happens, impulse arising is seen for what it is.

And what is it? It is the forerunner of insight because it carries within it a great deal of information. The surface of impulse arising contains a mental/emotional mix that sets off reactivity in the nonmeditating mind. Bare attention, by contrast, allows this surface to flow fully into awareness without engaging it in any way. This creates what is called spaciousness in the mind because the mind gives neutral, nonreactive, nonengaging space. When impulse arising enters that space, it has no option but to turn itself inside out and reveal its contents.

The consequence of this varies according to the nature of the contents. If, for example, there is repressed trauma, the result will be catharsis, integration, insight into an area of neurosis, freedom from neurosis, and growth. Growth in this instance is increased self-knowledge, wisdom, clarity, and compassion.

As meditation progresses, the results will be more in the nature of unfolding direct perception and understanding the nature of the mind and deep truths about the nature of existence.

ACCEPTANCE: THE GROUND OF MEDITATION

I hope this short comment will help meditators understand why it is so important to learn an attitude of acceptance and allowing in relation to impulse arising—this means all thoughts and feelings that flow into view. Once an attitude of acceptance and allowing is established, the basis for true meditation is in place.

Why?

Because this attitude is the basis of recognizing content. Impulse arising is content and thus has the potential to draw the meditator back into thinking and out of meditation.

But more than that. Without acceptance, the conditions for the natural unfolding of the mind's deep wisdom, compassion, and clarity are not there, so meditation becomes sterile and rigid. In this latter situation there is no resolution of psychological states because repressed material remains repressed. Thus there will be no growth at a psychological or spiritual level, and the mind becomes tight, narrow, and rigid instead of spacious, flexible, and joyful.

The rigid condition is sadly apparent among meditators who are too strict with themselves and try too hard. They may experience a little tranquillity but not insight.

Oddly enough, meditators who in their early years of practice go through what may appear as chaotic experiences seem to be the ones who move on into more open spaciousness. So if you think you are a bad meditator, that may not be a disadvantage—provided, of course, you are sustaining your practice.

Helping the Dying and the Dead

When people are dying, we can help them in special ways. If people are already dead, even long dead, we can help them, from a spiritual perspective, even more than we could have done in life. When we consider these teachings on living, dreaming and dying, then dying and being dead take on a positive perspective.

12

Helping the Dying

> In Tibetan, the word for body is *lü*, which means
> something you leave behind, like baggage. Each
> time we say lü, it reminds us that we are only trav-
> ellers, taking temporary refuge in this life and this
> body.
>
> —*Sogyal Rinpoche,* The Tibetan Book of Days

Perhaps you find yourself in the following situation: "I have never experienced death. I know nothing about dying. Now my mother is ill and
dying and I have no idea what to do."

I think this is how most of us would feel. We have such a culture of fear
and denial of death that we feel hopelessly inadequate in the face of it.

"Death is a subject that is evaded, ignored, and denied by our youth-
worshipping, progress-oriented society," says Elisabeth Kübler-Ross in
Death: The Final Stage of Growth.[1] Yet death fills television screens and
other media. Somehow there is a split in our psyche: Death is part of our
violent world "out there." But we don't accept it "in here" by coming to
terms with our own mortality, by preparing in life to meet death.

The mysteries around death and dying are unnecessary. There is no
reason for us not to learn to care for the dying. In fact, there is every reason we should, because caring for those we love, or for any person during
his or her final days, is the last and greatest gift we can offer the person.
The vast area relating to death and dying is covered in some excellent
books by, among others, Elisabeth Kübler-Ross and Robert Buckman.

Here are some principles we can follow.

ATTITUDE

We are all going to die. It's not a failure or a disaster. We will be sad to see someone move on and we will miss the person, but that's samsara, the way of the world, isn't it?

Modern medicine has made such advances in recent years that many people feel that virtually everything should be curable. Doctors may regard a patient's death as a failure, and this feeling rubs off on relatives and friends, resulting in an atmosphere of helplessness and failure around the dying person.

So the first thing we need to do is check our attitude toward death in general, both our own death and the death of the dying person. Learn to accept the situation, come to terms with mortality, and let go of sentimental or unrealistic notions that lead us to pretend it isn't happening. Becoming realistic about death and relaxing our attitude is very liberating and will result in our naturally finding the strength we need to deal with it. It will also enormously help the dying person.

Perhaps people feel that accepting and coming to terms with death indicate an insensitive and uncaring attitude. It's as though we should pretend right up to the end, avoid giving the impression that we somehow *want* the person to die.

A Reflection

We begin with attitude. We check our attitude to death.

At the end of a day sit quietly and watch the setting sun. As day fades to night and the light leaves the sky, observe the ending. "The day is done; it has ended. The bright promise of dawn blossomed into midday, then faded beyond noon. Silently evening crept upon us and now there is an ending. The day has passed." Reflect on this. Reflect on the impermanence of it all so that you slowly soften the edges of your mind with reality: Nothing lasts. Everything is impermanent. This too will pass.

These reflections may disturb you at first, but slowly they will bring you to accept reality. This is reality: We are impermanent, all of us. Don't make it into something morbid or turn your world into a place of gray despair. Rather, use it to liberate your intelligence so that you feel freer, able to flow with the great tide of change instead of thinking you should resist and hold everything immovably in place. Watch the clouds: great towering masses that are there, then gone. See the leaves on the trees: green and vibrant in summer, red and gold in autumn, then blown by winter's wind and gone, leaving the branches bare.

Wherever you are, whatever you are doing, allow your mind to attune itself to the all-pervading impermanence that surrounds us. Your mind will relax a little, loosen its urgent sense of grasping, and as the Buddha said, sit a little more loosely to life.

If you want to, you can help this process along by listing all the people you knew who have died. As you do this, keep reflecting, "I knew so-and-so, now she has died, gone. Yes, we die. We pass away. It is part of the human condition."

You will free your own mind from a lot of unnecessary confusion and morbidity that you would otherwise most likely project onto the dying person. You will be freer to be with dying persons physically and psychologically in a clear way, able to meet their needs, be there for them in their final hour in a real, human way.

Openness and Honesty

Now is the time to be honest, with yourself and with the dying person.

Many people become confused when someone close is diagnosed with a terminal condition. A frequent response is, "Don't tell him." And so a web of conspiracy is spun, with all the friends and relatives being told, while the dying person is treated to a barrage of well-meaning but transparent lies and pretence: "A few more tests. We don't really know what's wrong. Don't worry; you will soon be up and about. We will have you well and home in no time . . . ," and so it goes on.

This is cruel and unnecessary. It springs from our culture of denial, which prompts us to deny reality right up to the end. Supposedly this is for the benefit of the dying person, but in fact it's rarely so. Most people don't realize that it is often we who can't bear to face the suffering, in this case the suffering of the dying person, particularly if the person is close to us. It hurts us to see them suffer, so we don't want to allow them their suffering. How do we do this? By shielding them from the truth. So we settle into an uneasy charade, smiling, putting on a brave face, and avoiding the obvious.

The effect of this is to isolate the dying person; that's why it's cruel. Those who are dying usually know they are dying and will definitely detect the pretence. All those who should be there for them, comforting them, helping them face and come to terms with death, abandon them at the crucial moment. They are thrown into limbo and may not be able to define or articulate exactly what it is that is happening. All they may know is that they are increasingly lonely, rejected, confused, and frightened.

So tell the dying person the truth if you can. You may need help at this point, and perhaps an experienced counselor could advise you how best to broach and deal with the subject. Nowadays there are many excellent hospices around the world, with people who are trained to help the dying.

If you have difficulty coming to terms with the situation, you may need to spend a little time reflecting on it and allowing yourself to assimilate and adjust to all the implications. Take the time to do it, but don't forget the dying person. The dying don't cease to be human simply because they are facing death, and who knows? Maybe the best course would be to share your confusion with the dying person if he or she is mentally and emotionally strong enough to talk about it. If the person is close to you, he or she might well be distressed at the thought of leaving you and would welcome the opportunity to talk about it and create the situation where you can help each other.

Some people cannot bring themselves to face death. If this is the case, you don't force the issue. The best you can do is create an atmosphere of caring and support so that they feel they are still in contact with the human race.

I remember so clearly my father's death. He was in the hospital, dying of cancer, and had lingered on for many weeks. I used to go and see him every evening, and day after day he became weaker and more frail. I tried to raise the subject of dying, but he became afraid and flatly refused to talk about it, so I dropped it and turned instead to topics he felt comfortable with. He was in the process of selling a limestone mine and was planning to use the proceeds to build the dream extension to his house: a billiards room. So we talked about that. He had great difficulty speaking because the cancer had attacked his throat and his vocal cords. But he had a mechanical device my brother had made for him and he could whisper some words. We discussed the location and size of the room. There was the issue of lighting and the placing of windows. I contacted an agent in town who gave me information on suitable tables and sizes. Every day I would come with some new piece of information, so he would have something to look forward to and occupy his mind. And thus the days and weeks passed.

Finally one evening I went in quite late and the hospital was quiet. I entered his room and he was dozing, propped up on pillows. Something had changed. His breathing seemed precarious and I knew he was losing his grip on life. I found the ward sister and expressed my thoughts to her. She was one of those forthright English matrons not given to mincing words.

"Yes, Mr. Nairn," she said, "your father is going to die tonight."

I returned to his room. He was awake, and the night nurse was talking to him, plumping up his pillows and fussing around doing reassuring little jobs. I stayed a few minutes. We didn't talk about billiard tables that night, and soon I said I would leave. I said good-bye, knowing in my mind that it was final. He glanced up at the nurse, who had said something to him, and waved casually to me, as you would to someone you know you are going to see again in a few hours. I left. He died four hours later.

I have often reflected on that ending and strangely enough have always felt okay about it. I think the reason is that I understood that his death was his deal. I had to respect the way he wanted it. Maybe it was the only way he could do it, pretending right to the end. It certainly wasn't my way of doing things, but that wasn't the point. I had done what I could to help him on his terms, and that was what it was all about.

This is perhaps what Elisabeth Kübler-Ross refers to as allowing someone to "die in character."

So although we can identify the best way of doing things, it may not always be possible. We should bear this in mind and not try to force matters.

Akong Rinpoche was once talking about compassion. He said, "Accept others as they are. Help beings according to the way they want to be helped." So often we want to help others on *our* terms.

COMMUNICATION: LISTENING, TALKING, TOUCHING

Human psychology is a peculiar business. Mostly it's about energy: energy flow. If we have problems or difficulties, we sometimes seize up and go all quiet, tense, withdrawn. Psychologically this is dangerous because it stops the normal healthy flow of energy, like building a dam across a river. As the dam within us fills, tension and stress increase, causing great suffering. We know about this and instinctively know that it is necessary to let it out.

The most common way of doing this is talking.

People who are approaching death usually need to talk, to be spoken to and heard in a real and sensitive way. They also respond to touch, the holding of a hand, wiping of a brow. This helps them remain in touch with their life, to begin to come to terms with what lies ahead of them and accept the process as something normal that happens to all of us. Otherwise there could be a growing sense of foreboding, as though some disaster were about to befall them.

When listening, try not to focus on the words only. Try to hear why the person is voicing the words, to understand the feeling behind the words.

Reading selected passages from favorite books—selected by someone who knows the person's inner life and who is sensitive to where he is at—could contribute to a profound understanding and acceptance of the process.

Often people have unresolved issues in themselves and with others. Help them deal with these. Now may be a good time to help the person deal with issues such as grasping and resentment. Do the resentment exercise with the person if he is open to it (see chapter 9). If you have unresolved issues with the person, this could be the time to resolve them with sensitivity and compassion. The interesting thing is that doing this will help you as well as the dying person. So a death can be a gift to you as well, helping you to face yourself in a more real way.

Sometimes it is touch that is the communication. Recently an elderly friend of mine was dying. He and his wife never touched, although they really cared for one another. Yet somehow his wife couldn't resist stroking him as he was lying in his hospital bed. "Your hand is too cold!" he protested. And she intuitively, like a little animal, bent down and stroked his forehead with her warm cheek.

Savor the Past

Rejoicing is a healing and enriching emotion that we often neglect in life. As death approaches we sometimes allow problematic issues to overshadow us and our relationships. We can reverse this tendency in a beneficial way by reminiscing, by revisiting happy and positive periods with old friends. Talk about old times; acknowledge past happiness, joy, richness. Reawaken the sunny days and balance or banish any present tendency to doom and gloom. This is not to deny and suppress past unhappiness but to bring balance and happiness into the present. The happy mind is more relaxed, more at peace. The heart can know some gladness in the face of death.

Interestingly, this will echo a spontaneous process that is triggered when we die: The mind reruns the entire lifetime like a fast-wind movie. So there is value in the principle of revisiting the past to bring balance to the present. There are many touching stories of old friends doing this, and in the process freeing each other of apparently minor but significant issues from the past. Not infrequently this results in the dying person's finally being able to relax, let go, and die with his or her mind at peace.

Releasing the Dying

Many people lie in a coma for long periods. Not all regain consciousness before they die. The question is: Can we communicate with them? The answer is yes. There is a great deal of evidence proving that the person is "there," often hanging on to life for strange and unnecessary reasons.

Talk to her. Tell her what you think she needs to know, make your peace, help the dying person make her peace.

If there is no chance of recovery and the person is still not dying, it may be that she is hanging on out of concern for someone who is still alive. If this is the case and you are the person, you need to talk. Tell the dying person that you are okay, that she doesn't have to feel responsible for you. Allow her to go on and face her new future. Tell the person you love her and will miss her but that her passing is not the end of the world. You will survive and she must go on her way.

There are many accounts of this being done, of the dying person giving a sigh of relief and dying peacefully. This was illustrated in an old Tibetan story about Gampopa's wife.

Gampopa was a famous Tibetan meditator in the eleventh century. Before becoming a monk he was a physician, such a good one that his fame spread throughout Tibet. He was, in fact, often known as the Physician. He was also extremely handsome.

When he was relatively young his wife became ill and took to her bed. Gampopa employed all his healing skills to no avail. Her condition deteriorated until it was obvious that she could not recover. She lay, week after week, on her deathbed, in great pain.

Gampopa puzzled over this. "I have done all within my power to help her, but her condition is hopeless. She should have died months ago, yet she lingers on in pain and great suffering. What can be the cause of this?" He decided to speak to her about it.

"Dear wife, you know I have done everything possible to heal your sickness but have failed. Your malady is incurable. You should have died months ago, yet you cling to life and prolong your pain and suffering. This is causing great anguish to both of us. What can be the cause?"

"Dear husband, the cause is simple. I love you so much that I cannot bear the thought of some other woman becoming your wife. I will not die and allow that to happen."

The astounded Gampopa thought about this for a while. "My dear wife, this cannot go on. I will make a promise to you. Upon your death I will become a monk and be celibate to the end of my days. No woman will ever take your place."

His wife gave a great sigh of happiness and died peacefully.

Don't Play Games

We often say things like "Everything is going to be all right." This is usually not true in life and certainly will be a lie in death if it is suggesting that the dying person is heading into some wonderful state. We don't know what state his mind is in. We can do our best to create a peaceful environment for him and help him resolve issues, but it is not for us to tell him that wonderful experiences with rainbows and angels lie ahead. Honesty and practicality will help the dying person. If he has some knowledge of the bardo teachings, or if he is a meditator, you can remind him to focus and recognize. Discuss what is to come so that he can be clear in his mind. But don't spin fanciful stories that are of short-term comfort only.

NEGATIVE AND PAINFUL EMOTIONS

Sometimes we can help people to deal with negative and painful emotions that well up as death approaches.

The classic process of dying involves some of the following stages: denial, anger, bargaining, depression, and acceptance. Many other reactions are mixed into this: fear, anxiety, hope, and guilt.

The following example is from a little book entitled *Tuesdays with Morrie*, by a young man named Mitch who began visiting an older man who was dying. It illustrates how one might deal with a negative emotion. The meetings were clearly a rich experience for both of them. The author comments on self-pity.

> I asked Morrie if he felt sorry for himself.
>
> "Sometimes in the mornings," he said. "That's when I mourn. I feel around my body, I move my fingers and my hands—whatever I can still move—and I mourn what I have lost. I mourn the slow, insidious way in which I am dying. But then I stop mourning."
>
> Just like that?
>
> "I give myself a good cry if I need it. But then I concentrate on all the good things still in my life. . . . Mitch, I don't allow myself

any more self-pity than that. A little each morning, a few tears, and that's all."[2]

A dying person is experiencing the death of the body, not the mind. So we can help him or her right to the end, to strengthen and liberate his or her mind.

FINALLY, COMPASSION

Years ago when I was studying various methods and theories of psychotherapy, I asked Akong Rinpoche what he thought was the best method of therapy.

"Compassion," he said, without a moment's pause.

I think it's the same here. It's good and useful to know theories and techniques that can hone our skills in helping the dying, but it's worth nothing if we lack compassion and the desire to help. If you have the desire to help and care for others, you will instinctively do what is needed. Even if you feel inadequate, your caring and loving will communicate itself to the dying person as a great comfort and a blessing.

> The art of peace is a form of prayer that generates light
> and heat. Forget about your little self, detach yourself
> from objects, and you will radiate light and warmth.
> Light is wisdom; warmth is compassion.
> —Morihei Ueshiba, The Art of Peace

13

Helping the Dead

The radiant power and warmth of the compassionate
heart can reach out to help in all states and all realms.
— *Sogyal Rinpoche*, The Tibetan Book of
Living and Dying

A great deal can be done to help the dead, according to Buddhist teachings. When entering this area, most of us find ourselves in strange territory, because we are familiar only with the practice of saying prayers for
the dead and perhaps the offering of candles. In general people feel that
those who have died are beyond help. This is not the case. As Ringu Tulku
points out, this is where Buddhists—particularly Tibetan Buddhists—
really swing into action, far more so than for births or weddings.

I go every year to Samye Ling, the big Tibetan Buddhist center in Eskdalemuir, Scotland, which is where my teachers live. In fact, my tropical
blood froze through five Scottish winters there when I did my long retreat—four years in retreat and one year receiving preparatory teachings.
As this might indicate, there is something more compelling than my
Scottish ancestry that still drives me back year after year. For me it is a su-
percharged place of spiritual energy. The focus is a huge stupa—the
biggest in Europe—which was consecrated in 2000.*

Within the stupa is a chamber where the ashes of the dead can be
placed, thus connecting their minds to the immensely powerful spiritual

---

*A stupa is a bell-shaped structure imbued with great spiritual power.

forces that magnetize the place. As long as the stupa stands, their streams of consciousness will be influenced by the blessing, life after life, down through the ages. People who die may arrange for their bodies to be transported to the stupa to be kept in this chamber for the days of the death bardos, and upon request, monks and nuns will say prayers beside the coffin for this period.

This is only one of many practices that Tibetan Buddhists offer to the world as ways of helping those who have died. Of course, the strangeness and mystery of it is daunting to many people, because we tend to fear the new and unknown and thus project our superstitions onto them; we also assume the practices themselves are mere superstitions. Let's look at the subject of helping the dead again.

When we die, our stream of consciousness floats free and roams the death bardos, undergoing very powerful experiences. In this state a huge potential for liberation is present, because if the person's bardo mind were to focus on its spiritual reality, the realization and *experience* of that reality would be beyond anything we could imagine from our knowledge of spiritual practice here. The mind is nine times stronger and the environment in which it moves is less solid than this one. Thus, if it thinks of a place, *it will be there.* If it is able to focus on spiritual truth, it will immediately be drawn into it, experience it, and be liberated by it.

In the death bardos our enlightened reality appears to us over and over again, and by now we know the key. If the bardo mind can focus sufficiently to recognize the experience for what it is, instead of our fleeing in fear or falling into confusion, the result will be immediate enlightenment.

The problem is that although the mind is much stronger, it is also unstable, in the sense that the rational frameworks that held it in place have gone. Think of dream: An apparently simple thing like recognizing the dream as a dream while we are in it is almost impossible for most of us.

Thus the potential for becoming enlightened, which is so tantalizingly close all the time we are in the death bardos is constantly missed because we simply cannot get it together to focus and recognize.

All the practices to help the dead are based on a knowledge of the happenings in the death bardos, with the understanding that although the dead have lost the power to communicate with us, we have by no means lost the power to communicate with them. For one thing, they can hear us. The Tibetan title of the *Tibetan Book of the Dead* is *Liberation in the Bardo through Hearing*. Traditionally lamas and monks spend the forty-nine days of the death bardo reading to the dead person. They sometimes read beside the body or call the person by name. So no matter where the mind is, it will hear the call and come. Then, day after day the lama reads, saying to the person words to the effect, "Now you are dead, you have left your body and entered the bardo of death. You cannot return; do not attempt to go back; go forward. Today such and such will happen. There will be appearances, vivid lights, sounds. Do not fear. They cannot harm you. They are projections of your mind. See them for what they are and go toward the bright light. Merge with the bright light; it is your enlightened mind."

In this way the dead are constantly encouraged and helped to come into focus. Apparently we don't even have to speak to them. Thinking of them is like calling their name, so they will be drawn to us. Thus there is value in the old injunction, "Don't speak ill of the dead," because they hear and may be affected by what we say.

This is the first aspect of these death practices: making direct contact with the person and offering guidance, instruction, and reassurance.

The other aspect is the generation of beneficial spiritual forces to help the person. This can be done in many ways and at many levels. To obtain full details you would need to contact your nearest Tibetan Buddhist center, but following are a few examples.

INVOKE THE BLESSING OF UNIVERSAL COMPASSION

Through meditation and reflection we experience spiritual forces that go beyond the limited confines of the rational cognitive mind that is thinking these words. Whether there is value or benefit in trying to name those forces, I don't know, but I can say for sure that the common quality that always manifests is *compassion*. Compassion, like the sun, is an impartial and powerfully healing blessing that shines on all beings, whether they be "good" or "bad" and whether they believe in the power of compassion or not.

Compassion is expressed through the discerning ability to help in an appropriate manner. It manifests as an all-embracing caring that arises within the mind, a caring that sees all forms of life and beings as equal. It can arise only in a mind that is open and accepting of itself and others, a mind that is not stifled by preferences, judgments, intolerance, self-absorption.

Because of this I am prepared to live by the proposition that the universe is an expression and manifestation of compassion and that the essence of our enlightened nature is compassion. If this is the case, we can awaken and manifest that compassion to heal the world and ourselves.

Tibetan Buddhism works along roughly these lines, and it contains many practices that invoke and channel into our world different aspects of the universal power of compassion to benefit beings.

The most common of these is the Chenrezi practice, which has as its focus the Buddha of Compassion. We could use the term *universal archetype of compassion* instead, an archetype being a primordial principle that exists in each one of us but also exists independently. It is not the projection of our minds.

The mantra that goes with this practice is OM MANI PADME HUM (Sanskrit). The Tibetans give it a different spin and sing OM MANI PEME HUNG. But it's the same thing.

Right now, at this very moment, if you want to help someone, dead or alive, think of the person and recite the mantra for a few minutes.

Delogs who have entered the death bardos and spoken to people there report that the dead plead with them to say the mantra for them because the effects are so enormously beneficial and powerful.

Here's an interesting account I read some time ago:

A lady was stuck in a traffic jam caused by an accident. Feeling sure people must have been hurt, she sent kind and loving thoughts to whomever was involved.

Some weeks later she received a letter of thanks from one of the accident victims, who told this remarkable story. She had been knocked unconscious and found herself looking down on the scene, feeling frightened and disoriented. A comforting wave of love and caring swept over her, making her feel much better. She quickly traced the feeling to our woman sitting patiently in her car.

The unconscious victim was so powerfully impressed by this experience that she resolved to thank her benefactor and noted her car registration number. When she regained consciousness she remembered this number, traced the owner of the car, and wrote to her.

Mantras are words of power that focus very strong spiritual forces. If loving and kind thoughts can have such a tangible effect, imagine how much more effective mantras can be, especially when accompanied by a visualization.

So there is one option to consider: the mantra of universal compassion.

PRAYERS AND CEREMONIES

Most lamas will conduct prayers and ceremonies upon request. If you make this request, accompany it with a financial offering, as you would do if you were requesting the services of a cleric in another religion. Ordained nuns and monks also perform these services.

DEATH YANTRAS

A yantra is a picture, usually geometric, that brings into focus and magnifies spiritual forces. If we contact a yantra through one of our senses, including touch, the blessing is transmitted to our stream of consciousness. There is a set of yantras that can be placed within and upon a coffin prior to burial or cremation. It is said they will help the consciousness of the deceased to remember to focus. They create a beneficial atmosphere to ward off fear and confusion and connect the mind to its enlightened reality.

These are a few of the things you can do. If you want to follow up on them, contact an authentic Tibetan Buddhist center. Even though many lamas and monks will not charge to perform these services, it is appropriate to make a meaningful offering, especially if you are serious about wanting to help someone and if you value that person. These offerings are for the benefit of the person concerned, rather than a reward for the teachers. The teachers personally don't mind whether there is an offering or not.

In all the methods we have reviewed here there is a simple principle involved. When we die and enter the death bardos, we find ourselves in very strange territory where familiar reference points have vanished. Most people become confused and afraid, so they suffer and forget all the teachings about recognition. They are blown through the death bardo as by a hurricane.

To some extent we can reach them by speaking to them, and this may help. But in addition there are immensely powerful ways of helping, ways that involve bringing beneficial spiritual forces into focus upon them. Because their minds are so much more sensitive, there is a good chance they will respond and benefit. Even if they do not become enlightened, the benefit will carry over into the following and even future lifetimes.

This may seem very Tibetan and not acceptable to some people. In this book we are looking at the Buddha's teaching as preserved and transmitted to us within a Tibetan Buddhist context. But the fact that all of this may seem very Tibetan and not acceptable to some people doesn't mean we can't benefit from it, and neither does it mean we have to take onboard all the Tibetan "stuff." I am trying to extract the principles and give them to you in a way you can understand and use beneficially. You don't have to be a Buddhist, you don't have to be Tibetan. All you need is to have compassionate motivation and a bit of determination to go for it.

MAKING OFFERINGS

Hungry Shades Outside The Walls

Outside the walls they stand,
and at crossroads.
At doorposts they stand,

returning to their old homes.
But when a meal with plentiful food and drink is served,
no one remembers them:
Such is the kamma of living beings.

Thus those who feel sympathy for their dead relatives
give timely donations of proper food and drink
—exquisite, clean—
[thinking:] "May this be for our relatives.
May our relatives be happy!"

And those who have gathered there,
the assembled shades of the relatives,
with appreciation give their blessing
for the plentiful food & drink:
"May our relatives live long
because of whom we have gained [this gift].
We have been honored,
and the donors are not without reward!"

For there [in their realm] there's
no farming,
no herding of cattle,
no commerce,
no trading with money.
They live on what is given here,
hungry shades
whose time here is done.

As water raining on a hill
flows down to the valley,
even so does what is given here
benefit the dead.
As rivers full of water
fill the ocean full,
even so does what is given here
benefit the dead.

"He gave to me, she acted on my behalf,
they were my relatives, companions, friends":
Offerings should be given for the dead
when one reflects thus
on things done in the past.
For no weeping,
no sorrowing
no other lamentation
benefits the dead
whose relatives persist in that way.
But when this offering is given, well-placed in the Sangha,
it works for their long-term benefit
and they profit immediately.

In this way the proper duty to relatives has been shown,
great honor has been done to the dead.
— *from "Tirokudda Kanda"**

Offerings fall into two categories, food offerings to the deceased and offerings on behalf of the deceased.

Food Offerings

It seems that some people who have died think they still need food and drink even though they no longer have a body to support. This belief causes them suffering because they search for sustenance without finding it and experience the psychological equivalent of hunger and starvation without being able to find relief.

We can help them.

When you have a meal, think of the person and put a small portion of food aside on a plate for him or her. When doing so, say the mantra

---

* From "Tirokudda Kanda" ("Hungry Shades Outside the Walls"), in the Khuddakap-atha (The Short Passages), which is a part of the Khuddaka Nikaya (The Short Discourses), translated by Thanissaro Bhikkhu, "Access to Insight: Readings in Theravada Buddhism," www.accesstoinsight.org/canon/sutta/khuddaka/khp/khp.html. Reprinted with permission.

OM MANI PEME HUNG three or seven times (your choice) and think, "This is for you." After the meal, put the food outside where people don't walk, in a place where birds or wild animals will be able to eat it. This will give relief.

A more complicated procedure involves a bit of chanting. In this instance you burn the food and offer the smoke or smell of burned food. Evidently the smell of burned food offered in this way satisfies the hunger of those who have died — not only humans but a wide range of suffering beings. This is normally done at monasteries and is called *tsur* in Tibetan.

Offerings on Behalf of the Deceased

Helping people who are poor, hungry, or suffering generates good karma. What the lamas suggest is that we do beneficial acts for the living on behalf of a deceased person, thinking, "This is for you; I dedicate the benefit of what I am doing to your welfare," or words to that effect. The words aren't important. What matters is to undertake compassionate activity with the pure intention of helping the person who died. Best of all, distribute some of the dead person's wealth or possessions with this in mind. Practicing generosity, even on behalf of others, is a very powerful spiritual help for them.

In Buddhist countries it is common for relatives of the dead to make offerings to monasteries or to endow temples with this motivation. It is said that one way of generating spiritual energy, not only on behalf of those who have died but for everyone, is to make offerings to spiritual teachers or to support spiritual institutions. The teachers are not enriched by these offerings; in the Tibetan tradition they do not earn "salaries." The offerings contribute to the professional running and upkeep of the centers, the support of visiting teachers, and the printing of dharma texts and other literature.

So this is something we can all do; it's practical and in harmony with our Western philanthropic practices. Many of the West's greatest institutions — universities, hospitals, schools, churches — were founded and are supported by the endowments and bequests of ordinary folk as well as industrial billionaires. In the East there is also an extra spiritual dimension to this that can help the dead: that ordained Buddhists keep their vows of poverty, that teachers are not paid, and that the intention of the giver, not the size of the gift, is what counts. Dana benefits the giver as well as the recipient.*

I find the teachings concerning helping the dead very heartening and practical because it is so empowering. Instead of collapsing in grief and self-pity when someone close and dear dies, we know that death is not the end of the story. It is the opening of a new chapter where we can do things that will help the person as never before. We can do more for the person's true, long-term spiritual welfare than may have been possible in life. If we love someone, what more could we ask?

---

* *Dana* is an offering to a teacher or institution.

Training for the Moment

In part 1 I tried to present what I think of as a working understanding of living, dreaming, and dying and the underlying conditions that lead to happiness or suffering in our lives and in death. Having once understood them, we will naturally want to take steps to weaken the conditions that lead to suffering and free ourselves from them. It also makes sense to develop and strengthen those conditions that make it possible for us to find true, enduring happiness and freedom.

Hence part 4. What is offered in here is a series of very simple methods of training the mind for freedom in life, dream, and death. They are not complex, and anybody can do them.

A suggestion: Form a little group and do them together.

14

Stripping Away Masks

The way of cowardice is to embed ourselves in a
cocoon, in which we perpetuate our habitual patterns. When we are constantly recreating our basic
patterns of behavior and thought, we never have to
leap into fresh air or onto fresh ground.
—*Chögyam Trungpa*, Transcending Madness

If in daily life we embark upon an enterprise, we usually prepare for it.
Death is no different. The reason should be apparent by now: The mind
that experiences dying is a continuation of the mind that is reading these
words. Unless we have the aid of an accomplished lama, no external
force is going to manifest magically and whisk us away into a heaven
world when we die.

Although it is the same mind, and therefore the same me, it is not the
superficial daily me. It is the total me and includes the hidden, subjective, repressed, and not-faced aspects of my stream of consciousness. All
these will manifest and predominate in the death experience. The superficial, socialized, intellectual, and conceptual aspects will shatter, disintegrate, and dissolve.

Put bluntly, all the mirrors and smoke, lies, pretences, ideas, and images we have woven into our personality will fall away to reveal the
deeper truth of what we really are. That is what we will experience. It is
a theme used by some novelists who like to put their characters into
traumatic situations where their normal controls and supports are removed. This strips away a person's masks and reveals the first underlying

layer of "truth," which is usually different from the one presented to the world. It is an appealing theme, because at heart most of us want to be real, to get in touch with our inner reality, and equally to be in touch with others in a way that is genuine, true, and meaningful. But we usually don't want to face all that this involves, such as accepting and coming to terms with our shadow.

So much alienation in our so-called civilized societies is caused by the psychological isolation of individuals. People create and crouch behind their images of themselves, thinking that this will lead to happiness. It doesn't. It leads instead to loneliness, isolation, alienation, and misery. People get out of touch with themselves and cannot get in touch with others. So relationships at all levels become shallow, meaningless, unfulfilling—and so does life.

Death changes this. What disintegrates along with the death of the body is this superficial world mind. When we are dying we experience what we are, completely and directly. Dream gives us hints of how this will be, because in dream the underlying energies seep through into the dream state, usually making enigmatic but true statements about the deeper state of the mind.

So how does one prepare if so much of the mind is beyond the reach of our daily, conscious experience? There are ways, which I propose to explain. But first the overriding principle needs to be understood.

HABITUAL TENDENCIES

Our personalities are expressions of deep, underlying tendencies. Some are hidden, usually because we prefer not to acknowledge or know about them. Others peep through and surprise us in undefended moments, and others may be reasonably familiar to us on a day-to-day basis.

For example, we may be profoundly insecure, needy, grasping, and greedy. This is a common complex that rules the lives of most people who are driven to acquisitiveness. They won't acknowledge these aspects and seek to conceal them from themselves and from others. The superficial personality might be quite jolly and seem happy, an appearance that can be maintained while external conditions remain favorable. But if things go badly wrong—for example, if the person's wealth, possessions, or relationships are threatened—a complete change of personality could well manifest. This could take the form of uncharacteristically violent, ruthless, or destructive behavior that might even surprise the person concerned.

What is the source of this Jekyll and Hyde change? Simply the underlying and hidden state of the person's mind. All that varies from person to person is the degree of denial and repression, or the amount of understanding and insight present in the mind.

These underlying tendencies, like a skeleton of the psychological entity, are not all negative: Some are positive and others neutral. They give this psychological entity shape and form and thus largely determine the way it is. If we continue the analogy, the mind that presents itself to the world is very close to being cosmetic. It concerns itself with image, overt behavior, and survival within its environment. The average person thinks this mind is important, is "me," and identifies with it. But the deeper layers of the mind are more powerful and real, in the sense of being truer expressions of the person's energy system rather than pretences.

While we are alive we cling to this shallow mind and generally ignore, repress, or try to escape from the deeper layers, particularly the negative aspects. This is why so few people grow or mature psychologically or spiritually. The power and strength needed for growth lie within these depths. By blocking access because we fear the negative component or our deeper divine component (as discussed in Jung's understanding of "shadow" in chapter 9), we block the totality and become superficial, shallow people, cut off from our deeper potential.

When we die, the truth will out because the shallow mind disintegrates. The deeper tendencies are then experienced directly, determining the quality of our experiences in the death bardos. This is a crucial factor to understand because it contains the key to all death training.

However we train, the focus must be on getting in touch with and changing the underlying tendencies. In particular we need to face, come to terms with, and integrate negative predispositions. In addition, we need to bring positive tendencies into focus, strengthen them, and finally take the mind beyond opposites altogether, through purification and awakening of the enlightened potential.

THE IMPORTANCE OF TRAINING

Why is training so important? Because all forms of training are designed to affect more than just the superficial mind of this life, that is, the rational, cognitive, intellectual mind to which we humans attach so much importance. Some people feel that spiritual training, in order to be worthwhile, should be something exotic, secret, or special. If you are one of those, you will be disappointed, because training has to do with your immediate day-to-day life situation — the way you live each day as an ordinary person.

What Effect Does Training Have?

This mind can easily be changed, and in fact is changing all the time: Just think of the typical fluctuations of thought, feeling, opinions, and ideas we go through in the course of a day.

We can decide with this mind that we want to be one way or another. Many people make New Year's resolutions: "I will give up smoking, drinking," "I will be less angry and impatient," "I will be kinder and more polite to strangers." Almost invariably these resolutions are broken before the first day of the new year is out. Why? Simply because there is a deeper level of the mind that is stronger and more set in its direction than the superficial mind, and this deeper level has not participated in the resolution.

This deeper level is the mind of habitual tendencies, which we have cultivated and developed over billions of lifetimes of thinking and reacting egocentrically. So deep and powerful are these tendencies that they have become instinctual. They naturally and automatically come into play and determine how we think, feel, and behave. We cannot change this mind simply by taking on new ideas or even beliefs. Something more has to be done, involving several factors.

First, we become aware of and acknowledge the existence of the underlying or habitual tendencies. We must accept and come to terms with them. This step is difficult for many people because it challenges or contradicts their self-image. Most self-images contain a good dose of lies we have told ourselves about ourselves. When we start being honest with ourselves, we are forced to acknowledge the lies, let go of them, and face the unsavory realities behind them. This means coming to terms with ourselves as we really are instead of as we have pretended we are. We humans are all a mixture of positive, neutral, and negative mind states. They arise in our minds not only as a consequence of conditioning in this life but also because of the aeons of conditioning that created our habitual tendencies. There is no point in trying to pretend that negative tendencies are not present.

So the first step is to face and come to terms with ourselves as we are at this moment and let go of self-blame and perfectionism. Unless we do this, we can do nothing to bring about change in our minds.

Second, we embark upon some form of training that is going to penetrate and have an impact upon the habitual tendencies that have the status of instinctual thought/feeling responses. Cognitive, intellectual, rational methods (such as brainwashing, analysis, acquiring new beliefs) have little or no effect on this level. We need something deeper.

We need to invoke counterforces that already exist in the mind and naturally operate at the same level as or deeper levels than the habitual tendencies. This process begins with training in mindfulness, which is a faculty that lies more or less dormant in every human mind. Because it has been left dormant, its power and force are not known to us.

As we train in mindfulness, many profound changes begin to take place naturally within the depths of our mind because this faculty is an expression of our enlightened wisdom nature, which naturally dispels negativity and ignorance when it begins to stir, just as light dispels darkness. The development of mindfulness operates as an antidote to the habitual tendencies.

But note what is happening. We are not mindfully formulating conceptual countermeasures to defeat the habitual tendencies. Rather, an unconscious process stirs and comes into being as a consequence of our training in mindfulness. Changes and insights spontaneously arise, sometimes in surprising or unexpected ways or areas of the mind. Mindfulness does not invoke in us a process over which we have rational control. Rather, it awakens deeper wisdom energy beyond our comprehension, and this energy progressively takes over. Increasingly there is a sense of being witness to the unfolding of a deeper, seemingly autonomous process.

This training in mindfulness is the ground that enables all other forms of training to be effective.

The third step is to strengthen the liberating forces within the mind while simultaneously weakening the mind's tendency to grasp. Any training that develops compassion and altruism will do this. All the training methods presented in this book fall into these categories.

Although the training methods are expressed in conceptual forms — for example, I have used words to describe how you do them, and you use words to get them going in your mind — they are not used as means of directly attacking specific mind states. If we did that we would be working at a superficial level. What we are doing instead is using the training methods to awaken and strengthen the manifestation of the enlightened qualities within. As these are strengthened they automatically weaken egocentric grasping and enhance compassion.

These changes have many beneficial effects in life and constitute the path to enlightenment. More important from the perspective of death training, they enormously enhance the chances of liberation in the death bardos, where the mind we experience is a much more immediate and direct expression of the habitual tendencies. The superficial mind is no more. In a certain sense we are another person in the bardo: the person who arises directly out of and faithfully reflects the karmic stream, or habitual tendencies.

Once we understand this, it becomes easier to undertake and sustain the long and sometimes seemingly unrewarding training. We learn to look beyond the superficial short-term rewards to the deeper purpose of freeing ourselves forever from the wheel of endless births, deaths, and suffering.

15

Reflecting

Life from the Buddhist perspective has no need of
meaning, because if we are in touch with ourselves
inwardly, the need to seek meaning evaporates. A
self-revealing significance is found, and this is profoundly meaningful.

ABOUT REFLECTING

There are ways of developing greater understanding of our psychological
processes. Reflecting is one of them.

Carl Jung said that common sense, reflection, and self-knowledge are
the only means of clearing away the clouds of projections and unconscious contents. He went further to assert that where insight into projection accompanies reflection, one approaches *metanoia*—deep moral
change. This is a radical change of character and even of the way one
thinks, which leads to an irreversible alteration of the entire personality.
In our terminology, we would say it leads to irreversible spiritual growth.

The mind that can reflect is very different from the nonreflective
mind, which is like hard soil, brittle and limited to intellect alone. Such
a mind is unable to experience true inner growth because it is cut off
from the sources of its deeper nature: wisdom and compassion. These lie
beyond intellect.

Our technological culture is dominated by the physical sciences,
which have enabled humans to accomplish amazing things. But the

emphasis is all external, on learning to understand and manipulate outer phenomena. The criteria for dealing with the external world are not the same as those for the internal.

Straddling the Inner and the Outer

The external world, until we enter the realm of quantum physics, which approaches the mystical, is rational, logical, mechanical. To be effective here, the mind works in a sequential, linear way. Observation and manipulation of phenomena are conducted according to predetermined techniques and postulates. Scientific method is applied, and results are externally demonstrable and measurable. To state the obvious, focus is entirely external, and meaning is sought and thought to lie within external factors, or at least scientifically verifiable factors. This has led to the assumption that everything in life must be testable, measurable, provable, or disprovable. Anything that does not conform to these criteria is dismissed as unreliable and untrue. "Seeing is believing" has produced a culture of materialism.

Our inner world differs radically from this one. Contrast the world of sunshine and searchlights with the world of moonbeams and starlight. Inwardly we are quieter. Our energies move within darkness. We intuit, sense, perceive, and understand without need of reason or logic.

In the inner world the mind does not move in straight lines or have sharp angles. Time is not linear; it is all there at once. A memorable line from a film script springs to mind: "Everything has already happened, but you don't find out about it until it catches up with you." Understanding is not sought or pursued; it presents itself in its own time. This inner world cannot be tested or measured. It is vast and lies beyond the reach of the cognitive, rational mind. Because we identify with the latter, we feel lost to and out of touch with this inner realm, which indeed most of us are. Technological humans attempt to probe this elusive inner world with the tools of the outer world. They have prescribed scientific method as the authentic means of exploration. Many psychologists have bought into this. As a result, our culture views the human as technological, or measurable with the tools of the external world.

This approach has a limited validity and works only in such border-lands as behaviorism, drug therapy, or conditioning. It fails to reach the true depths, just as we cannot weigh moonbeams—that doesn't mean they don't exist. My perception is that by fixating on scientific method as the only authentic means of enquiry, we have trapped ourselves in a culture of scientism. We have developed a shrunken, limited perception of our humanity, so we ourselves have become shrunken and limited. We have lost touch with much of our being, the spiritual part of ourselves. The result is alienation.

When we are alienated, life becomes empty and meaningless, leading to depression, stress, suicide, and a growing list of psychological problems. In response we search for meaning externally, where it cannot be found. This worsens our situation because the sense of meaninglessness stems from inner fragmentation, which is aggravated by external fixation.

Life from the Buddhist perspective has no need of meaning, because if we are in touch with ourselves inwardly, the need to seek meaning evaporates; a self-revealing significance is found, and this is profoundly meaningful.

Humans are constantly searching, but few seem to find. We search in the wrong way, using reason and intellect alone. We have failed to develop the means or tools for accessing true inner experience. Of all the tools we can develop for this purpose, reflecting is one of the most effective. By using it we learn to straddle the inner and the outer, thus enabling the wisdom of the inner to filter into the outer.

As Jung points out, this leads to irreversible growth and change.

Impatience

Perhaps the major obstacle to reflection is impatience. When we do things in life, we usually expect quick responses. When we deal with problems, we want to resolve issues at once, with quick, simple solutions. If they don't present themselves, we become agitated and think something has gone wrong.

When we reflect, we engage an inner process that works in its own time and way. It does not respond to conscious commands to perform.

In fact, such a command and the attitude accompanying it would block the reflecting process. Reflecting requires letting go. We bring the rational mind to a particular place, focus it, then let go and wait because the job at that level is complete. We wait for a response from within, so the process requires patience.

Reflecting helps in many situations, such as problem solving or trying to understand life. Any issue in life that we want to understand more deeply, or resolve, can be brought into reflection. Some people solve their problems in a similar way by thinking about them when going to bed at night and then sleeping on them. A solution often pops up next morning. The principle is the same: Formulate a question, drop it into the mind, and then leave it alone—that is, disengage from the normal, rational thinking process.

In order to reflect we need to settle our minds, and unless we have the natural capacity to do so, this must be learned.

SETTLING THE MIND

Mostly our minds are unsettled in that they are active, seeking distraction, externally focused, jumpy and reactive. If we try to meditate or reflect with an unsettled mind, it will be difficult not to be carried away into thinking and distraction. So we learn to settle the mind at the beginning of any reflecting session.

EXERCISE: Settling the mind

Sit comfortably in a chair or on the floor in a place where you won't be disturbed. Focus on your breath.

Breathe in through the nose for a count of four or five. Find out for yourself which is comfortable and fits the rhythm of your body-mind.

Hold your breath for the same count.

Breathe out through the mouth for the same count.

Do this for seven breaths. Then, as you continue, with each out-breath imagine you are breathing out all negativity, restlessness, confusion, and pain in your mind and body. Keep breathing and imagining in this way until your mind and body gradually begin to relax and you feel at ease. When breathing in and holding, push the breath deep into the lungs, as though you were trying to push it down against the diaphragm.

If you feel anxious during the breathing, focus more on the out-breath. Breathe out for longer and shorten the holding time. Allow your mind to relax and feel easy about being present in the same room as your body.

After about five minutes, end the exercise and allow your breathing to return to its normal rhythm.

Having settled your mind, you should now be ready to proceed with the reflecting exercise. If your mind becomes agitated or distracted during reflecting, repeat the settling exercise.

HOW TO REFLECT

It takes a while for most people to learn to reflect. But it's cumulative: The more we do it, the more it works—so the more we do it. It's a quality or faculty that gradually grows in us and becomes part of our way of being in the world. We find ourselves slipping into it more and more until we no longer "do" it; it becomes part of us. We become more reflective and therefore more intelligent and insightful, less reactive. Wisdom and compassion grow out of this quality.

The Key Lies in the Question

When we start to reflect, the mind engages the problematic issue as soon as effort is made to formulate a question. If you do this reflecting exercise a few times, you will see why it is so. The act of formulating the question requires the mind to sift out all irrelevant and extraneous issues. In doing this it gradually exposes the main issue or issues, and then a conclusion isn't far away. Krishnamurti used to say that "the answer lies in the question." The question is the key. Once you learn to ask the right questions, those that relate to the heart of the problem and emerge only when you have intelligently stripped away all the irrelevant side issues, solutions will fall into place. This is because an honestly put question points the way to uncompromising solutions. But be prepared: Often they are not the solutions our emotionally reactive minds would like.

Big Issues

If we understand reflecting, we can ask big questions that deal with life, with who we are and what we are. The procedure here is exactly the same.

There is a further step: We can go on to reflect upon material that isn't even expressed in the form of a question. It may be a statement that stirs us because it contains profound truth or significance that we can sense but not understand. By reflecting on this type of material, we engage inner forces that free and profoundly transform the mind. This is the path that Buddhists call penetrating insight. We train progressively to penetrate illusory outer appearances and understand what lies behind them. It may not always be possible for the rational mind to comprehend fully what is "seen," but this doesn't matter. We can still know and understand it.

The Essence of Reflecting

What has been outlined above works best if we understand the essential principles of reflecting. It is not a rational process, so we don't try to work it rationally. We are learning to open up to the profound wisdom that is within us, wisdom that is usually ignored. The route involves presenting ourselves at the door, handing over the question, then sitting down to wait. Patience is needed.

We may be unfamiliar with this idea of getting a response from within, but that is what it is all about. Putting the question, then disengaging the rational mind, is essential. Picture an archer: The arrow is fitted to the string, the bow is drawn, then string and arrow are released. The job is done. The arrow is free to fly to its target. We have posed the question; let it go. Then keep on relaxing. We have nothing left to do.

The response may not come in any sort of logical, sequential form. So it's essential to catch what the mind throws up. We do not attempt to impose order, sequence, logic, or any criteria of outer mind. Inner mind must be left free to express in its own language. We don't inhibit this by trying to make sentences or even words if they are not what is being presented.

We work gently and sensitively. If we apply force, pressure, or time scales, we will inhibit or block the process. It must be left to go at its own pace. That is why relaxation and the casual approach are important.

TOPICS FOR REFLECTION

Now we are ready to begin reflecting. Within the context of this book, an appropriate topic is to identify our habitual tendencies. Take each one in turn and follow the steps outlined below, beginning with the reflecting exercise, then settling the mind.

EXERCISE: Reflecting

Have paper and pen handy. Simply relax for a while and allow your mind to play with the topic you want to reflect on. Suppose it concerns your work: Should you change jobs? As you play, you notice that most issues in life are complex. We usually fixate on only one dimension and consequently miss the others. In this instance, a string of questions will begin to present themselves: Do I want to change? Is the new work the kind I would like to do? Do I really want to leave the present job? What is my reason for wanting to change?

Don't write anything down yet. Simply let your mind tease out the main elements of your issue. Do this without putting pressure on yourself to find an answer.

When you have mulled over the issue, formulate it as a question, or perhaps more than one question, which can be considered sequentially at separate sittings. In this instance the questions might be: Should I quit my present job? Should I apply for *x* job?

Write the first question down at the top of your sheet of paper.

Now sit and settle your mind (see the previous exercise). Do the settling exercise for five or ten minutes. During this time, pay no attention to the question.

When you have settled your mind, drop the question into it, like dropping a stone into a pond. Put it into your mind without any sense of having to seek an answer or struggle to solve or analyze it. It's essential now to let go of the question. This means that you don't consciously work at it. You don't analyze, reason, probe, work out—anything. Just leave it in your mind like that stone at the bottom of the pond.

Now relax. You can remain sitting or lie down. The most important thing is to be comfortable and relaxed. Don't direct the mind into any specific thinking activity. Let go of having to solve a problem or work something out. You may daydream for a while or even doze off for a few minutes. That's okay. If it happens, drop the question again when you come to.

Soon thoughts will begin popping into your mind. Write them down. Some will relate to the question, some won't. Others will seem very vague and perhaps even irrelevant. Some people are bothered that in the beginning they get a lot of thoughts that are obviously purely rational. Don't let this bother you. Simply write them down and continue reflecting. Slowly the balance between inner and outer will change.

Whatever arises, write it down, quickly, without thinking about it or analyzing it. It's important at this stage to write without any form of censorship. Your rational mind is not part of what is happening now, so try not to engage it. Simply write. You don't even have to make coherent sentences. It's okay to write words, half-completed phrases—even make marks or draw pictures. Anything to record the meaning that is welling up within your mind. How you do it doesn't matter, and each person will devise his or her own methods. What does matter is that you record in some way the flow of ideas without conscious, rational intervention.

After a while the flow will dry up. When this happens, take a short break, stretch, look out the window, relax. Then drop the question again—*plop*—and repeat the process of dropping and then writing. Do this three or four times during a session, until you begin to feel that, for the time being, your mind has presented you with whatever is there.

Finally, read through what you have written and allow your mind to piece it together. It's like mulling over a dream, looking at the different images and events. Don't try to impose a meaning on the material. Rather, play with it and see what presents or reveals itself. Interestingly, at this stage the underlying resistances and prejudices in your mind come into play and you will find yourself trying to block out and ignore certain revelations or conclusions about yourself. These reactions won't be obvious or consciously articulated: They manifest as negations. The mind will simply negate a line of thinking, conclusion, possibility. Emotional resistance lies behind it. When you begin reflecting, these obstacles—which is what they are—will not be seen, and your reflecting efforts may not seem to bear fruit. This is to be expected because you are learning to use your mind in a new and unusual way. Don't be discouraged. Keep at it, but always be sure that your main mode is relaxed, casual. The mind that wants to achieve, find answers, get to solutions, is not the mind that reflects; that mind must be given a way to drop out of the picture so that the reflecting mind has a chance to be heard.

After a while you will discover that some sort of answer is emerging. You will know that you are getting to it when your deep inner sense of the situation begins to come into the same focus as the emerging answer or solution.

REFLECTION: Identifying habitual tendencies

TOPIC 1: What are my hidden strengths?

It may seem strange to reflect on this topic. Most people assume that they know their positive qualities. This is not so. Many people ignore or conceal them because they feel too unworthy to have good qualities or that acknowledging them would be vain. Yet the "I," or ego, that is to be transcended ultimately needs first to have a psychologically healthy and well-integrated sense of self.

Some positive qualities are not very obvious—such as tolerance, patience, and kindness—so they are easily overlooked. Positive qualities create beneficial forces in the mind, which result in favorable conditions in the death bardos. If these conditions are present, it is easier to recognize and become enlightened. There will also be less fear and confusion.

In life, positive qualities tend to stabilize and balance the mind, counteracting the effect and growth of negative qualities. A positive mind is happier than a negative one. For these and many other reasons it makes sense to optimize the positive in the mind.

We begin by identifying the existence of positive states. Having done so, we proceed to consciously strengthen them.

For example, you might discover that you are inclined to be generous. Strengthen this by increasing your practice of giving, and reflect on the beneficial effects of generosity. If everyone in the world practiced generosity, there would be no poverty or starvation, just for a start. A mind that is strong on generosity will be more open, free, joyful, and naturally happy and at peace.

When one understands the value and importance of generosity, it becomes easier to overcome the mind's inherent tendency to grasp and hold for "self." Where greed is present in the mind, giving is difficult because the mind is locked in a sense of lack and neediness and a feeling that it is somehow wrong to share with others. Even minimal giving may become impossible.

To strengthen generosity we must consciously practice it, never passing up an opportunity to give, be it materially or in other ways, and no matter how small.

This training flows out of the exercise in reflecting.

TOPIC 2: What positive qualities have I not yet developed?

In the beginning this reflection might produce a fairly long list. Don't worry. You have within you the capacity to develop and perfect all known positive qualities.

Begin by reflecting on and sensitizing yourself to these qualities so that they awaken in your mind as specific points of awareness. They will then draw energy to themselves and gradually strengthen. Use the attitude suggested for the previous topic to strengthen awareness, and never pass up an opportunity to put the quality into practice.

Some people feel that they are losing out by practicing positive qualities, almost as though they were somehow missing the fun by being a goody-goody. This is not true. Nothing worthwhile is being missed or lost. On the contrary, enormous benefit and a sense of liberation from the narrow ego-limited world are gained.

TOPIC 3: What are my hidden negative tendencies?

To begin identifying negative tendencies, reflect on how your mind typically reacts when confronted by unexpected, threatening, or painful situations. The energy underlying your reaction will reveal your fundamental negative tendencies. It may take a while to see through your psychological smoke screens.

Remember, this is not an exercise in self-torment. If you are human, there will be negative tendencies in your mind. There will also be positive and neutral ones. The negative ones are the chief source of your sufferings in life and will most certainly cause you suffering when you are dead. So it makes sense to deal with them now.

Negatives may be blame, rationalizing, justifying, judging, or plain "hanging on to," as in harboring a grudge. Once you have discovered your main negatives, don't dwell on them and become morbid. Rather, be pleased that you have discovered the source of your difficulties. Then make it your discipline throughout your life to be alert to their manifestations. If you do this without fear, blame, or avoidance, you will gradually learn about them. You will learn how they are triggered—and there will be many triggers. You will learn how you unwittingly sustain them once they have been triggered, and then how they subside and leave the mind. This understanding will strengthen your mind and become the basis for freeing yourself from negative tendencies and the mental and physical behavior they arouse.

This is your life's work, so prepare to learn patience!

These three reflecting exercises may seem far removed from dreaming and dying. They are not. The texts emphasize over and over again that in the bardo of becoming, one is entirely at the mercy of the winds of karma. What does that mean? Every single action of this life echoes there and produces a specific mind state that may be horrifically nightmarish, benign, or heavenly. And no day dawns to awaken us from it.

So the choice is ours. We can begin training immediately to improve the quality of our living experience and enhance our chances of gaining enlightenment when we die. Or we can continue going around in circles.

We deepen our training through reflecting and learning to uncover our projections. In short, we train to get in touch with and transform the deeper levels of our mind.

16

Compassion:
The Wish-Fulfilling Jewel

This is not a question of religious practice, but a
question of the future of humanity.
    —*The Dalai Lama*, The Power of Compassion

Compassion is the most powerful force in the universe, and the cultivation of compassion is the surest means of liberating the mind. The reason is simple. All our difficulties come into being because of egocentric grasping. This grasping and its attendant negative mind states dissolve in the face of compassion.

Compassion seems to be a much misunderstood concept. It is not a sentimental emotion. It is the discerning ability to help in an appropriate manner; it is vital, active knowledge of what is appropriate in a given situation and the wisdom to apply it skillfully. Many people assume that to be compassionate one must become some kind of wimpish, sentimental doormat, always smiling and being nice to people. Huge misunderstanding follows this assumption because it implies suppression of one's aggression and a ban on standing up for oneself.

This is a clear mistake.

Compassion begins with being open first to ourselves, to our inner experience, and thus accepting ourselves—realistically so. If this is not done, we won't be able to be compassionate to others, because we cannot be what we are not. If we try (and many do), we get caught up in pretence, hypocrisy, and secretly harmful activity.

We apply this openness to the world around us: to people, to events, to situations. Compassion is all-embracing caring that arises within the mind of an enlightened being, a caring that sees all forms of life and of beings as equal. It can arise only in a mind that is completely open, a mind that is not narrowed by preferences, judgments, intolerance, or blocking off. We can all reach the stage of enlightened compassion: We start accepting ourselves and others without judgment.[1]

HEARTS LIKE LITTLE IRON BALLS

One of Akong Rinpoche's students at Samye Ling gave this account:

> When Akong Rinpoche came back from Tibet after his first visit, he came into the shrine room like a mountain. While he was away, people had been disagreeing and arguing, but everyone was so glad to see him safely back. He had, wrapped in a cloth, the skull cups of his father and mother, which had somehow been saved for him and given to him in Tibet. He said, "This is my father, this is my mother."
>
> I felt all my stupid sentimentality washed away, drowned by his presence, so real and intense, like standing under a waterfall.
>
> He said, "You all have such nice exteriors, such smiling faces, but inside you have hearts like little iron balls. You do not know the meaning of true compassion."

Question: What does being compassionate really mean?

Akong Rinpoche: The practice of compassion should not be accompanied by any expectation of receiving something in return. To regard one's practice of loving-kindness as some kind of business transaction only reinforces the sense of ego and separate self. Unselfish compassion, however, will expand our horizon beyond the scope afforded by such an isolated, impoverished view of reality and our place in it, so putting us in touch with the essential unity that pervades everything. The right attitude is neither to hope for success nor to fear personal failure but simply, and humbly, to proceed with the liberating effort to care for everyone.

Throughout human history there have been many great saints and masters whose lives were devoted to working hard for the benefit of others. Their achievements were not based on study, the ability to wage war, or on the accumulation of material possessions, but on their kindness to all beings. By following their example, we too can fulfill the promise of our precious human birth and awaken that limitless compassion in ourselves.[2]

AWAKENING THE HEART

> Awaken the heart by opening the mind.
> —*Ringu Tulku, slogan of the Bodhicharya association*

There is a wonderful Sanskrit word that embraces heart and mind: *bodhichitta*. But what is bodhichitta? *Bodhichitta* means "awakened heart" or "courageous heart." "Bodhichitta has the qualities of gentleness, precision, and openness, being able just to let go and open up."[3] This roughly means the mind determined to rediscover its enlightenment so that it can truly help and benefit others. One who is working to awaken his or her bodhichitta is a bodhisattva, a spiritual warrior. True, lasting happiness cannot find its way into a mind that is solely concerned with its own welfare.

Within some schools of Buddhism, training in compassion is given priority over most other trainings. Students are trained to develop bodhichitta, to take a vow to become a bodhisattva. A student on this path learns to dedicate every aspect of life and spiritual practice to the welfare of others. If this is done, the mind gradually becomes oriented to others rather than to self. Unselfishness begins to replace selfishness, and the mind becomes more open, caring, and loving. True happiness arises in such a mind and communicates itself to others.

Following are three methods of training that all emphasize the simplest and profoundest principle of liberation—compassion:

- Being kind
- Loving-kindness meditation
- Taking and sending—tonglen

BEING KIND

Kindness and an open, tolerant acceptance of life are essential ingredients of compassion. All the lamas emphasize this. The Dalai Lama said that we should try in life to be kind. Then he said, "But if you cannot be kind, at least avoid doing harm." This sounds so simple that one may be tempted to discount its power. Don't. Instead, try it out.

We begin with ourselves—be kind to ourselves. This does not mean become self-indulgent. Indulgence is generally harmful. Rather, we find out what we do in life that harms us unnecessarily. Curiously enough, most of us have the odd streak of self-destructiveness, masochism, or martyr complex in our makeup. We may think we have to sacrifice ourselves for the benefit of others. This is nonsense, and it is nauseating to be on the receiving end of this sort of behavior. We may need to *make* sacrifices, for example to provide for our children, but not sacrifice ourselves.

We extend to others the feeling of kindness to ourselves. Again, this is not indulgence but, rather, openness and acceptance of the other's being and point of view.

I remember a striking incident that happened years ago when I first began visiting Samye Ling. The place was a bit wild in those days and the people who lived there didn't often display the characteristics one would expect from spiritual practitioners.

When things got too out of hand, Akong Rinpoche would appear in the dining room during lunchtime. This was a smart move because the only thing that brought most of the community together was food. One would certainly never find large numbers in the meditation hall.

This was one such occasion. Rinpoche appeared and an expectant hush fell.

"I want you to think about how you are behaving," he said.

"I don't mind if you stay in bed late. I don't mind if you forget to sweep the floors or wash the dishes. All I ask is one thing: Be kind to one another."

That's all he said. Then he left.

Here are two reflections to check the status of your kindness to yourself and to others.

WHAT DO I DO TO MYSELF?

Begin by reflecting on what you do to yourself—how you relate to yourself. Gradually identify unnecessary unkindnesses and start letting go of them.

If you are an uptight, tense, anxious, sensitive person, this is particularly important. This line of reflecting will reveal that your inner environment is probably presided over by a maniacal tyrant who censors your every thought and action, threatening you constantly with the pit of doom. This tyrant needs to be befriended and disempowered.

HOW AM I WITH OTHERS?

Next reflect on how you are with others, and here is a crucial factor to look out for. It's not so much how you relate overtly but, more important, your *attitude* to others. Often our attitudes are predatory, superior, self-seeking, proprietary, manipulative, defensive. We may not realize the existence of these underlying but powerful forces in our minds, but they will be affecting others more than our words and actions, and they will also reveal a lot about ourselves and our habitual tendencies.

A simple way to begin this exercise is to put yourself in other people's shoes. Again and again ask yourself, "What is the other person experiencing? What effect am I having? What does he need? Where is she coming from?"

This simple training is surprisingly powerful and will teach you a lot about yourself, others, and the way your life works out—or doesn't work out. With this understanding will come a natural inclination to be kinder, because you will begin to appreciate the sufferings and difficulties of other human beings.

The second step is to reflect on how you are with those closest to you and begin an attitude of being kind to them—preferably without telling them or talking about it. Just do it. Work toward a situation where you don't pass up an opportunity to be kind, but don't turn this into a formula for self-torment.

Finally, extend your range of activity to all beings you meet. Then, in your mind, to all the beings you can think of.

Being kind naturally leads to restraint of our selfish and harmful tendencies (not in the form of repression but, rather, by our becoming aware of them and not acting them out). This naturally gives rise to consideration of the needs of others. Don't be tempted to underestimate the power of this training even though in the beginning you don't feel different. With time you will begin to notice subtle but stable, deep changes, a deepening sense of contentment and restfulness in the mind, a natural caring for others. These forms of training are not quick-fix techniques; they are ways of profoundly changing our lives forever.

This is specific training for death, because if it is done throughout life, the mind will soften and change. You will become happier and more peaceful in life, and the mind that passes out of life will have an easier time and be more prepared to recognize in the death bardos. Remember, life and death are not unrelated events. They form links in a great tangle of interrelatedness.

LOVING-KINDNESS MEDITATION

Loving-kindness meditation works on the principle of accessing whatever natural love and kindness we have in our mind, bringing it into focus, like a magnifying glass focusing the sun's rays, and then progressively generalizing it from a few chosen subjects to all beings in the universe, not forgetting oneself. When we do it, we discover that our love and predisposition to kindness tend to be selective. We are prepared to love and be kind to certain people or groups but not others. Sometimes we are definitely *not* prepared to be nice to some, and would in fact rather harm them if we had the chance. Compassion training is designed to take us beyond this selectiveness so that we begin to be like the sun: shining equally upon all sentient beings without preference or precondition.

So it works at two levels: consciously strengthening and deepening whatever feelings of love and kindness are already within us and widening our scope of care from a few chosen beings to all beings in the universe—in short, developing unconditional love.

If you are attracted to meditation and want to bring loving-kindness into your period of daily or weekly practice, you could begin with loving-kindness meditation. Start with the focus on kindness for yourself. We open our heart to accept ourself as we are and then we extend this openness to others. The following guidelines by my friend Beryl Schutten are a good start. You will develop your own imagery and words as you do this practice.

LOVING-KINDNESS MEDITATION, PART ONE

Take the attention into the body. Not my body — *the* body.

Allow yourself to relax deeply. Let the breath come and go naturally. No control.

Begin to imagine a beautiful white light flowing all through the body, within and without, like a soft summer shower. As it flows, feel the body becoming soft and warm and deeply relaxed. It's like a balm, soothing and comforting as it flows.

Gradually the concreteness of the body begins to dissolve, the hard outline of the body disappears. There seems to be little difference between the outside and the inside. You are very calm, very relaxed; there is a gentleness.

This is compassion, kindness toward the body.

Now we take this same kind, accepting attitude toward the mind. We look within and if there's anything that takes us away from the calm, peaceful mind — any anger, resentment, jealousy, feeling of rejection, loneliness, grief — with the greatest gentleness we simply place the feeling in the compassionate heart — which is so vast, so spacious, so limitless that there is room for everything. We see that it is just a part of our humanness. Not condoning, just accepting. So we rest in the compassionate heart.

We can look, if we want to, at forgiveness, particularly for ourselves — to let go of the unkind heart that doesn't allow this. To forgive ourselves for anything we may have done, said, or thought in the past or present. We simply take this immense gentleness and place it in the compassionate heart and let it rest there . . . forgiveness for ourselves.

Spend a few minutes experiencing the feeling of forgiveness: the gentleness, the softness, the kindness to self.

Finally we let go of everything and just rest the mind in the body, the body in the mind. . . . Just rest.

LOVING-KINDNESS MEDITATION, PART TWO

Begin by thinking of a being that you really love.

It could be a human or an animal, or it could be somebody or something who is no longer alive; it doesn't matter. Just let your mind rest thinking of this being and allow the love to arise in your heart. You love that being. You are capable of love. Think of the being. Let yourself feel how you love the being and how you want to ensure the being's happiness. You would give a lot to promote the being's happiness. If you like, you can say to yourself words such as:

May you be happy. I'd really like you to be happy.

May you be free from suffering. Think how often suffering comes upon people. But we love them so we don't want them to suffer.

May you be free from the causes of suffering. Think how people often do things that are obviously going to make them suffer. And they do this out of ignorance and confusion. You don't want them to do that, to create the causes for suffering.

You feel this very strong love and caring.

Now that you've established this in your heart, think of others whom you love in the same way. You really want them to be happy, free, joyful. In this way it's as though that feeling grows bigger and encompasses more people and more beings.

Then let your mind go out to all the beings you know in this city, this country, this continent, in the world. May they all be happy. *May they be free from suffering and the causes of suffering.*

Radiate that same sense of caring and loving to them.

Then all the beings you don't know: billions and trillions of humans, animals, reptiles. They all feel suffering, they are subject to pain, they all seek happiness. They all want to escape pain.

May they be happy. May they be free from suffering.

Your love has no limit. Your caring and kindness are not limited—they are as wide as your mind can think.

Now think of enemies, or people whom you dislike. And think how in the bigger scheme of things there's no real point or value in hating them, holding enmity, resentment. Think in your heart: I could forgive them. I can forgive them. Despite my feelings, I would like them to be happy. So you let this feeling go to them.

Finally you encompass the whole universe, the countless beings in the universe. May they all be happy. May my love and caring go to all of them, touch their hearts and bring them happiness.

End by thinking of yourself. *May I also be happy. May I be at peace and may my life be joyful.*

Rest for three or four minutes with this sense of expansive, limitless love and caring that knows no limits. The universe is at peace.[4]

TAKING AND SENDING—TONGLEN

> When the world is filled with evil, all mishaps should be
> transformed into the path of enlightenment.
> —*Old Tibetan teaching*

Within Tibetan Buddhism there is a profound system of training called the Seven Points of Mind Training, and the heart of the training is tonglen: taking and sending. The principle it teaches is that all suffering and the unenlightened state are the result of egocentric grasping, which is the basic habitual tendency of the human mind. Any erosion or weakening of this state will therefore naturally begin to liberate the mind.

The training is practical, and many of the exercises focus on helping one work skillfully with negative and conflicting emotions in daily life situations. The practice is easy to understand and apply in life, while at the same time it is very powerful and will bring about long-term changes in the mind.

The essence of tonglen is compassion. The training is to develop a mind that naturally wants to give happiness and joy to all beings while simultaneously taking away their suffering and unhappiness.

The Practice of Tonglen

You can regard tonglen practice as a meditation, a devotional exercise, or simply a way to train your mind to free itself from egocentricity, to develop bodhichitta.

The practice originates in Tibetan Buddhism, so some of the format reflects that tradition. If this does not work for you, substitute equivalent imagery and words from your spiritual system that are meaningful to you.

If you are going to do tonglen, you will need to spend a little time familiarizing yourself with the steps. A full session consists of four steps, with a fifth step integrating the practice into everyday life.

- Preparation: setting up a visualization and invoking a spiritual power
- Motivation: contemplating four reminders
- Loving-kindness: a short meditation
- The actual tonglen: taking and sending
- Integration into everyday life: postmeditation practice

In emergencies, and when you do not have the time to do the first three steps, you can start instead with simply "flashing absolute bodhichitta," which Pema Chödrön describes as "just opening up . . . flashing some sense of openness and spaciousness,"[5] and then continue with actual tonglen.

Preparation

Visualization

Sit comfortably and settle your mind. Imagine your body is not solid. It's made of light—like a hologram. Picture in the middle of your chest a very beautiful space. It's very light; gold and white predominate. The space contains a seat that is beautiful and pure like crystal. If you want to follow Tibetan Buddhist imagery, you imagine an open white lotus flower. In its heart lies a two-dimensional full moon, flat: This is the seat.

Now imagine a clear glass funnel or tube standing upright within your body. Again, it is not solid; it's made of light. The lower end hovers above the beautiful seat in your chest and the upper part ends with a mouth like a trumpet at the top of your head, at the Brahma aperture, which is a magical spot.

Picture above you in space something that symbolizes or represents the source of spiritual power for you. If you are Christian, it might be God or Jesus. If Muslim, Allah or Muhammad; Hindu—Brahma or Krishna. If you have no religious focus, a ball of white or golden light might work. You can imagine invoking the forces of universal compassion, the source of your creativity, or whatever works for you.

A Buddhist would visualize his or her guru, maybe the Karmapa, the Dalai Lama, another guru, or the Buddha.

This completes the first stage of the visualization.

In these next few paragraphs I have used the terminology of the mind training text for convenience.[6] If this Buddhist system doesn't work for you, it's important to substitute, from your preferred spiritual system, equivalent imagery and words that are meaningful to you.

Invocation

You want to invite the enlightened presence into yourself and become one with it. To do that you say a prayer from your heart:

> I pray for your blessing, my guru,
> Great and completely worthy spiritual friend.
> I pray that you will cause love, compassion, and bodhichitta to
> arise in my mind.

Perform the invocation by reciting this prayer or your variation at least three times. You may wish to recite it many times so as to build up a strong feeling that a powerful spiritual being or force is present.

In response to your prayer, the guru descends into your body via the light tube and becomes seated in your heart in a pavilion of light, in that space you visualized earlier.

You think: "Now my guru and I are one and inseparable. I am united with the enlightened mind. Whatever happens from now on is happening from a source of enlightenment, not from my egocentric personality."

Nothing in this universe can harm the enlightened mind.

Thinking in this way will give you strength and confidence.

Now think of the universe. It contains billions of trillions of sentient beings. They are all essentially like you: They want to be happy and avoid suffering. But out of ignorance they create the causes of suffering, so they are unhappy and experience pain. You want to help them.

Motivation: The Four Contemplations

If we are fully motivated to do something, we will do it and complete it. If we are not motivated, we will give up when difficulties get in our way. An understanding of this principle is fundamental to Tibetan Buddhist training, which teaches a way of contemplating four specific topics in order to develop unshakeable motivation. If we do the reflections time and again, we develop a mature long-term perspective on our lives that we would not have otherwise. Once we have this perspective, we know without doubt that spiritual training and helping others are more important than anything else. This knowing keeps us going more and more strongly right to the end of the path.

We reflect that:

- We are very fortunate to be born as humans with a predisposition and opportunity to follow a spiritual discipline. This is in contrast to billions of beings who do not have these predispositions and therefore waste precious time and opportunities. We call this a precious human birth.

- All things are impermanent, including this life of ours. It could end at any moment, so we resolve to make good use of it now instead of delaying for even a day.

- Everything in the world is governed by karma—cause and effect. We do not know what karma awaits us. Our lives could end at any moment, and we cannot be sure we will have another human birth next time. So we see that it's important to train now, use this chance while we have it, and among other things, increase our chances of having not only another human birth but a better one where we will be able to help more beings.

- Samsara—this universe we live in—is a mixed bag. Many of the existences within it are subject to extreme stress, much more than anything we are experiencing. We don't want to have a hard time in the future, nor do we want others to have a hard time, so we strengthen our resolve to work toward enlightenment now, because we have the chance.*

Loving-kindness Meditation

Do a short meditation, along the lines of the loving-kindness meditation, parts 1 and 2 above.

Tonglen Practice

"Train in taking and sending alternately. Put them on the breath."[7]

Move on now to the actual tonglen. Focus on your breath but don't interfere with your breathing

Begin with yourself. Imagine all your sadness, depression, anxiety, stress, unhappiness, negativity, whatever, in the form of black smoke or tar. Think not only of states you are experiencing now but of all suffering that is due to come to you karmically in the future. With your in-breath draw this into your heart, into that special place where the spiritual force has been visualized and now presides. If you wish, you

---

* This is a very brief summary of the four contemplations. If you want to cover this aspect fully, read Jamgon Kongtrul's *Torch of Certainty* (Boston: Shambhala, 2000); or *Great Path of Awakening* (New York: Random House, 2000); or Khentin Tai Situ Pa's *Way to Go* (Newcastle, Scotland: Kagyu Samye Ling, n.d.).

can think that the suffering is purified or transformed here into pure light like moonlight. Then you breathe out, again to yourself, pure light that makes you happy and peaceful and awakens your spiritual potential.

You do this at the beginning until you feel that you are okay and ready to move on to exchange your happiness for the suffering of others.

Sending. As you breathe out, imagine white or golden light—that is your love, compassion, happiness—streaming out of your heart. You are like a cosmic candle. The light goes in all directions at once. It fills the universe and touches the heart of every being within it. As this happens, all beings become happy and at peace. You have sent them your happiness and it has made them happy.

This doesn't mean your happiness is diminished. Think of a candle. If you have a lighted candle, you can light any number of other candles from it. Your flame never fades. Instead there are more and more lights. So you are a very, very powerful source of light, happiness, and blessing. This light goes out to all beings in the universe.

This is the sending visualization.

Taking. Then you breathe in. As you do this you take suffering from all beings. This is the receiving. Imagine that all their mental and spiritual suffering leaves them in the form of black oily smoke and comes to you. It enters your heart and is transformed there into the white or golden light of compassion. So the more black you can take in, the more golden light you will be able to give, because this is a process of transformation. In this way you become an increasingly powerful source of blessing with each breath.

Remember, you are doing this exercise with the guru in your heart. It's not the small egocentric you doing it. It's the enlightened you, so no harm can befall you.

This description of how to do this aspect of the practice is a little different from the traditional text. I have varied it slightly to try to make it easier for you, but this has not changed the principle of how it works.

Continue with this sending and receiving for most of your session. You may find it too hectic to visualize lights and black smoke going and coming with every single breath. If so, pace yourself and discover what rhythm works for you; you may do it with every second or third breath.

As you approach the end of your session, begin to think you have now taken all the suffering in the universe. All beings are happy, free from suffering. Picture this. See faces gradually becoming peaceful and happy wherever they are.

When you end this session, think of the task as complete: You have removed the suffering of all beings and given them happiness in its place.

End the session by dedicating whatever positive energy you have generated to all beings in the universe.

Do the first four steps of this exercise daily for a month, spending about twenty minutes on each session.

Thereafter do it at least once a week for the rest of your life, unless you decide to make it your main training, in which case do it daily or as often as you can.

Special focus. If you know any person or being or group of beings who are experiencing particular difficulty or suffering and you want to help them, you can focus specifically on them for the entire session.

Integration into Everyday Life: Postmeditation Practice

When in hot water, bathe.

By integrating tonglen practice into everyday life, we turn the tables on our usual tendencies and turn them into practices to benefit others.

What we call formal meditation is very valuable, that is, meditation where we sit down and do nothing except meditate. But most of us have busy lives and are unable to allocate much time to this. So we look for ways to bring our meditation into daily life. We call this postmeditation.

Postmeditation focuses on the state of the mind while we are walking around and doing things. Most of us are engaged in a surprising amount of emotional thought-feeling activity in the course of our average day. Some of this is clearly negative, such as mild irritation, anger, or envy, or we may indulge in passionate longing for someone or a situation—one could think of many examples. We normally pass these experiences off as unimportant because they don't stand out as major disturbances or obscurations. But they are not unimportant, because they continually reinforce underlying emotional tendencies, which therefore become stronger instead of weaker. These tendencies are called mind poisons, because they poison the mind and disrupt our potential for equilibrium and compassion. How do we deal with them?

We learn a new approach, which appears in traditional texts under the unlikely title "three objects, three poisons, three seeds of virtue."[8] The three poisons are greed, hatred, and delusion, which are the most common disturbing emotions.* The three objects are the things in relation to which we typically experience the poisons: the things we desire and feel comfortable with, the things we don't want or hate, and the situations where we behave inappropriately or with indifference. The "three seeds of virtue" means turning those situations around so that when they arise we use them as a way of freeing ourselves from attachment to our habitual way of reacting and cultivating compassion, instead of reinforcing the poisons. This area of training has a lot of potential because we experience the mind poisons many times every day, and therefore we can train in compassion many times a day.

When in Hot Water, Bathe

When you realize you are experiencing a mind poison, pause and reflect. See how anger, for example, is disturbing, painful. A mind that is angry is suffering. It can lead to negative consequences for you and others. There is no benefit in the situation—and so it is with all the negative emotions.

Now we introduce what I call the "When in hot water, bathe" principle. A situation has come upon us and at the moment there is no way out of it, so use it to advantage. Being stuck in one of the mind poisons is like being in hot water. Normally what we do is strengthen the poison. Now we turn the table on it. So what do I do? I bathe. I turn it into a positive practice. And I say: This is suffering. I can't deny it—I'm in the middle of it. Now I know about suffering. And this is what happens in

---

*The three mind poisons—greed, hatred, and delusion—can also be called passion, aggression, and ignorance. Traditionally pride and jealousy are added, making five. Lamas say Westerners have invented a sixth: guilt.

other beings' lives. And when they have it, they suffer just like this. So now since I am stuck in it, I'm going to experience it for everybody. So the suffering of all beings is contained in this suffering of mine. So I suffer for them all. As long as I'm experiencing it: *May other beings be free.*

Whatever emotion is causing the suffering, we imagine we are suffering for the whole universe. As long as the negative emotion persists, we think in this way and use the otherwise negative situation to advantage by developing compassion where we would otherwise have strengthened negativity.

It doesn't mean we suppress, deny, act out, or nurture the excessive emotion. We simply change our attitude: It is not a problem; it is a chance to practice. The emotions are there, we allow them to be there, but we introduce a new perspective into our normal self-pitying round, this completely new element: Wonderful, I'm in hot water for others. And if it gets too steamy and burning: Good, I am in a burning bath for others. So we turn a poison into the seed of a virtue.

Interestingly the texts mention pleasurable and enjoyable or horrific and terrifying emotions and influences. We can share these equally with all beings: *May they be happy. May they be free from suffering.* The perspective is to accept any situation as it is, and as "a stimulus to wakefulness and an opportunity to express compassion."[9]

This is postmeditation training: integrating the training into everyday life. To me it is the most useful of all the practices, and many have testified to the amazing transformation it has brought about in their lives.

In the beginning this method may feel strange or contrived, but after a while it changes our outlook. And it goes further. We know this principle for ourselves. When we are with some people, we just start feeling better. They have a vibe that frees us. Whereas other people seem to be like vampires sucking our vital energy. So we train to be a beneficial force, learning to help by our mere presence.

Comment on Tonglen Practice

Two crucial principles are being woven together.

The first is the importance, when doing profound spiritual training, of invoking and working with powerful spiritual forces that can help us. This principle is central to Tibetan Buddhism, which is why serious practitioners seek a qualified teacher or guide. The teacher will introduce them to one of the great lineages so that their practice can be inspired and sustained by the accumulated spiritual force of the lineage. These two factors (guru and lineage) enormously strengthen spiritual practice and enable the student to accomplish levels of training and development that would not otherwise be possible. This principle is given effect and illustrated in the preparation for tonglen described earlier.

Second, egocentric grasping is what stands between us and enlightenment. It's easy to say this but difficult to understand because self-cherishing is so all-pervasive in our minds. It would be a hopeless task to attempt to identify and root out every instance of it. So the training offers a general approach that automatically covers all instances. It works on a simple principle: *Put others first*; cultivate an increasingly genuine concern for the welfare of others. In doing this we don't invite the world to walk on us; we simply focus on the welfare of others and in doing so begin to free ourselves from our obsessive preoccupation with our own desires, concerns, and welfare. This naturally liberates us and allows the spontaneous arising of goodwill, kindness, and compassion. It also strengthens our motivation to become enlightened, not so much for ourselves as for others—in making others our focus of concern, we become increasingly aware of how they suffer and need our help. Slowly it's as though all beings become our children. We watch over them and genuinely care for their welfare. We want to help in every way possible and realize that if we become enlightened we will naturally manifest skills and abilities to help that are not available to unenlightened beings.

So we cultivate a specific attitude or mind state: bodhichitta—the mind determined to become enlightened so that it can genuinely help and benefit others by leading them to enlightenment, which is freedom from suffering and any further possibility of suffering; it is also the manifestation of all positive and "divine" qualities.

Bodhichitta is commonly referred to as the mind of awakening. Tonglen embodies bodhichitta. Bokar Rinpoche recommends it as one of the most powerful practices to do not only in life but as we are dying: "This mind of awakening is full of great power by itself. It implies a compassionate mind directed toward all beings. The person living in the mind of awakening wishes to take on others' suffering, and to give them happiness in exchange. Egocentric vision is abandoned. The only remaining thought is for the benefit of others and love directed toward them."[10]

Because tonglen is such a powerful practice, it is generally recommended as a primary discipline to be adopted for life. Some people make it their only practice. In the context of dying, it is said to be about the most effective way of ensuring that we enter the death experience in the best possible state of mind. So you can put it at the top of your list of training options.

THE WISH-FULFILLING JEWEL

The hands joined in prayer at the heart of Chenrezi hold a special gem known as the wish-fulfilling jewel. This sounds magical. What is this wish-fulfilling quality? Compassion.

Compassion is the fuel of the universe. It is like the sun emanating rays from this jewel or the heart in which it is burning. It offers the potential for anything we could wish for—beyond measure, unthinkable.

By awakening the heart we can all become bodhisattvas who practice bodhichitta—in touch with our own inherent jewel of infinite potential to benefit all beings.

> May all beings always have happiness and the causes of
>   happiness.
> May they be free from suffering and the causes of suffering.
> May they know the true happiness that is sorrowless.
> May they be free from attachment to some and aversion to
>   others and know the great impartiality of life.
> — *The Four Limitless Contemplations*

Conclusion

Of course we will die, and it really doesn't matter. But what does matter is whether we choose to make our death beneficial. It's up to us. Most people I have met prefer not to face the inevitable and end up just hoping for the best. We don't have to be like that.

Life, dream, and death are bardos we visit on our endless, circular journey through samsara, and they are all connected. Our destiny is to become liberated from this cycle, but when this will happen is a matter we each have to decide for ourselves. The sooner we do it, the sooner we can help free others.

So we decide: In this lifetime I will begin seriously training. This does not mean pie-in-the-sky idealism. It means practical, down-to-earth coming to grips with what it's all about: the state of my mind.

Our mind is not a simple reflection of this life's experiences. It is molded by the force of habitual tendencies we have established over countless lifetimes. So we have to contend with them and set in motion new forces to free ourselves from them. These forces arise in the mind in response to specific forms of training that go deep, beyond intellect and rational thought, and their effects will manifest in all the bardos along the way—not just life. Training for freedom in life is the basis for freedom in dream and death. No effort is wasted.

I have suggested five areas of training: mindfulness, reflecting, being kind, loving-kindness, tonglen. If you are inclined by temperament to meditative types of training, then you can start with mindfulness and loving-kindness meditations. If you are of a more active disposition, I would recommend mind training and trying to be kind to yourself and the world—all the time. But also try a bit of mindfulness. Everyone will benefit from learning to reflect.

Don't compartmentalize. When you first read of these training methods, you might feel a little overwhelmed and wonder where to begin. Start with the one that seems easiest to you. Spend time with it and master it. Then move on to another one. In the end you will be able to incorporate them all into your life, and you will never regret it.

After a while you will realize that the training is not something special or disconnected. It has to do with your immediate day-to-day life situation: the way you live each day as an ordinary person — but it's not just the ordinary living of acting out needs, desires, routines. It is characterized by the introduction of new attitudes and disciplines into your life that make living worthwhile, meaningful, and beneficial.

There is no need to adopt strange or unusual lifestyles. Simply give up harmful activity and try to benefit others in the world.

Afterword

When we die we do it alone, and how we do it is up to us. Our dying will reflect how we have used our mind in life.

As a generalization this is true, but not so if we have a connection with a lama who is accomplished in one of the meditations related to death. A lama can help us a great deal.

There is the story told in *The Bardo Guidebook* by Chokyi Nyima Rinpoche of a lama who was traveling in Tibet to meet His Holiness the Sixteenth Karmapa.

In the party was a particular lama's younger brother, who was not at all spiritually inclined. In fact he was a bit rebellious and reckless, but he had a connection with the Karmapa. This brother fell off his horse one day and chipped a piece off one of his front teeth. A short while later he became ill and died.

After completing the death arrangements, the party moved on, reaching the Karmapa's monastery a week or so later.

When the lama was admitted to the Karmapa's presence, His Holiness said, "Oh, I saw your young brother last week." His Holiness then pointed to his front tooth and said with a chuckle, "He had lost part of his tooth."

Needless to say the lama was pleased that his brother's mind had made it to their destination and asked after his welfare. His Holiness said he thought he had been able to help him and then explained: "I am a Karmapa. Certain qualities have developed due to past aspirations and practice, but there is no need to mention them. But one thing always happens: All those whom I have met during this lifetime, whether we have a good or bad connection, always come and visit me after they die before continuing on. I can help some, but not everybody."[1]

What an eye-opener for us Westerners. There are beings who have great spiritual power—and they don't exist only within Buddhism—who can help us in unimagined ways. All we have to do is make a connection.

There is a mantra, KARMAPA CHENNO, which means "Karmapa, think of me." You could try saying it often, and if you are able to circumvent skepticism, you will make a connection with the Karmapa.

We never know when death will knock at our door. When we are young we tend to imagine that years of life lie ahead, so we postpone our preparations.

If we understand the great cyclic nature of our existence, we will view ourselves differently. Not young, not old, just at one or another point on the great wheel of life, moving ceaselessly through the illusion of time and space. Sometimes we have moments of joy, peace, tranquillity. But for most beings those are rare and soon end. *There is no final resting place in samsara.* Samsara is the six bardos, and our fate is to drift endlessly through them like a wraith driven by our karma. Driven on by our grasping and desire, we desperately seek the impossible—final peace and rest. What we long for is not there. It's like a bad soap opera, just going on and on and on, playing out the same old themes. And according to the lamas, most of the possible births in samsara are much more painful and awful than the human theme park.

Vicki Mackenzie sums it up so neatly in her book *Reborn in the West: The Reincarnation Masters:* "As to the Buddha's answer to why we keep on being reborn, he replied that the only point of it all was to learn how to stop. When disenchantment with continuous travelling sets in, when the fascination with our mind dramas, both tragic and comic, ceases, then we yearn for peace. That's when we begin our final journey to discover our true nature and the absolute reality of all things."[2]

The great message of the *Tibetan Book of the Dead* is one of hope and inspiration—*we do not have to go on this way.* If we get our act together now, while we are "alive" and have a chance, great things are possible. We can free ourselves from the wheel.

So we get ready. We deal with grasping and resentment. We train in mindfulness, compassion, tonglen—whichever fits our temperament. If we have a connection with a lama, we can learn phowa, or transference

of consciousness. We can take initiations, do the purification meditations, and plant the seeds of profound liberation.

Above all, we can begin, from this very moment, training in compassion. It's simple:

Step 1: *Face yourself as you are now.* Come to terms with and accept
yourself.

Step 2: *Allow others to be as they are and accept them.* Remember
what Naropa said: "Samsara is finding fault with others."

Step 3: *Be kind.* Be kind to yourself; be kind to others.

Imagine you have three feet, because you take all three steps at once.

I think by now I must have said all I have to say. Be well; seek your
peace.

Acknowledgments

We wish to thank the many people who have made the publication of this book possible:

His Holiness the Seventeenth Karmapa for inspiration, blessing, and the foreword

Tai Situ Rinpoche for his encouragement and blessing

Thrangu Rinpoche, Akong Rinpoche, and Lama Yeshe, who removed obstacles and made it all possible

Ringu Tulku Rinpoche, who was kind enough to share

Maria Hündorf-Kaiser of Bodhicharya in Hamburg, Germany

Lama Phuntsok and Lama Tenam at Gyuto Tantric University, India

Pieter Carst, who facilitated our archetypal pilgrimage to His Holiness the Seventeenth Karmapa in India to receive the blessing

My old friend John Taylor, who was so patient and helped so much

Judith Finn and Sister Ellen Finlay in Tulsa, Oklahoma—two busy people who kindly spent many precious hours helping

Beryl Schutten and Miles Mattson for contributing gems

Adam Pinos for sending help from Mongolia

Mark Greenwood, Achim von Arnim, Mike Peacock, and Moyra Keene

Desmond and Soozi Rice, in whose Kalk Bay home much of this book happened

For this edition, we would like to thank Jonathan Green, Emily Bower, Ben Gleason, and all at Shambhala Publications for their support

And especially our anonymous sponsor, without whose generosity there could have been no book.

—*Rob Nairn and Erika van Greunen*
Kairon Press
Kalk Bay, South Africa
December 2003

Appendix A

A Perspective on Living and Dying

Ringu Tulku.

In the Tibetan tradition, dying is the busiest time. Usually in Tibetan society, nothing much happens at a person's birth except that a lama might be asked to give a name for the child. A marriage is a social contract, with social celebrations. A lama may come to give a blessing, but that takes only minutes and isn't essential; the monasteries have no role at all. But at the time of death, the lamas become busy because religion or spiritual practice remain the only things that might help the person go through the process of dying. It was very interesting for me to hear from the Japanese that nowadays in Japan they celebrate birth according to the Shinto system, marriage in a Christian church, and with death they go to the Buddhists.

In Buddhism, you will find various methods to help the dying and the dead, and the *Tibetan Book of the Dead* is among them. It is believed that the consciousness of a person can be guided and directed in the right direction. Although it is important to try to help someone at the time of death, the real preparation for death has to be done while we are still alive. It is understood that to be prepared for death is the best way to learn how to live, and to know the nature of life is the best preparation for death.

This life, the life we are living now, is considered to be a transitional period, or *bardo* in Tibetan. From the Buddhist point of view it is important to understand this because death is not the end. Life itself is a transition, a process of change. If we consider it carefully, we find that change does not occur just over the course of long periods of days, months, and years, but it occurs in every moment.

According to Buddhist thought, everything is a continuum of dependent arising. This moment of my consciousness arises out of the last moment of interactions, and the interactions of this moment give rise to the next moment of my consciousness. This and the next are not exactly the same, and yet not exactly different. Take the example of yogurt. When milk turns into yogurt, are the milk and the yogurt the same or different? The yogurt is not the milk, but without the milk, there would be no yogurt.

This is how what we call our "being" continues, and the sense of "I am" arises out of this continuum. This "I" or "self" has joy, fear, many different kinds of experiences, but it is not one solid thing. It is a continuum of a process that is made of many changing elements of body and mind. We are like a river; there is no river without the water, but the water is always flowing and never remains the same, although the river seems to remain same. The way we see ourselves influences the way we relate to and react toward everything around us. In one sense we die every moment. In another sense there is no death but only transitions. That is why the whole cycle of life and death is described as the four or the six bardos. When we talk of four bardos, we have the bardo of living plus those of death, which is divided into three stages: the bardo of dying, bardo of *dharmata*, and the bardo of becoming. When we talk of six bardos then we also divide the bardo of living into three areas of being awake, dreaming, and the meditative state. The process of dying is just the reverse of the process of a life forming in the mother's womb. The bardo of becoming is similar to that of a dream. In a deep meditative state we can experience dharmata or clear light. Each of these states is seen as a challenge, an opportunity, and a practice. We have a chance to be liberated from samsaric sufferings at any of these stages if we can see and experience the reality or true nature of ourselves and know how to react. It is also believed that if we have some understanding and training now it would be easy to be liberated when we die. Therefore the bardo of life becomes the most important for us at the moment.

The main thing for us to do now is to try to understand and experience the true nature of the world around us to learn how to react through that reality. As a step toward that we also try to cultivate a habit of seeing and feeling and reacting in a positive way, inspired by compassion toward ourselves and others, which will bring more benefit and less harm to ourselves and others. The cultivation is called accumulating wisdom and the benefit is called accumulating merit. Wisdom and compassion become the essence of Buddhist practice.

SEEING BEYOND PROJECTIONS

First we look at how strongly our mind is colored by our projections. If we look deeply we will see that each of us is more or less a process with many elements, all of them always changing. But we do not normally see that way. We tend to see ourselves as one and the same from birth to death. We see everything around us in the same way and we react with aversion or attachment. With that attitude and habitual tendency we are usually either running after something or running away from something. There is no peace and satisfaction in our mind. Once we experience how our concept of reality causes us to see things, then we are ready to understand two more liberating principles: (1) the way we view things determines how we experience them; and (2) the way we see reality is not necessarily the only way it can be. These principles point out how relative reality is. Hell, heaven, and the rest of the six realms are created by the habitual ideas that got impressed in our mind. It is easy to create hell and it is also not that difficult to create heaven, if you have accumulated those kinds of perceptions, attitudes, emotions, and habits.

If we were to learn how to see ourselves clearly and directly without any projections, we would be liberated, which means that the appearance of hell or heaven does not need to bother us because we know our true nature. This is called realization, liberation, awakening, enlightenment, buddhahood. The main purpose of Buddhist practice is to actualize this realization for yourself and then to help others toward that. Until that happens we try to create a more positive situation for ourselves and help others to create a positive situation in their lives as well.

UNDERSTANDING, EXPERIENCING, REALIZATION

How do we attain this realization? First, we try to find good teachers and receive proper teachings. We study, reflect, and meditate on these teachings. The first stage of realization would be a clear understanding. We might get a very clear and doubtless understanding of how we are and how things are and how we could do our practice. This understanding can sometimes be mistaken for experience, but it is only a clear understanding of the reality, a conceptual knowing. This is the first step.

As we continue to meditate and train with this understanding, there comes a stage during which we can experience different levels of clarity, peace, nondual experiences, and other signs of realization—but it does not last. This is the second step, called the stage of experience.

If we continue to practice without getting attached to these experiences, then these experiences can mature and deepen and become our normal experience. Nothing can disturb or distract us from this experience of seeing things completely clearly and we become free from fear and attachment. There is no need to run away from or after anything. Great peace and relief and joy arise spontaneously. We overflow with limitless and unstained compassion. This is the third step, the step of insight. In Tibetan these three steps are called Gowa, Nyongwa, and Togpa. This is the first level of true realization. One does not have any fear of death or birth. One is freed from the cycle of birth and death so that one can take whatever appearances one needs to take and create all sorts of miracles for the benefit of beings.

This realization can be accomplished in one lifetime and this is the greatest preparation for death. Even if we do not become that realized in this lifetime the practices we do now can help us to get the realization when we go through different stages of death.

IMPERMANENCE, INTERDEPENDENCE, EMPTINESS

The most important principle in understanding these ideas is interdependence, or dependent arising. The true nature of everything is interdependent, which means that everything—all entities in the whole universe, mental and material—are completely dependent and completely impermanent. If you tried to find an example of a functional entity that is independent and permanent, you would not be able to find one.

Interdependence means that anything you look at is caused by many things and it will disappear if one cause is missing. An entity appears only when all the causes and conditions come together. Whatever I am is caused by my previous moments. And that moment is caused by the moments that preceded it. Our actions and reactions and habitual tendencies that cause and condition our next moments and next lives are called karma. When we are not realized and do not fully experience our true nature, our next birth is conditioned by our karma. When we are enlightened, our continuum is not discontinued but we are not forced by our karmic conditions any more. We can make our own decisions where and how to take the next birth.

Actually, emptiness and interdependence are one and the same. When we understand impermanence and the interdependent nature of phenomena, it is easier to understand emptiness. Take one thing and see what it is made of. It is made up of many parts. You look at an atom and it also has many parts. Scientists say that a water particle is made of hydrogen and oxygen and if we took these two apart the water particle would disappear. Each entity is made of many things but each of these parts may not have an independent existence. Therefore, all are like a rainbow, a mirage, a dream. This is what we call the nature of emptiness. When we realize this experientially we are freed from the material imprisonment. For example, a great yogi of Tibet named Milarepa once entered a yak horn. His disciples saw him sitting in it comfortably. The yak horn had not grown bigger than its normal size. Milarepa had not become smaller.

Many great masters can go into what is called the rainbow body at death. Their body just dissolves into light and no remains are left, except sometimes the nails and hair. This also comes from seeing the nature of emptiness clearly and completely.

If we can understand this then we can also understand that time and space are relative — there is nothing absolute about them. A whole universe can be on one speck of dust. It is possible because the world is created from nothing permanent.

This also clarifies the famous Zen parable of "the gateless gate." When you pass through it, you realize that there has never been a gate. When you realize what you really are, then you know that there has never been any delusion. But till then there is samsara, delusion, karma, and rebirth.

KARMAPA: THE FIRST REINCARNATIONS

In the Buddhist view, everybody is a rebirth of somebody. We have had countless lives before us and probably will have many more. It is also true that buddhas and bodhisattvas always reincarnate and appear in many and various forms to help beings. But the tradition of recognizing tulkus or reincarnations started in Tibet.

In the twelfth century there was a lama called Karmapa Dusum Khyenpa. In his life he built two monasteries. When he was around eighty years old he said, "I must go and build that third monastery that I promised to my guru." Although he was quite old, he went to central Tibet, built a little hut, and then he died. Before he died, he said, "Do not dismantle any of the things I have done, and do not give away my books and other things; keep them. I will come back."

After a few years, a small child came and said, "I am Karmapa." He became an extraordinary lama called Karma Pakshi, who performed various miracles at the court of Kublai Khan as stated by Marco Polo and became one of the teachers of the Mongol emperor. He built the Tsurphu monastery that his predecessor started. Orgyenpa, one of the main students of the second Karmapa and a great master who brought the lineage of the three vajra practices from India, recognized the third Karmapa, Rangjung Dorje. He was a student of Karma Pakshi and a great sage and scholar. When this Karmapa was in his mother's womb, Orgyenpa said to the lady, "You will have a son and he will be the reincarnation of my teacher, Karmapa." A special child was born. This child remembered not only his past but he also remembered his experience in his mother's womb. He also wrote an autobiography of his life in the mother's womb.

This is how the tradition of tulkus started. For the first time in Tibetan history, maybe in the history of the world, a certain child was recognized as the tulku of a lama by another revered master. Soon after that the Dalai Lamas and Panchen Lamas and many other tulkus started to be found. When a respected lama died his students sought and found his reincarnation. Tibet became full of tulkus and almost every monastery had a tulku. The tulku tradition is now about nine and half centuries old but Tibetan people continue to respect the tradition and many great meditation masters live among them.

LOVE WHOLEHEARTEDLY WHILE IT IS POSSIBLE

Sometimes we fight with the people we love—and we are devastated when we lose the fights. Understanding impermanence also teaches us how to love. The following story is from the Jataka tales. There was an old father and mother with a grown-up son who had a wife and child. They were very loving to each other, caring and close. Their family was the symbol of love and harmony for the whole village.

Suddenly one day, the son died. All the people in the village were shocked. They thought, "Now we must go and console this family because they must be devastated. They were so close and loving." When they arrived they found that nobody was mourning. The family was living happily as if nothing went wrong. They explained to the villagers, "The secret of our mutual love and harmony was that we knew we would have to part one day. When that would happen was and is uncertain. So we lived as if we could part anytime. We live together the best way we can. Now that the time has come, we are prepared. We have no regrets." We need to learn to love each other and give our best to each other when we are alive and be prepared to let our loved ones go when the time comes.

Nonattachment and compassion are the guiding principles in Buddhist practice. When we die the most important thing is to try not to get attached to our body, our family, and our property. There is great difference between love and attachment. Attachment is totally conditional while compassion is not conditional. If I say I love someone, but my loving her is based on whether she loves me back or she does what I want, then it is attachment because my love can immediately turn into hatred. If I love her and my love does not depend on what she does or does not do, then it is unconditional and true love. The first is only thinking of "me" and my needs, while compassion is when others' welfare is more important. Attachment is for one; compassion is for many, which includes one. Attachment is trying to grab and cling to things that cannot be kept. Compassion is trying to find out what is most beneficial to everybody and trying to accomplish that.

Rob Nairn's psychological approach to depicting the six bardos is so clear and practical that there is no need to say any more. I would like to thank Rob for writing this book and I would like to urge people to read and study this book. May these words bring understanding and benefit to many people.

Appendix B
About Buddhism

As with all major religions, Buddhism has a number of schools and lineages. These developed over many centuries, first in response to the needs of the laity in the southern countries. As Buddhism moved northward the teachings took on cultural and psychological coloring appropriate to the country, while remaining faithful to the core doctrines: new ground, new growth, but the same seed.

There is no centralized world Buddhist authority, and different groups throughout the world are autonomous. Some groups are large with branches throughout the world; others are small and localized.

There are three main groups: Theravada, Mahayana, and Vajrayana.

THERAVADA (THE TEACHING OF THE ELDERS)

Theravadin schools constitute the Southern Transmission, and are found in Burma, Indonesia, Cambodia, Laos, Sri Lanka, and Thailand. They trace their origin to the period immediately following the passing of the Buddha when eighteen schools of early Buddhism developed. Of these, Theravada is the only modern survivor.

Theravadin Buddhism has two main areas of focus:

First is the observance of strict ethical rules and the avoidance of all harm to others. As a result, it markedly emphasizes the monastic life, and great respect is accorded monks and nuns.

The second area of focus is understanding, through meditation and reflection, of the inherent emptiness of the personality. This is not an easy area of Buddhism to understand. The danger of failing to comprehend its subtleties has been likened to that of wrongly grasping a snake.

MAHAYANA (THE GREATER VEHICLE)

This school developed in the first century C.E. The term *Greater Vehicle* distinguishes it from the contemporary Theravadin schools which were monastic and focused chiefly on self-liberation and thus came to be called Hinayana (Lesser Vehicle).

The Mahayana schools incorporate the teachings of Theravada, but in addition regard the bodhisattva ideal as of primary importance. A bodhisattva is one who does all for the benefit of others. He or she vows not to enter the state of final liberation (nirvana) but instead returns to the world to help others. Compassion and wisdom are emphasized. The place of lay practitioners is given importance.

On the subject of emptiness, Mahayana includes the Theravadin view of emptiness of personality, but goes further and teaches emptiness of object, or "nonself of phenomena": that to be empty of a separate enduring identity means to be full of everything in the cosmos. Emptiness does not mean nonexistence. It means coexistence with everything. It is impermanence; it is change; it is life.

Mahayana schools are found in Taiwan, Japan, China, Tibet, India, Nepal, Indonesia, and Korea. Within Mahayana are many well-known subgroups such as Zen.

VAJRAYANA (THE DIAMOND VEHICLE) OR TANTRA

Tantric schools developed in north India between the third and seventh centuries C.E. They incorporated the other two schools but added a further feature: rapid attainment of Buddhahood through specialized forms of meditation that used visualization and mantra (the chanting of sacred words). They developed and flourished chiefly in Tibet and thus Vajrayana became known as Tibetan Buddhism.

In Vajrayana a major shift of perspective is involved. The practitioner trains to recognize the fundamental purity of all phenomena, even though they appear otherwise. We are now in the realms of the most paradoxical Buddhist teachings on the nature of reality.

TIBETAN BUDDHISM IN THE MODERN WORLD

There are four main lineages or schools in Tibetan Buddhism: Nyingma, Sakya, Karma Kagyu, and Gelugpa. The present Dalai Lama (the fourteenth), the best-known Buddhist in the modern world, is the spiritual head of the Gelugpas. He is also the political head of the Tibetan government-in-exile. He was granted political asylum in India after the Chinese takeover of Tibet in 1959 and established a Tibetan village in Dharamsala in northern India.

The Karmapa is head of the Karma Kagyu lineage. The Seventeenth Karmapa, Ogyen Trinley Dorje, escaped from Tibet in 2000 at the age of fifteen and currently has "refugee" status in India, where he is living as a guest of the Dalai Lama at the Gyuto Tantric University. The main seat of the Karmapa in India is Rumtek Monastery in Sikkim, and in the West it is Karma Triyana Dharmachakra (KTD) in Woodstock, New York.[1]

Appendix C
Aunt Palo

She was still dancing at eighty-five
And singing at ninety.
She aged gracefully
And died peacefully.

In her ever smiling face,
You would never notice
The painful life that she lived
In the bloody twentieth century.

She lost her husband
To the Chinese bullet
And both her sons
One after another

She lost everything
That she considered hers
Including the country
And the civilization that she loved.

What she didn't lose was her spirit.
"There is no time to be miserable," she laughed,
"If we can't do something useful,
At least live it joyfully."

She always had a candy
For everybody she met
Whether old, young or a baby
She offered a candy and a smile.

—Ringu Tulku
Gangtok, Sikkim

Appendix D
Contemplation On No-Coming, No-Going

This body is not me.
I am not limited by this body.
I am life without boundaries.
I have never been born
and I have never died.

Look at the ocean and the sky filled with stars,
manifestations from my wondrous true mind.

Since before time, I have been free.
Birth and death are only doors through which we pass,
sacred thresholds on our journey.
Birth and death are a game of hide-and-seek.

So laugh with me,
hold my hand,
let us say good-bye,
say good-bye, to meet again soon.

We meet today.
We will meet again tomorrow.
We will meet at the source every moment.
We meet each other in all forms of life.

— *Thich Nhat Hanh*

Notes

1. Being Fully Human

1. Graham Coleman, ed., *A Handbook of Tibetan Culture: A Guidebook to Tibetan Centres and Resources throughout the World* (London: Rider, 1993).
2. Ringu Tulku, "The Four Bardos" (teachings given at Thrangu House, Oxford, England, 1997, based on *The Mirror of Mindfulness* by Tsele Natsok Rangdrol).
3. Sogyal Rinpoche, *The Tibetan Book of Living and Dying* (London: Rider, 1992).
4. Francisco J. Varela, ed. and narr., *Sleeping, Dreaming, and Dying: An Exploration of Consciousness with the Dalai Lama* (Boston: Wisdom Publications, 1997).
5. Jamgon Kongtrul, *The Great Path of Awakening: The Classic Guide to Using the Mahayana Buddhist Slogans to Tame the Mind and Awaken the Heart*, trans. Ken McLeod (Boston: Shambhala Publications, 1987).
6. Varela, *Sleeping, Dreaming, and Dying.*
7. C. G. Jung, "Psychological Commentary," *The Tibetan Book of the Dead*, ed. W. Y. Evans-Wentz (Oxford: Oxford University Press, 1927).
8. Ibid.
9. Padmasambhava, *Natural Liberation: Padmasambhava's Teachings on the Six Bardos*, with commentary by Gyatrul Rinpoche, trans. B. Alan Wallace (Boston: Wisdom Publications, 1998).
10. Ibid.
11. James H. Austin, *Zen and the Brain: Toward an Understanding of Meditation and Consciousness* (Cambridge: MIT Press, 1998).
12. C. G. Jung, "The Relations between the Ego and the Unconscious," *Two Essays on Analytical Psychology (Collected Works of C. G. Jung, Vol. 7)*, 2d ed. (Princeton: Princeton University Press, 1953).

2. Freedom through Recognizing

1. Tai Situpa, *Awakening the Sleeping Buddha*, ed. Pema Donyo Nyinche and Lea Terhune (Boston: Shambhala Publications, 1999).
2. William Wordsworth, "Ode on Intimations of Immortality from Recollections of Early Childhood," *The Complete Poetical Works of William Wordsworth* (London: Macmillan, 1888).

3. Dreams and the Path

1. Varela, *Sleeping, Dreaming, and Dying*.
2. Ibid.
3. Ibid.
4. C. G. Jung, *Dreams*, trans. R. F. C. Hull (Princeton: Princeton University Press, 1974).
5. Ibid.
6. Varela, *Sleeping, Dreaming, and Dying*.
7. Ibid.
8. Ibid.
9. Robert Moss, *Conscious Dreaming: A Spiritual Path for Everyday Life* (London: Rider, 1996).
10. Varela, *Sleeping, Dreaming, and Dying*.
11. Ibid.
12. Ibid.
13. Bokar Rinpoche, *Death and the Art of Dying in Tibetan Buddhism* (San Francisco: Clear Point Press, 1993.

4. The Process of Dying: Outer and Inner

1. Khenchen Thrangu Rinpoche, *Everyday Consciousness and Buddha Awakening*, trans. and ed. Susanne Schefczyk (Ithaca, N.Y.: Snow Lion Publications, 2002).
2. Sushila Blackman, comp. and ed., *Graceful Exits: How Great Beings Die* (New York: Weatherhill, 1997).
3. George Grimm, *The Doctrine of the Buddha: The Religion of Reason and Meditation* (Delhi: Motilal Banarsidass Publishers, 1973).
4. Ibid.

5. Dying Skillfully

1. Sogyal Rinpoche, *The Tibetan Book of Days: A Journal with Thoughts from Sogyal Rinpoche* (London: Ebury Press Stationery, 1966).

6. Now We Are Dead

1. Bokar Rinpoche, *Death and the Art of Dying*.
2. Jung, "Psychological Commentary."
3. Bokar Rinpoche, *Death and the Art of Dying*.
4. Ringu Tulku, "The Four Bardos."
5. Ibid.
6. Sogyal Rinpoche, *The Tibetan Book of Living and Dying*.
7. Bokar Rinpoche, *Death and the Art of Dying*.
8. Ibid.
9. Ibid.
10. Jung, "Psychological Commentary."
11. Ibid.
12. Bokar Rinpoche, *Death and the Art of Dying*.

7. The Six Psychological Orientations

1. Chögyam Trungpa, *Transcending Madness: The Experience of the Six Bardos*, ed. Judith L. Lief (Boston: Shambhala Publications, 1992).
2. Daniel Noistadt, "Money: The Mirror of Mind," *Tricycle* (winter 1996).
3. Bokar Rinpoche, *Death and the Art of Dying*.
4. Kalu Rinpoche, *The Dharma: That Illuminates All Beings Impartially Like the Light of the Sun and the Moon* (Albany: State University of New York Press, 1986).

9. Breaking the Cycle of Illusion

1. C. G. Jung, *Analytical Psychology: Notes of the Seminar Given in 1925*, ed. William McGuire (Princeton: Princeton University Press, 1991).
2. Robert A. Johnson, *Owning Your Own Shadow: Understanding the Dark Side of the Psyche* (San Francisco: HarperSanFrancisco, 1993).

10. Fear

1. Dalai Lama, *The Power of Compassion: A Collection of Lectures by His Holiness the Fourteenth Dalai Lama*, trans. Geshe Thupten Jinpa (London: Thorsons, 1995).
2. Ibid.

11. Impulse Arising and the Furies

1. Ringu Tulku, "The Four Bardos."

12. Helping the Dying

1. Elisabeth Kübler-Ross, *Death: The Final Stage of Growth* (New York: Touchstone, 1997).
2. Mitch Albom, *Tuesdays with Morrie: An Old Man, a Young Man, and Life's Greatest Lesson* (London: Warner Books, 1997).

16. Compassion—The Wish-Fulfilling Jewel

1. Rob Nairn, *Tranquil Mind*, (Kalk Bay, South Africa: Kairon Press, 1997).
2. Akong Tulku Rinpoche, *Taming the Tiger: Tibetan Teachings on Right Conduct, Mindfulness, and Universal Compassion* (London: Rider, 1994).
3. Pema Chödrön, *The Wisdom of No Escape* (Boston: Shambhala Publications, 1991).
4. My friend Beryl Schutten wrote this meditation specifically for this book.
5. Pema Chödrön, *Start Where You Are* (Boston: Shambhala Publications, 1994).
6. Jamgon Kongtrul, *The Great Path of Awakening*.
7. Ibid.
8. Ibid.
9. Ibid.
10. Bokar Rinpoche, *Death and the Art of Dying*.

Afterword

1. Chokyi Nyima, *The Bardo Guidebook* (Ithaca, N.Y.: Snow Lion Publications, 1996).

2. Vicki Mackenzie, *Reborn in the West: The Reincarnation Masters* (New York: Marlowe and Co., 1996).

About Buddhism

1. From Rob Nairn, *Tranquil Mind*.

Recommended Reading

Dawa Drolma. *Delog: Journey to Realms Beyond Death*. Translated by Richard Barron under the direction of Chagdud Tulku. Junction City, Calif.: Padma Publishing, 1995.

Khenchen Thrangu. "Four-Month Course of Bardo Teachings." Unpublished teachings given at Samye Ling Tibetan Centre, Scotland, 1980. Attended by the author.

Lodö, Lama. *Bardo Teachings: The Way of Death and Rebirth*. With a foreword by Kalu Rinpoche. New York: Snow Lion Publications, 1982.

Nairn, Rob. *What Is Meditation: Buddhism for Everyone*. Boston: Shambhala Publications, 2000.

Noistadt, Daniel. "Money: The Mirror of Mind." *Tricycle* (winter 1996).

Tai Situpa. *Relative World, Ultimate Mind*. Edited by Lea Terhune. Boston: Shambhala Publications, 1992.

Thubten Yeshe. *Introduction to Tantra: A Vision of Totality*. Compiled and edited by Jonathan Landaw. Boston: Wisdom Publications, 1987.

The Tibetan Book of the Dead. Translated by Kazi Dawa Samdup. Compiled and edited by W. Y. Evans-Wentz. Oxford University Press, 1927.

The Tibetan Book of the Dead: The Great Liberation through Hearing in the Bardo. Translated with commentary by Francesca Fremantle and Chögyam Trungpa. Boston: Shambhala Publications, 1987.

The Tibetan Book of the Dead: Liberation through Understanding in the Between. Translated by Robert A. F. Thurman. New York: HarperCollins, 1994.

von Franz, Marie-Louise. *Dreams: A Study of the Dreams of Jung, Descartes, Socrates, and Other Historical Figures*. Boston: Shambhala Publications, 1998.

———. *On Dreams and Death: A Jungian Interpretation*. Boston: Shambhala Publications, 1998.

Wilber, Ken. *One Taste: The Journals of Ken Wilber*. Boston: Shambhala Publications, 1999.

About the Author's Teachers and Their Organizations

RINGU TULKU

Ringu Tulku is an eminent Buddhist teacher whose scholarship, fluent English, and responsive teaching style have become much appreciated throughout the world. He is founder and president of Bodhicharya, an international non-profit educational and cultural association.

Ringu Tulku was recognized as the reincarnation of the abbot of Rigul Monastery in Tibet and was the first Kagyu lama to obtain the Acharya degree at Varanasi University in India. The title of Khenpo was awarded to Ringu Tulku by His Holiness the Sixteenth Karmapa. He has also received the Lopon Chenpo Ph.D. title from the International Nyingma Society.

His Holiness the Sixteenth Karmapa and Dilgo Khyentse Rinpoche were Ringu Tulku's root gurus, and he has studied and practiced under the guidance of many distinguished lamas from all the traditions of Tibetan Buddhism. He was professor of Tibetology in India for seventeen years.

Bodhicharya

Awaken the heart by opening the mind.

— *Bodhicharya slogan*

The objective of Bodhicharya is to contribute toward revealing the ancient wisdom of Buddhism to the modern world for the generation of peace and harmony and to help preserve this wisdom in Tibet and the Himalayas, where it has been kept alive for centuries. Ringu Tulku's style is the Rimé approach of Jamgon Kongtrul: All the teachings of Buddha are of one taste — all leading to the truth. However, according to Ringu Tulku, "Rimé is not a way of uniting different lineages. It is rather an appreciation of their differences and an acknowledgment of the importance of having this variety for the benefit of practitioners with their different needs."

Ringu Tulku travels for much of the year and teaches in many countries, including Samye Ling Tibetan Centre in Scotland and Naropa University in the United States. His itinerary and the Bodhicharya activities can be accessed at: http://www.bodhicharya.org.

Contacting Bodhicharya

> Bodhicharya General Information
> Rue d' Edimbourg 23
> 1050 Brussels, Belgium
> Tel/Fax 00 32 2 514 1449
> office@bodhicharya.org

> Bodhicharya UK Coordinating Office
> 28 Carrick Drive, Coatbridge
> Lanarkshire ML51JZ, Scotland
> co-ordination-uk@bodhicharya.org

AKONG RINPOCHE

Dr. Akong Tulku Rinpoche is the founding president of Rokpa International and the spiritual guide to many dedicated Western meditation practitioners. Rokpa International functions in the following areas: dharma teaching (including meditation), charity work, and therapy. Akong Rinpoche has developed a therapy program based on principles of spiritual growth to meet the needs of people in high-stress cultures.

Akong Rinpoche was born in Tibet, where he received spiritual and medical training, and is a fully qualified Tibetan doctor. He escaped to India in 1959 together with Chögyam Trungpa Rinpoche. They both went to England in 1963 and later established the Samye Ling Tibetan Centre in Scotland. Akong Rinpoche has since established centers in Europe, southern Africa, and the Democratic Republic of the Congo.

Akong Rinpoche is Rob Nairn's root guru.

Rokpa International

> Helping where help is needed.
>
> —*Rokpa slogan*

Rokpa International is an family of charities founded by Dr. Akong Tulku Rinpoche that includes humanitarian aid, healing arts, and spirituality.

The spiritual activity of Rokpa and its many centers is maintained by Akong Rinpoche and Lama Yeshe Losal, abbot and retreat master at Samye Ling.

Specializing in the living lineage of Kagyu teachings, perfectly preserved in Tibet for almost a millennium, the centers offer meditation and general counsel to people of all faiths, with the aim of promoting peace, spiritual well-being, and compassion throughout the world. For information on Rokpa International, see: http://www.rokpa.org.

Credits

Photograph of His Holiness the Seventeenth Karmapa by unknown photographer.

Photograph of the Karmapa and the Dalai Lama by unknown photographer.

Photograph of Akong Rinpoche by June Te Water.

Photograph of Ringu Tulku from Bodhicharya archives, photographer unknown, used with permission of Bodhicharya.

Chenrezi, the Bodhisattva of Compassion used with permission of Samye Ling Center, Scotland.

Death Yantra used with permission of the Ethnographic Museum of the University of Zürich.

"Aunt Palo" by Ringu Tulku, reprinted with permission.

Lines from "Choruses from 'The Rock'" from *Collected Poems 1909–1962*, 5th ed., 1970, reprinted by permission of Faber and Faber.

"Contemplation On No-Coming, No-Going" from *Plum Village Chanting and Recitation Book* by Thich Nhat Hanh reprinted by permission of Parallax Press.

Index